THE PRO-BOERS

Studies in Imperialism

Robin W. Winks, EDITOR

The Anatomy of an
Antiwar Movement
THE PRO-BOERS

Edited and with an Introduction by
STEPHEN KOSS

THE UNIVERSITY OF CHICAGO PRESS
Chicago_____London

THE UNIVERSITY OF CHICAGO PRESS, CHICAGO 60637
THE UNIVERSITY OF CHICAGO PRESS, LTD., LONDON

© 1973 by The University of Chicago
All rights reserved. Published 1973
Printed in the United States of America

International Standard Book Number: 0-226-45134-8
Library of Congress Catalog Card Number: 73-77135

For E., again and always

STEPHEN KOSS is professor of history at Columbia University. His books include *Lord Haldane, Scapegoat for Liberalism* and *Fleet Street Radical; A. G. Gardiner and the 'Daily News'*.

Contents

Contents

Series Editor's Preface

Imperial historians may well be prime imperialists themselves, if by "imperialism" one means, in part at least, the expansive questing after that which traditionally has been thought to belong to others. For imperial history, as written and taught today, must embrace political science, economics, anthropology, sociology, and law, and may well require formal training in one of these disciplines in the future; and imperial history, and those who profess it, must be immersed in areas conveniently and even fashionably labeled African, or Southeast Asian, or West Indian, or South Asian History. For the imperial experience was a shared one, between the Western, thrusting, encroaching power, and the cultures and people thrust upon, who in turn—whether through collaboration, primary resistance, or collapse—were shaped by the imperial experience. Indeed, it is the thesis of this series of volumes that the imperial experience is one best approached as an aspect of intellectual history, of what European and indigenous peoples came to think was true of each other, fully as much as being aspects of economic or political realities. An hypothesis buried within the conception of the series as a whole (although not necessarily explicit in each volume) is that the imperial experience, as a meeting between high- and low-technology cultures, turned predominantly upon four variables present in all such encounters: the cultural baggage borne by the encroaching white settlers, administrators, missionaries, or traders; the incredibly various natures of the indigenous cultures themselves, which helped promote widely different responses; the degree of commitment the imperial power had to the retention or exercise of power over an area, which changed; and the physical nature of the landscape in which the confrontation between the cultures was to be played out. It is, further, an implicit conclusion of this series that it might be well were we to call a moratorium on further generalizations and broad theories about imperialism, until a sufficient number of case studies are available to make such theorizing more fruitful than it has proven to be in the past.

The series will, therefore, admit of volumes limited to the responses of the indigenous societies to the European and of volumes which appear to be almost solely about the Europeans themselves; of volumes which might, for those who must have

vii

tidy minds, appear to be more anthropological than historical; and of volumes which, while pointing toward theoretical conclusions concerning racism, or the exercise of power in a capitalist economy, or the problem of decolonization, are rooted in the sources. It follows that the series must contain contributions assembled in a variety of ways: works of original scholarship which grow from doctoral or postdoctoral research; translations of important statements about empire and colonies from German, or Afrikaans, or Portuguese originals; new collections of source materials not previously assembled in a single place; edited memoirs of district officers, native chiefs, and other men truly on the spot; or reprinted works of otherwise unobtainable scholarship and observation. The series taken as a whole is intended to be comparative, in that all modern imperialisms are appropriate to its purpose. No broad theory of "comparative history" is intended, however, and the series carries the bias that, baldly put, comparisons are useful only when made between the genuinely comparable: to play the nineteenth-century British game of comparing the Pax Britannica with the Pax Romana seems scarcely creditable in the twentieth century, for surely today we realize that to compare two experiences so utterly unlike in technology and the availability of resources is to engage in a fruitless metaphysical game about power and some unproven notion about the psychic unity of mankind. In short, volumes will not be self-consciously comparative, although taken as a whole, the series should provide new insights into the idea of comparative history.

Certainly Professor Stephen E. Koss's volume does this. As he notes in his Introduction, the Boer War was Britain's Vietnam in a variety of ways, and a study of pro-Boer sentiment in Britain during the Anglo-Boer War will provide any perceptive reader with much to think about as he contemplates American imperialism. But Professor Koss feels no obligation to draw these parallels fine, partly because they are, in fact, not lines likely to meet at the horizon, and partly because only certain aspects of the two situations of domestic protest and defiance prove to be comparable. The present collection of materials is therefore happily representative of what the series hopes to achieve. Even though a collection of documents, it is a work of meticulous scholarship and clear originality, treading unfamiliar ground, appealing to the American conscience in 1973 while never failing to serve a larger concern, that of illuminating a discrete historical situation, domestic as well as imperial, which arose at the end of the nineteenth century. The chapters reveal a variety of interpretations present at the time and preserve that variety while nonetheless suggesting certain conclusions about opposition to government, the role of the apathetic as well as the activist element of society in bringing change, and party politics—conclusions capable of being generalized and of having comparative utility. The infinite variety of mankind documented here should remain for us—even as we search for general statements about political behavior—a source of wonder and delight.

ROBIN W. WINKS

Acknowledgments

I should like to express my gratitude to those who, by stout arguments and wise counsel, helped me to focus my ideas and to hone my prose: Bernard Barber, J. M. W. Bean, F. M. Leventhal, Robert McCaughey, Peter Stansky, Chilton Williamson, and, not least of all, Robert K. Webb. Miss Patricia Auspos, my student, brought several selections to my attention and shared with me the conclusions of her research. My wife expertly helped to ferret out source materials and to organize the volume for publication. Among the many librarians and archivists who assisted me, I must give special thanks to those at the British Library of Political and Economic Science, the Trades Union Congress Library, and the British Museum Newspaper Library at Colindale.

Acknowledgements

Introduction

I

A dozen years after its conclusion, the Boer War (1899–1902) was already something of a curiosity, an event from a bygone age which had stirred passions that were easier to recall than to explain.[1] In less time than contemporaries would have anticipated, the victorious British conceded a constitutional settlement that denied them many of the gains hard won on the battlefield. In 1914, the Boer armies reassembled, often under their former commanders, to defend the British Empire from which they had unsuccessfully struggled to withdraw. Jan Christian Smuts, fifteen years after he led a Boer commando raid into Cape Colony, sat in the Imperial War Cabinet alongside Lord Milner, once the personification of all that he detested. Why, then, had there been such a vast expenditure in money, lives, and national reputation?

The events of later decades provide us with clues, if not answers. England, which charted the course of political revolution in the seventeenth century and industrial revolution in the nineteenth, can claim the dubious distinction of being the first of the great nations of the twentieth century to be locked in brutal combat with the determined forces of a small and backward state. The Dutch eventually encountered much the same situation in the East Indies, the French in Indochina and Algeria, and the Americans first in the Philippines and, more recently, in Vietnam.[2] Like the British at the turn of the century, each of these powers initiated a police action that escalated; they thereupon resorted—in desperation—to military tactics that belied the principles they professed, that incurred international disapprobation, and that savagely divided domestic opinion. The parallels are striking and need not be labored.

1. In recent years, this episode has come to be identified as the South African War or, more passionately, as the Second War of Freedom (*Tweede Vryheidsoorlog*). The designation used here, perhaps old-fashioned, is nonetheless the only one that would have been recognized by the subjects of this study.
2. Ernest R. May argues that Americans, at the time of the Philippine insurrection, looked to the British experience in South Africa as a precedent. *American Imperialism: A Speculative Essay* (New York, 1968), pp. 321–22.

It is domestic opinion, and specifically that segment of it that was opposed to the war, with which the present volume is concerned. Here the similarity to latterday events is at once most obvious, and, to use the jargon of recent times, most "relevant." The critics of the British effort in South Africa resemble the opponents of American involvement in Southeast Asia in their intellectual diversity, if not necessarily in their social backgrounds; in the intensity of their rhetoric, if not necessarily in their frames of reference; in their ambitions, if not necessarily in their strategies; and, not least of all, in their distrust of authority and disillusionment with institutions of government. Both movements, if either may be considered as a collective entity, were pitted against and frustrated by essentially the same forces.

The pro-Boers—as their enemies disparagingly called them, and as they, with a perversity reminiscent of the early Christians, took to identifying themselves—were individuals of disparate personalities and persuasions. There was fundamental agreement among them that the war was unnecessary and could have been averted; but they were more united in their condemnation of past policies than in either their appraisals of the present predicament or their prescriptions for the future. Some agitated to "Stop the War," immediately and regardless of the consequences; others campaigned for meaningful negotiations and the promulgation of moderate war aims. Some were more concerned with the justification of the war, others with its conduct. Some were most outraged by civilian suffering in South Africa, others by the loss of equanimity at home. Some sought to evolve new political alignments, others to redefine imperial relationships. Some feared the consequences of their country's reduced standing in the eyes of the world, others in the eyes of God.

The last ingredient cannot be too much emphasized. The pro-Boers derived much of their inspiration and organization, and even more of their rhetoric, from a fervent Christianity. That, above all else, distinguishes them from the opponents of later wars who become progressively more secular in their aims and attitudes. Yet the pro-Boers often combined their evangelism with strong anticapitalist sentiments, which critics of future "imperialist aggressions" might appreciate and, indeed, find serviceable. And, upon occasion, they denounced the exploitation and oppression of subject peoples, black as well as Boer, in a style that has a distinctly modern ring.

But historical analogies, like mirrors in a carnival sideshow, tend to distort the images they reflect: they amuse, but do they instruct? Indisputably, British opposition to the Boer War was the product of a particular set of historical circumstances. Among other things (the list can be expanded indeterminately), it was a response to the aspirations and anxieties of late Victorian society, to the dislocation of the Liberal Party after W. E. Gladstone's belated retirement from its leadership, and to a chain of international developments that individual statesmen were powerless to control. That American society in the 1960s came to exhibit similar characteristics was not historical inevitability, but the result of diverse factors, including the challenge posed to the country's technological and military supremacy, the distress of the Democratic Party (although it retained office) after the tragic loss of John F. Kennedy, and the extent to which the United States had assumed the place in global politics and commerce that Britain once occupied. The parallels cannot be carried too far, however, without serious injury to the respective situations. One may only speculate whether America's Vietnam experience has had as chastening an effect as the British intervention in South Africa.

Causality in history can be determined with neither certainty nor universal satisfaction. It is submitted here that the Boer War was a major contributing factor to the rejection of Toryism at the polls in 1906, to Liberalism's phoenix-like recovery, and to the emergence of a parliamentary Labour Party. Even sooner, the war brought a popular reaction against the jingo enthusiasms that had reached their climax at the close of the old century; it fostered a rigorous reappraisal of Britain's world position, leading by steps to the retreat from splendid isolation, to the formation of the Committee of Imperial Defence, to the Fisher navy reforms and the Haldane army reforms; it transformed the image and also, arguably perhaps, the ethic of empire by bringing into question not only the policies but also the motives of imperial statesmen. If the pro-Boers did not succeed in their primary objective—preventing or terminating hostilities—

they nonetheless managed to provoke a widespread reaction against the outlook that had made for war and the government that had waged it. Perhaps, under the circumstances, that is the most that any antiwar movement can reasonably hope to accomplish.

II

The political opposition to the war, like the war itself, had its roots in the issues and events of preceding decades. The last quarter of the nineteenth century had witnessed the growth of an imperialist sentiment that attended the expansion, not always with government approval, of the far-flung boundaries of empire. While South African affairs cannot be considered without reference to these earlier proceedings, neither can they be viewed as their culmination. As the century ebbed, there was one final "surge" of imperialist emotion, more intense than any that came before it; according to Richard Koebner and H. N. Schmidt, this manifestation,

> though prepared by manifold antecedents, . . . was . . . remarkably sudden. Attempts to interpret it in terms of sociology and to trace it back to literary influences have been made by the same contemporary writers who directed attention to it. But no explanation can be adequate which does not take full account of the one fact that the waves of "imperialism" between 1897 and 1899 were not only in the nature of a social phenomenon, but also in the nature of historical events.[3]

The present work assumes no obligation to explain the origins of the South African War, except as perceived by contemporary minds. Yet it is necessary, if one is to gauge the weight of critical arguments, to understand context and chronology. The British captured Cape Town during the Napoleonic wars and retained it—along with its outlying regions—in the peacemaking of 1815. This extended their rule over the Boers, a people basically of Dutch descent, who by then had evolved their own language (Afrikaans) and national characteristics. As the Boers moved inland, in quest of new pasture lands and freedom from governmental

3. *Imperialism: the Story and Significance of a Political Word, 1840–1960* (Cambridge, 1964) , p. 215.

interference, they were actively pursued by the British, whose
strategic considerations included the prevention of conflict
with the native tribes and the extirpation of slavery. This
policy was reversed in the 1850s, when the British abandoned
control of the Boer territories in the interior. But in 1877,
in the face of an acute Zulu threat, Britain again extended
her unwelcome protection. Gladstone, campaigning at
Midlothian in 1879, vowed to undo the injury, but there were
delays. He did not allow the defeat of British troops by
Boer forces to deflect him from his purpose, and, in 1881, the
Transvaal was granted self-government "under the suzerainty
of the Queen," with no precise determination of what this
meant. It was not until the close of the century that a
definition became imperative.

There were those who later complained that the Boer War
would not have occurred if Gladstone had been more alert
to the interests of empire. Others strenuously countered
that the crisis was due to Gladstone's inability to act as
swiftly and as generously as he would have liked and to the
failure of others to follow his noble example. Neither view
takes into account the fact that the South African situation
was radically altered soon after Gladstone dealt with it. In
1886, gold was discovered on the Rand, bringing an influx of
aliens to the Transvaal. The president of the Boer republic
was Paul Kruger, a patriarchal figure and the obdurate
opponent of the pernicious forces of modernity that found
their headquarters at Johannesburg. His antagonist, both
figuratively and literally, was Cecil Rhodes, the virtual
proprietor of the Kimberley diamond mines, whose consum-
ing ambition was to see the extension of British influence
northward from the Cape. Not that Rhodes was an imperialist
out of altruism. Sir Edward Grey, the future Liberal foreign
secretary, met him at Lord Rosebery's house back in 1892 and
wrote to his wife: "Rhodes is not exactly what you call a
Liberal: he has a new version of 'one man, one vote' for
South Africa, viz. that he, Rhodes, should have a vote, but
nobody else should."[4]

It is now generally agreed that the British Government
exercised as little control over Rhodes, its self-accredited

4. November 2, 1892, quoted in G. M. Trevelyan, *Grey of
Fallodon* (Boston, 1937), p. 69.

agent, as over Kruger, who resisted the unauthorized encroachments made in its name.[5] Rhodes's strategy hinged upon the Uitlanders, the foreign settlers in the Transvaal, who were overwhelmingly British in origin. Denied the political participation to which their wealth allegedly entitled them, they might rebel and thereby provide the pretext for the absorption of the Transvaal into an Anglicized confederation, receptive to commercial influence. Like many idealists (and he well qualifies for that designation), Rhodes lacked the patience to let history take its course. On December 29, 1895, at his instigation, Dr. Leander Starr Jameson launched an abortive raid on the Transvaal, which was intended to induce a widespread uprising against Kruger. Rhodes's culpability was readily apparent, and his public career suffered accordingly; he resigned the premiership of Cape Colony and, for a time, the directorship of the chartered company. But was the British Government, and particularly Joseph Chamberlain at the Colonial Office, in any way implicated?

Kruger, whose success in withstanding the assault won him a congratulatory telegram from the German emperor, had seen his worst suspicions confirmed. More than ever, he was resolved to defend Boer integrity against the twin threats that emanated from Johannesburg and London. It made no difference that Chamberlain, quickly and categorically, disavowed Jameson. "That repudiation by itself," one historian has recently explained, "did not satisfy all his contemporaries that the British Government was innocent of the charge of complicity at worst, connivance at best."[6] A select committee of the House of Commons was appointed to inquire into the circumstances of the raid. Although it included five members of the Liberal Opposition (Sir Henry Campbell-Bannerman, Sir William Harcourt, Sydney Buxton, J. E.

5. "By 1895 South Africa had passed beyond the British government's direct control. . . . Power and initiative lay with Rhodes on the one hand and with Kruger on the other, not with the Colonial Office." Ronald Robinson and John Gallagher, with Alice Denny, *Africa and the Victorians* (London, 1963), p. 427.

6. Jeffrey Butler, *The Liberal Party and the Jameson Raid* (Oxford, 1968), p. 12.

Ellis, and Henry Labouchere), its report, issued in July 1897, failed to allay public and private doubts. "The S[outh] A[frican] Committee was certainly a scandalous mess," John Morley confessed to Lord Spencer, "and I shall never have a more vexatious job than the lame vindication of it which I felt bound to attempt, for the sake of W. V. H[arcourt] and C[ampbell-] B[annerman]."[7] The persistence of such doubts, even in the minds of members of the committee, did much to determine the Liberal response when war eventually broke out.

While the South African Committee conducted its investigations, the nation was celebrating Queen Victoria's Diamond Jubilee. On June 25, 1897, Beatrice Webb returned to London, and noted in her diary: "Imperialism in the air—all classes drunk with sight-seeing and hysterical loyalty."[8] Neither Jameson's escapade nor the humiliation it incurred in any way dampened public ardor. Further imperial exploits only served to raise the pitch of excitement. "Khartoum and Fashoda," Harcourt predicted with gloomy accuracy to Morley, "will rally the popular sentiment as much as Trafalgar and Salamanca. . . . We shall either see the submission of France which will be popular or a war with France which will be more popular still."[9] Early in 1899, the French relinquished their claim to the Upper Nile. *The Times*, in a leader on January 18, proclaimed that "the Empire . . . is now the mainstay of civilisation and progress, the refuge of freedom, intellectual, political, and commercial, in every part of the globe." On February 11, the *Spectator* approvingly quoted Rudyard Kipling and concluded: "The duty of the white man is to conquer and control, probably for a couple of centuries, all the dark people of the world, not for his own good, but for theirs." Needless to say, it was not an atmosphere conducive to a thoughtful examination of South African problems.

7. Morley to Spencer, October 15, 1897, Spencer Papers, Althorp, Northants.

8. Quoted in *Our Partnership*, ed. B. Drake and M. Cole (London, 1948), p. 140.

9. Harcourt to Morley, October 10, 1898, Harcourt Papers, Stanton Harcourt, Oxon.

Concurrently, attitudes were hardening in the Transvaal. In February, 1898, Kruger was reelected to the presidency with almost double the vote he had received five years earlier. Furthermore, he now commanded considerable sympathy and support in the Orange Free State, the Transvaal's sister republic, and among the Dutch in Cape Colony. Sir Alfred (later Lord) Milner, whom the British had dispatched to South Africa as high commissioner, did little to ease tensions. From May 31 to June 5, 1899, he met with Kruger at Blomfontein on the subject of Uitlander grievances, and "his clear super-civilized mind lost patience with the tedious and devious obstinacy of the Arcadian president."[10] Further proposals to reform the Transvaal franchise and naturalization laws were rejected by one side or the other. By autumn, passions ran high and troops were mobilized. On October 9, the Boers issued their ultimatum, which was tantamount to a declaration of war.

III

By this time, British opinion was already divided. On one side, there was the bellicosity of the public at large, still under the intoxicating influence of Khartoum and Fashoda; on the other, there was the moral outrage of an articulate minority who saw the abyss that lay ahead. Frederic Harrison, writing in the issue of the *Positivist Review* that appeared in late September, conceded that Boer obstinacy "may be unreasonable, hotheaded, unwise," but he argued that "it affords no just *casus belli*."[11] G. P. Gooch, who considered *The War and Its Causes*, agreed. He could understand, if not approve, the Boers' refusal "to revolutionise their old polity. Old-fashioned and unprogressive as their civilisation was, it was their own, and they were profoundly attached to it."[12] Dr. G. B. Clark, a critic of British policy in

10. R. C. K. Ensor, *England, 1870–1914* (Oxford, 1963), p. 248. First published in 1936, Ensor's history relies on memory as well as research. During the Boer War, its author was a student at Oxford and later a junior member of the *Manchester Guardian*.
11. *Positivist Review* 82 (1899): 171–72.
12. London: The Transvaal Committee, 1900.

Parliament and in print, offered documentary evidence that Kruger, far from being intractable, had offered significant concessions.[13]

In any case, Kruger was seventy-five years old. There was every reason to believe that the British, had they acted with tact and forbearance, would soon have been dealing at Pretoria with someone more accommodating. It did not go unnoticed that in the presidential election of 1893, before the unsettling experience of the Jameson Raid, P. J. Joubert— the "liberal" candidate—had run Kruger a close second. Boer progressivism was therefore not necessarily a contradiction in terms. "Who is there," G. P. Gooch demanded to know,

> who would venture to assert that a new President and a Colonial Secretary with a better record than Mr. Chamberlain (and for these in the ordinary course of things there could not be long to wait) would not be able to effect a settlement?

"Not I," John Morley would have answered. "I have no love of Boers, and I am not for peace at any price," he assured Lord Curzon, the proconsul of empire,

> but the notion of committing us to these immense operations for objects that were sure to be realized without them in two or three years with the death of an old and broken man like Kruger, makes me sick.[14]

Those who attempted first to stave off war and then to end it ascribed paramount importance to the role of personality: if Kruger had not spent a lifetime as a fugitive from British law and culture, if negotiations had not been entrusted to a man of Milner's authoritarian temperament, if Chamberlain were less ambitious and his cabinet colleagues stood less in awe of him, the war would not have occurred.

---

13. Clark, ed., *The Official Correspondence between the Governments of Great Britain, the South African Republic, and the Orange Free State which Preceded the War in South Africa* (London, 1900).

14. Morley to Curzon, November 26, 1900, Marquess Curzon of Kedleston Papers, India Office Library, London.

Those who supported the military effort saw it as unavoidable and, indeed, necessary: it was the result of long-standing differences which could not be settled satisfactorily except by force. In between, there was an amorphous group that regretted the outbreak of war but accepted it as an established fact and agreed to its effective prosecution: either they deferred to those who were supposedly in a better position to know the facts, or they took refuge in the doctrine of "my country, right or wrong."

It took courage to speak out against prewar statesmanship; it took even more to persist as a voice in the wilderness after the first shots were fired. Some were fortunate, in that their response was dictated by their actions (sometimes even their fathers' actions) earlier in the century: at the time of the Crimean War or, more usually, in the 1876 agitation against the "Bulgarian horrors." These veteran crusaders, either by instinct or inheritance, belonged to a proud tradition of resistance to the spirit of swagger. But their experience was not without its liabilities. No longer young, some of them had exhausted their energies in previous struggles. Often they were handicapped by an inability to perceive the extent to which times had changed. Almost a quarter century before, they had helped Gladstone rouse the country, and particularly its Nonconformist conscience, against the baleful influences of Beaconsfieldism. This time, however, they conspicuously lacked a Gladstone, and Nonconformity had lost its political thrust.

There were political reasons, not necessarily discreditable, for becoming a pro-Boer. Some wished to save the Liberal Party as a viable alternative to the Unionist government: Liberal Imperialism, so far as Morley was concerned, was only "Chamberlain wine with a Rosebery label." Others sought to save or advance their own positions within that party. Usually, however, the decision was taken to satisfy the dictates of conscience; as such, it was not taken lightly. "No problem in the ethics of citizenship," G. P. Gooch wrote many years later,

> is more difficult than the duty of men and women who disapprove of a conflict in which their country becomes engaged. Shall they content themselves with registering protest and then stand aside till the storm is over, or shall

they strive to combat the agencies and ideologies which in their opinion helped to produce the catastrophe?[15]

Gooch did not exaggerate the seriousness of the matter. To criticize publicly national policy during wartime, even during a war in which national survival was never at stake, was to invite imputations of disloyalty. Those who allegedly sympathized with the enemy were subjected to ridicule and, upon occasion, physical assault; their opinions cost them friendships and, sometimes, employment; those who sat in Parliament ran considerable risk of losing their seats.

This is not to deny that there were those who opposed the war out of pique, or as a gesture (and not always a logical one) against the prevailing system. "What I hated about it," G. K. Chesterton recalled with his characteristic blend of bombast and ebullience,

> was what a good many people liked about it. It was such a very cheerful war. I hated its confidence, its congratulatory expectations, its optimism of the Stock Exchange. I hated its vile assurance of victory. It was regarded by many as an almost automatic process like the operation of a natural law; and I have always hated that sort of heathen notion of a natural law.[16]

Chesterton went on to boast that he was never ashamed to be classified as a pro-Boer: "It expressed exactly what I meant much better than its idealistic synonyms."[17] But to others, eager to accomplish something constructive, the label was more a stigma than a badge to be worn with pride. It was not the least inconsistent for one to condemn British policymakers without championing the Boers. Nor (as Chesterton observed with some annoyance) did all his fellow pro-Boers share the same objectives and priorities. A homogeneous group in the eyes of their adversaries, they were individuals with a strong individualistic bias. Their agitation incorporated pacifists and inveterate anti-imperialists (although far fewer of either than one might suppose); "economists," who wished to reduce government spending, but also enthusiasts for costly welfare programs; isolationists,

15. *Under Six Reigns* (London, 1959), p. 75.
16. *Autobiography* (London, 1937), p. 113.
17. Ibid., p. 115.

but also dedicated internationalists. We shall meet them all in due course.

IV

The pro-Boers knew one another and therefore deserve to be known by the company they kept. A succession of committees, with overlapping memberships and sometimes mutually exclusive aims, sprang into existence. An examination of these groups will help to account for the nature of the agitation and also its limitations.

The Transvaal Committee had begun operations before the outbreak of the war, sponsoring meetings and publishing pamphlets first to warn the British public of the imminence of war, and second to argue the justice, moral and constitutional, of the Boer position. In its membership and avowed objectives, the Committee was an offshoot of the old Transvaal Independence Association, which had been founded early in 1881 to repeal the 1877 annexation. When war came, many of the committee's arguments, and indeed its name, were no longer acceptable to a wide public. Although it remained in existence, it fed in turn into other groups, most notably the South Africa Conciliation Committee.

Ironically, the group most responsible for the popular image of the antiwar movement was least representative of the movement as a whole. On Christmas eve, 1899, the Stop the War Committee was called to life to challenge "a policy which we regard as criminal as it is suicidal." It was Silas K. Hocking, "a bestselling author of healthy fiction"[18] as befitting a former member of the Methodist ministry, who took the initiative; but the moving force behind the enterprise was unquestionably W. T. Stead, the veteran journalistic crusader and physician to the nation's moral health. With its fire-and-brimstone quality, the new committee was incapable of any halfway measures. Its very name was a deliberate affront to popular sensibilities; its slogan, "Stop the War and Stop It Now!" even more so. The committee had no affiliation with any political party, and, except for the Almighty, recognized no higher authority. Its leaders included some of the most gifted controversialists and

18. *D.N.B.*

skilled rhetoricians of the age, but these were men who eschewed discipline and whose rigid ideas defined implementation. "Stead's *Stop the War* campaign was worse than useless," Gooch concluded more in sorrow than in anger.[19] Instead of educating, it incited passions, ones often antagonistic to its purpose.

Given the moribundity of the Transvaal Committee, the South Africa Conciliation Committee was galvanized into action to retrieve the antiwar movement from the hands of doctrinaires and extremists. More self-consciously respectable than the Stop the War people, the S.A.C.C. sponsored meetings, not rallies, which were addressed by some of the most distinguished figures in contemporary letters and politics and which drew relatively small crowds. Leonard Courtney, universally acknowledged as a man of principle, was president, and his associates were men of equally high calibre. Willing to concede to the government that the war, once begun, could not be halted by a unilateral act of withdrawal, they nonetheless pressed for negotiations to bring the war to a speedy conclusion. In this respect, the committee occupied a middle ground: it did not preach peace at any price, nor did it join in the popular cry for war to the finish. Its leaders knew well enough that the Boers, given no alternative to terms of unconditional surrender, would resist as long as humanly possible. The S.A.C.C. urged a compromise solution not only to save lives and money, but also—as its name implied—to save South Africa for the Empire and to save the Empire as a venture founded on principles of mutual trust and common loyalties.

With remarkably few exceptions, the key figures in each of the various committees belonged to the Radical wing of the Liberal Party. Courtney was an apostate, but it was clearly the Liberal element in his Liberal Unionism that he now wished most to emphasize. The affinity between Liberalism and the antiwar agitation was, in all respects, a natural one: as Her Majesty's Opposition, the party was the legitimate parliamentary agency for action against the government; as the party of the left, it was a haven for those with grievances and dissenting opinions; and as a tradition it

19. *Under Six Reigns*, p. 75.

had an abiding sympathy for subject nationalities. But the Liberal leadership, deeply split over the issues of the day, was in no shape to mount a concerted offensive. Sir Henry Campbell-Bannerman, who replaced Harcourt at the helm eight months before the war, experienced the same difficulties that had driven his predecessor to resignation. Of his private sentiments, there can be little doubt: "I am very much in harmony with your views," he wrote to F. A. Channing, a pro-Boer M.P., "although I am not at liberty to speak out quite so freely."[20] But he could ill afford to widen the breach within the party by giving the Liberal Imperialists a pretext for open rebellion. The pro-Boers, therefore, were denied use—or, at least, exclusive use—of the party organization and had to content themselves with those channels that remained in the possession of the Gladstonian regulars: the National Reform Union and, to a lesser extent, the National Liberal Federation. In addition, there emerged a new party ginger group dedicated to the campaign for peace and especially to the reelection of those M.P.'s who constituted a party of peace. This was the League of Liberals against Aggression and Militarism, whose members were nicknamed "Lambs." With a broad base in the constituencies, it was conceived as a direct response to the Liberal Imperialists (called "Lib-Imps" or "Limps," depending upon the severity of one's view). Separately organized, the imperialist faction worked to deliver the party to Lord Rosebery, who might have had the prize for the asking, but who somehow could never bring himself to ask.

In parliamentary votes and personal credentials, the Liberal Imperialists could not be discounted. They included three of the dominant members of the next Liberal administration: H. H. Asquith (who ascended to the premiership in 1908), Sir Edward Grey, and R. B. Haldane. Men of talent and creativity, they preached doctrines of national efficiency and, to varying degrees, flirted with theories of collectivism. Their aim as politicians was nothing less than to remake their party's image, which was diametrically opposed to the

20. Campbell-Bannerman to Channing, November 10, 1899, Campbell-Bannerman Papers, British Museum Add. MSS. 41,213, fol. 20.

pro-Boer aim of salvaging as much as possible of the Gladstonian heritage.[21]

The Liberals, with their commitment to Home Rule for Ireland, their aversion to armaments, and their limited enthusiasm (bordering on disdain) for colonial acquisitions, invited misrepresentation as a party of separatists, defeatists, and even traitors. The situation was nothing new. Disraeli, in his 1872 Crystal Palace speech, equated Liberalism with "the disintegration of the empire of England" and with the consequent sacrifice of national greatness; Gladstone, in the first of his Midlothian speeches, eloquently defended the Liberal record against imputations of "want of patriotism." Their political heirs, decade after decade, leveled the same charges and issued the same denials. The Liberal Imperialists sought to put an end to the embarrassing business by professing their own imperial instincts and by discarding those attitudes and policies that laid the party open to attack.

To those who took seriously their spiritual descent from Cobden, Bright, and Gladstone, the Liberal Imperialist strategy reeked of opportunism. A moral issue was at stake, and it had to be defended whatever the personal or political consequences. Lord Rosebery had apparently forgotten, but others could still remember, Gladstone's stirring words to the electors who welcomed him to Midlothian in 1879:

> It is not particularly pleasant for any man, I suppose, to spend the closing years of his life in vain and unavailing protest; but as long as he thinks his protest may avail, as long as he feels that the people have not yet had their fair chance and opportunity, it is his duty to protest, and it is to perform that duty, gentlemen, that I come here.[22]

It was in the same spirit that John Bryn Roberts rose to address the House of Commons on February 19, 1901: "We have suffered a great deal for our opinions," he said in reply to catcalls from the ministerial benches,

21. Sidney Webb, who took Campbell-Bannerman to task for "piecing together the Gladstonian rags and remnants," celebrated "Lord Rosebery's Escape from Houndsditch" in the *Nineteenth Century* 50 (1901):366–86.

22. Speech at the Music Hall, Edinburgh, November 25, 1879, *Midlothian Speeches, 1879* (New York, 1971), p. 50.

but we stick to those opinions, because we believe that the best interests of our country depend upon those opinions being expressed and adopted by the country. We are willing to sacrifice ourselves to save the country. Honourable Gentlemen opposite, on the other hand, have been ready to sacrifice the country to save themselves.[23]

Gladstone, of course, had sensed a ground swell of electoral support in 1879; in 1901, however, a Liberal victory was at best a remote prospect. Nevertheless, pro-Boer backbenchers continued to make themselves heard.

As Bryn Roberts's statement would suggest, the question soon acquired a new dimension. No longer a simple matter of license to criticize the war, it became a conscientious attempt to vindicate historic rights of free speech. Was the British Government, avowedly engaged in a struggle to safeguard the liberties of the Uitlanders, prepared to allow the stifling of opinion at home? Were individuals to be insulted, threatened, and attacked for holding minority views? Was there to be a free debate of issues and a free exchange of information so that objective decisions could be made?

Government spokesmen, if they did not condone the disruption of peace meetings, nonetheless offered fulsome excuses for those whose "patriotism" had got the better of them. The Irish Nationalists gloated to see the British, for all their pretensions to civic propriety, capable of hooliganism. As in Ireland, there were recurrent reports that the police were always on hand to interfere with a demonstration, but never to protect a demonstrator against the fury of the mob. Worst of all, there was a prevailing notion that one could not question any aspect of the war without giving aid and comfort to the enemy. Sir Wilfrid Lawson, whose pro-Boer activities lost him his seat in the House of Commons, told the story of a Scotsman on a London omnibus who turned to a fellow passenger and declaimed: "Kruger ought to be hanged." His neighbor replied: "Kruger, perhaps, might have something to say to that," and the Scotsman, furious, summoned the conductor and demanded, "Put yon man out. This is no debating society."[24]

23. *Parliamentary Debates*, 4th series, LXXXIX, col. 536.
24. *Manchester Guardian*, April 5, 1900.

Lawson, one must concede, hardly helped matters when he contemptuously referred to supporters of the war as "Union Jackasses"; nor did David Lloyd George, when he cavalierly remarked that, "after all, the Boers are the Liberal Forwards."[25] Indeed, there were occasions when the pro-Boers, far from being the innocent victims of popular prejudice, employed strong-arm tactics (not necessarily in self-defense) and prevented the expression of contrary views on the floor of their meetings. To be sure, many more pro-Boer than prowar editors and journalists were turned out of their jobs; but surely this fact is more a commentary upon the structure of the press than testimony to the tolerance of pro-Boer publishers: was H. W. Massingham's ejection from the imperialist *Daily Chronicle* in November, 1899, any worse than E. T. Cook's dismissal from the anti-imperialist *Daily News* thirteen months later?

V

All in all, the opponents of the war were guilty of much of the same intemperate behavior and narrow-mindedness that they deplored in their adversaries. If the ministerial press featured outrageous reports of Boer atrocities, the antiwar press doubtless exaggerated the brutality of the jingo hordes.[26] If one side depicted Kruger as a fiend, the other portrayed Chamberlain, in equally lurid colors, as the devil incarnate. If one saw the war as a conspiracy (possibly hatched in Berlin) to menace the vital sea route to India, the other saw it as a plot perpetrated by cosmopolitan (almost invariably Jewish) financiers in search of cheap dividends. It was by hyperbolic language that each side sought to rouse indignation and win support. There were three arenas in which contemporaries waged this war of words: in Parliament, in the pages of the partisan press, and in innumerable pamphlets.[27]

25. Quoted in F. W. Hirst, *In the Golden Days* (London, 1947), p. 207.
26. See, for example, Stead's account of Mafeking week in the *Review of Reviews*, June, 1900.
27. John S. Galbraith has provided an excellent survey of "The Pamphlet Campaign on the Boer War," in the *Journal of Modern History* 24 (1952) : 111–26.

To probe any more deeply into the dissension between and within parties would alter the scope and nature of this collection. Nor, given the limitations of space and subject, can one hope to do justice to such complex questions as the relationship between politics and the press, the ways in which opinion was influenced, and the ways in which it in turn helped to shape policy. Yet the sources that have been assembled will speak, at least indirectly, to these and other related subjects.

Parliament is sufficiently well known as an institution to require no introduction. But the structure of the press and, particularly, the function of the pamphlet may require explanation.

That the vast majority of British newspapers, Tory-connected, would support the war was a foregone conclusion. But what about the minority of Liberal dailies? There was no shortage of Liberal properties in Fleet Street, but in either readership or influence (as the *Westminster Gazette* proved, the two factors did not invariably go hand in hand) most were inconsequential. The *Morning Leader* and the *Star*, for what they were worth, were vigorously pro-Boer. But the more important Liberal papers were, in varying degree, committed to an imperialist position: J. A. Spender, editor of the *Westminster Gazette*, shared a Balliol background with Asquith, Grey, and Milner; the *Daily Chronicle*, in the early weeks of the war, was purged of its pro-Boer staff; and the *Daily News*, until it changed hands, tried its best to discern and follow Lord Rosebery's lead. This left the pro-Boers the *Manchester Guardian*, which ought never to be underestimated. Its editor, C. P. Scott, doubled as a pro-Boer M.P. But, as its banner boldly proclaimed, it was neither London-based nor London-oriented; the railway did not deliver copies to the metropolis until nearly noon, when its news was already slightly stale and its arguments perhaps less persuasive. Not until January, 1901, when they captured the *Daily News*, did the pro-Boers possess an effective voice in London.

Neither the *Manchester Guardian* nor the converted *Daily News* had an easy time of it. Both sacrificed circulation by espousing an unpopular cause. Both were threatened with reprisals against personnel and plant, which sometimes made

it necessary to operate under a virtual state of siege. One
Guardian old-timer

> recalled how as an apprentice in the composing room in
> 1900 he used to bring a large parcel of sandwiches with
> him to work. Several times he was challenged by the police
> who had been put on to guard the building and had his
> parcel searched to see if it contained a bomb.[28]

There was a shower of abusive letters in every mail. Some
correspondents, however, were more bewildered than irate. A.
G. Gardiner, newly installed as editor of the *Daily News*, heard
from "a clergyman's wife, a most enthusiastic Gladstonian,
& a reader of the *Daily News* for 30 years," who asked him to
refute the rumor that his salary was secretly paid by President
Kruger.[29] A former employee proffered the information
that the paper enjoyed "enormous influence" over General
Botha, an avid and appreciative reader.[30] Patently absurd,
such stories had a disastrous effect upon sales at a time when
the *Daily News* had yet to establish its base among the
suburban middle classes. The *Manchester Guardian*, on the
other hand, was comparatively fortunate in that it could
depend upon the patronage of the Lancashire cotton trade,
which may have detested its politics but could not afford
to dispense with its commercial news. It was said that the
morning trains and trams steamed into Manchester

> full of men who expressed their attitude by crumpling the
> paper into a ball and throwing it away ostentatiously,
> when they had read the telegrams from New York,
> Galveston, and New Orleans.[31]

But the *Manchester Guardian* slowly brought round the
business community, to which it astutely put its case in terms
of "expanding currency, . . . rising prices, and . . . diminished
profits."[32]

28. Quoted in David Ayerst, *Guardian: Biography of a Newspaper* (London, 1971), p. 280.
29. Emily A. Maddy to Gardiner, June 28 [1902], quoted in
Stephen Koss, *Fleet Street Radical, A. G. Gardiner and the 'Daily
News'* (London, 1973), p. 52.
30. J. Saxon Mills, letter to the editor of *The Times*, July 6, 1901.
31. R. H. Gretton, *A Modern History of the English People,
1880–1922* (New York, 1930), p. 526.
32. See, for example, December 31, 1901.

The two major pro-Boer newspapers did not participate directly in the pamphlet campaign, although items from their columns were frequently reprinted under other auspices. The *Morning Leader* issued a series of leaflets, available from its offices in Stonecutter Street at rates of "1 d. for 6; 1½ d. for 12; 1 s. for 120; 10 s. for 1,200." Among them were "When and Why the Boers Armed," "Pushful Diplomacy," and "The Real Motive for the War." The *Review of Reviews* produced several sixpenny tracts, written by Stead, its editor, and distributed by the Stop the War Committee. The *New Age* and the *Speaker* rendered weekly service to the cause, as each of them perceived it, but neither had the facilities to publish pamphlets. The National Reform Union issued some, as did the League of Liberals against Aggression and Militarism. The Liberal Publication Department made sporadic contributions, especially at the time of the 1900 general election, but party divisions militated against vehemence or even consistency: Harcourt and Morley were quoted (as opposed to Lloyd George and John Burns), but so were Asquith and Rosebery. The overwhelming number of pamphlets bore the imprint of private groups, the most prominent being the Stop the War Committee and the South Africa Conciliation Committee.

Until the advent of the penny press (after the repeal of the newspaper tax in 1854), the pamphlet was one of the crucial media of national debate: theological, social, and political. Thereafter, its importance declined but did not disappear. England, "perhaps to a greater extent than in any other country,"[33] boasted a tradition of pamphleteering that stretched back to the Puritans, who had regarded the pamphlet not as a weapon to be wielded on its own but as a complement to activity in Parliament and pulpit. In this respect, the pamphlet campaign against the Boer War followed precedent. The difference was that there had recently emerged a "new journalism," typified by the *Daily Mail*, against which the pamphlet could not compete. The penny press had weakened the tradition; the halfpenny press killed it.

If the pro-Boers grasped the situation, they did not acknowledge it, except to rail against the excesses of the

33. Galbraith, p. 111.

"yellow" or "gutter" press. They poured out a stream of pamphlets and leaflets that hammered relentlessly at the same overworked themes: the war was inexcusable in its origins and immoral in its prosecution; it was inspired by alien capitalists; the British Government was hypocritical and unwilling to negotiate a just settlement; and the British public had been hoodwinked and its soul corrupted. There were, of course, variations: the exploitation of labor and "inferior races," the effect upon international relations, and the threat to civil rights. These were the same general issues to which M.P.'s addressed themselves in the House (many pamphlets were reprints of parliamentary speeches), but the pamphlet often provided a less restrictive forum.

There was a close relationship between style and content: uniform type and balanced format promised a reasoned argument by a respected authority, while an overindulgence in italics denoted an exercise in extremism. Some pamphlets added to their appeal with villainous portraits of Rhodes or Milner, or cartoons of Chamberlain, whose monocled countenance lent itself to caricature. The most scurrilous tended to be published anonymously. Few made any pretense to originality. Stead wrote a "Catechism for the Constituencies" in the manner of a Talmudic discourse, and Frank Harris contributed a playlet (*How to Beat the Boer*) in which six characters—George Washington, Samuel Johnson, Thomas Carlyle, Charles Stewart Parnell, Lord Randolph Churchill, and a stray Fenian—carry on "a conversation in Hades."

We cannot tell for certain how widely any pamphlet was read, by whom, and with what results. The people who published and circulated them enjoined readers to pass them on. Presuming their logic to be irresistible, they failed to consider the fact that "a pamphlet read is not necessarily a pamphlet accepted."[34] Although the different antiwar groups shared the same basic concerns and often distributed one another's literature, they concentrated their fire upon particular levels of society and chose their styles accordingly. The South Africa Conciliation Committee, as one would expect from the quality of its leadership, appealed to the intellect with arguments based on history and social theory: it was inclined to give the benefit of the doubt to Chamber-

34. Ibid., p. 112.

lain and his confederates, whom many of its members
knew personally. The Stop the War Committee appealed
unabashedly to the emotions, specializing in fiery rhetoric
and prognostications of divine retribution: it posited the
existence of shady dealings, financial and diplomatic, to
which Chamberlain was allegedly a party. Who is to say which
approach was the more effective?

VI

Social classes and professional groups did not necessarily
respond to the crisis as recent experience might encourage us
to expect. On this occasion, for example, university communities did not aspire to serve as consciences of their
society. With the extraordinary exception of the struggle
against Hitler's Germany, the Boer War probably commanded
unsurpassed acceptance among intellectuals. The fellows of
Oxford and Cambridge colleges showed little of the humanitarian zeal that their predecessors had demonstrated during
the 1876 Bulgarian agitation,[35] and there was none of the
pacifist sentiment that was found, at Cambridge especially,
during the First World War.[36] (That the war in South Africa
was fought on the basis of voluntary recruitment is admittedly significant, but does not itself explain the acquiescence
of the universities: British students have since demonstrated
vigorously against the American involvement in Vietnam,
for which they obviously stood no danger of conscription.)
When Morley or Campbell-Bannerman visited the university
towns, they addressed party meetings, not academic assemblies.
There was no undergraduate protest movement worthy of
the name, although some recent Oxford graduates (like

35. "Though the prevailing tone of the universities, especially
Oxford, was, not surprisingly, antagonistic to the agitation [of 1876],
the more strictly academic section of the intelligentsia did itself
fair justice in the list of conveners of the Eastern Question Conference." The participants included twenty-two fellows of Cambridge
colleges, twenty Oxford fellows, and nineteen professors from
outside Oxbridge. R. T. Shannon, *Gladstone and the Bulgarian
Agitation, 1876* (London, 1968), p. 220.

36. See G. H. Hardy, *Bertrand Russell and Trinity* (Cambridge,
1970).

Introduction

J. L. Hammond and F. W. Hirst) took an active part in
the national committees. There were, of course, dons who
emerged from their cloisters to oppose national policy (like
Gilbert Murray, the Oxford classicist), but their agency
was the Liberal Party. Those academics who brought the
war into their lectures or scholarship tended to be its
supporters: Karl Pearson, then Goldsmid professor of applied
mathematics and mechanics at University College, London,
justified the war as a step toward the fulfillment of a Dar-
winian plan;[37] and Professor J. A. Cramb, an historian at
King's College, London, exulted in "the intensification of
life" which was war's gift to man.[38] There is no evidence to
suggest that these teachings met with the least resistance.
At the Scottish universities, which boasted a long tradition
of training young men for imperial commerce and administration, students engaged with conspicuous ardor in such
extracurricular pursuits as breaking up pro-Boer meetings
and pillorying suspected subversives.[39]

Others, too, failed to behave in the manner of persons of
comparable status, before and since. All but a fraction of
Church dignitaries supported the war. Lord Rosebery had
assiduously cultivated the Nonconformists, who reciprocated
either by preaching imperialism (the Reverend Hugh
Price Hughes, the Methodist Boanerges, now thundered
against Kruger as he had once thundered against Parnell) or
by maintaining an uneasy silence.[40] There were of course Free
Churchmen, ministers, and lay officials, who decried the
sinfulness of national policy (like Dr. John Clifford, the

37. Bernard Semmel, *Imperialism and Social Reform* (London,
1960), p. 41.
38. A. P. Thornton, *The Imperial Idea and Its Enemies* (London,
1959), pp. 102–3. Cramb's response contrasts with that which
prevailed in his discipline in 1876, when J. R. Green thought it
"certainly well worth remarking that every conspicuous historian
in England goes with Gladstone." L. Stephen, ed., *Letters of
John Richard Green* (London, 1901), p. 466.
39. Reports from Aberdeen, Glasgow, and Dundee, quoted in
Richard Price, *An Imperial War and the British Working Class*
(London, 1972), pp. 150–53.
40. Elie Halévy, *A History of the English People in the
Nineteenth Century* (London, 1961), 5:104.

Baptist leader); but, again, they acted as individuals or as members of the Liberal rank and file, not as the spokesmen for an organized Nonconformity, which did not exist. The situation gradually changed, as we shall see particularly in the case of the Congregationalists, as the war dragged on and became discredited by its own methods.

Organized labor was, on the whole, equally belated in its response. Aside from certain left-wing militants, trade unionists did not range themselves against government policy until the war had ended, and the decision was taken to import Chinese indentured labor to work the Rand mines. At this point, and not before, trade unionists united to condemn the war as a conspiracy of the "Randlords" to obtain "Chinese slavery" and to depress wages.

There remains one other major interest group to consider, the largest in mass base and potential adherents. British feminists, pursuing more ambitious social and political goals, were the natural allies of those who opposed the war. This it not to suggest that a majority of the nation's women were either feminists or pacifists, but the two causes tended to find joint advocacy. Women's organizations, which cut across the horizontal lines of class, often revealed a tactical sense that was conspicuously absent elsewhere in the antiwar movement, as well as a welcome ability to relate the issues of the war to larger themes. The chief feminist contribution was in the person of Emily Hobhouse, who toured the ravaged areas of South Africa and then returned to describe the shocking conditions to countless audiences at home. Wilfrid Scawen Blunt, himself a celebrated traveller, sat next to her at a lunch given by Frederic Harrison: "She is an amiable middle-aged woman," Blunt wrote in his diary, "much persecuted on account of her action in the concentration camps. People are rude to her, refuse to shake hands, and they get up to go when she enters a drawing-room."[41] It is unlikely that the redoubtable Miss Hobhouse minded in the least these calculated insults, which only testified to the fact that she was taken seriously.

Emily Hobhouse belongs to the last phase of the war. More than any other individual, she publicized the "methods of

41. Entry for March 2, 1902, Blunt, *My Diaries* (London, 1919), 2:19.

barbarism"[42] that revitalized the Liberal Opposition and awakened the popular conscience. But these methods, however odious, soon brought victory. Britain had been a bully, perhaps an inefficient bully, but superior force ultimately prevailed. The pro-Boers had been unsuccessful first in their attempt to avert the war, then to stop it, and finally to effect any significant change in the way it was fought. What had they accomplished?

Their achievements, some perhaps difficult to recognize as such, were not immediate. On October 12, 1903, Lloyd George presciently advised C. P. Scott that "the work of the 'Pro-Boers' is only beginning."[43] Their influence was apparent in the spectacular Liberal victory of 1906 and in the party's reorientation thereafter. Campbell-Bannerman, without excluding the Liberal Imperialists, gave office to such veterans of the antiwar movement as John Morley, James Bryce, Sir Robert Reid (Lord Loreburn), Lloyd George, Lord Ripon, John Burns, Augustine Birrell, and L. V. Harcourt (Sir William's son). Bonds were forged during the Boer War, and suspicions were planted, that strongly influenced the course of Liberal politics for the next quarter century. To the end of their days, Liberal politicians

> were still to distinguish among themselves between those who had kept the pass and those who had sold it, between those who on public platforms had swayed patriotic audiences to enormous applause and those who had been compelled to duck out the back door of halls under police protection in order to escape the consequences of the righteous fury of the people, and their baying cry of "Pro-Boer."[44]

When the next war came in August, 1914, the pro-Boers (with a few obvious exceptions) reverted to type, to even less avail.

42. The phrase was Campbell-Bannerman's, used in a speech to the National Reform Union on June 14, 1901. A few days before, the Liberal leader had had a two-hour interview with Miss Hobhouse. Spender, *The Life of the Right Hon. Sir Henry Campbell-Bannerman, G.C.B.* (London, 1923), 1:335.

43. Quoted in Trevor Wilson, ed., *The Political Diaries of C. P. Scott, 1911–1928* (London, 1970), p. 29.

44. Thornton, p. 102.

It is tempting, but fundamentally a mistake, to think that the Boer War triggered an anti-imperial reaction. Like Dorian Gray in the Oscar Wilde story, the British Empire remained surprisingly vital; only its image was impaired. Indeed, one may argue that the war provided a stimulus to imperial cohesion in the areas of trade and defense. Despite their reputation, the overwhelming majority of pro-Boers had never sought to dismantle the Empire, merely to avoid the assumption of further burdens. They could therefore take satisfaction that the Empire survived, but that "its dynamic of self-confident expansion was dead,"[45] as Curzon soon learned when Whitehall put the brake on his Forward Policy in Tibet. In addition, by showing that Englishmen were not incapable of humanitarian impulses, the pro-Boers paved the way for a self-governing South Africa to return to the imperial fold.

At their best, the pro-Boers deserve credit for raising the level of popular debate; even at their worst, for widening its scope. They forced the British democracy, enfranchised but yet without a sense of self-esteem, to confront serious issues and to acknowledge a responsibility for actions taken in its name. They raised crucial questions about imperialism as a doctrine and a practice, about the priorities of patriotism, and about the demands of conscience. To be sure, they dissipated a good deal of energy and sometimes generated more resentment than enthusiasm. But they rendered honest service to principles of humanity and international justice, which, however inconvenient, ought never to be forgotten. It is hoped that the following selection from their writings (public and private) and speeches will provide a sense of the dynamics of their agitation, their competing activities and sometimes conflicting ambitions, the intellectual and social resources at their disposal, and the context in which they operated. Their dilemma must be perceived and understood as a product of the age to which they belonged. The reader may choose to ascertain a wider significance: that, of course, is the prerogative of any student of history.

45. Ibid., pp. 109–10; also Max Beloff, *Imperial Sunset* (New York, 1970), 1: 75–80.

Chronology of Events

1877	British government (Conservative) annexes the Transvaal.
1879	Zulu War.
1880	Outbreak of Anglo-Boer hostilities.
1881	
Feb.	Boer troops defeat British at Majuba Hill.
Aug.	British government under Gladstone restores qualified independence to the Transvaal.
1886	Discovery of gold in the Transvaal; Uitlanders flood in.
1895	
June	Unionist government takes office in Britain: Lord Salisbury, prime minister; Joseph Chamberlain, colonial secretary.
Dec.	Jameson launches his "Raid," surrenders on January 2, 1896. German emperor telegraphs congratulations to President Kruger of the Transvaal.
1897	Sir Alfred Milner appointed governor of the Cape and high commissioner for South Africa.
1898	Kruger re-elected president of the Transvaal.
1899	
May	Milner and Kruger meet at Blomfontein to negotiate differences. Talks broken off on June 6.
Aug.	Further negotiations. Chamberlain delivers an uncompromising speech at Birmingham on the twenty-sixth.
Oct.	54,000 signatures collected in Britain for a National Memorial Against War in the Transvaal. On the ninth, Kruger delivers his ultimatum (which expires on the eleventh), tantamount to a declaration of war.
Dec.	Boers defeat British attacks at Colenso, Stromberg, and Magersfontein, take offensive. Lord Roberts appointed commander-in-chief of British army in South Africa, Lord Kitchener his chief-of-staff.

1900

Feb.   Relief of British garrison at Kimberley.

March Roberts enters Blomfontein.

May   Relief of Mafeking.

Aug.   Kruger goes into exile.

Sept.   Transvaal is formally annexed.

Oct.   "Khaki" election in Britain returns Unionist majority.

Dec.   Roberts returns to England proclaiming that the war has been won. Guerilla warfare ensues.

1901

Jan.   Queen Victoria dies on the twenty-second.

Feb.- Boers consider Kitchener's terms; peace hopes rise.
March

Spring Circulation of reports on farm-burnings, concentration camps.

June   Sir Henry Campbell-Bannerman, Liberal Party leader, decries "methods of barbarism."

1902

May   Negotiations at Vereeniging with Boer commandos; treaty of peace signed on the thirty-first.

July   A. J. Balfour succeeds Salisbury as prime minister.

1903   Chamberlain resigns as colonial secretary.

1904   Chinese Labour Ordinance.

1905

Apr.   Milner leaves South Africa.

Dec.   Balfour resigns; Campbell-Bannerman forms a Liberal government.

1906

Jan.   Liberal landslide in general election.

Dec.   Transvaal constitution.

1907   Orange Free State constitution.

1910   Formation of the Union of South Africa.

THE PRO-BOERS

1: The Prospect of War

On March 24, 1899, nearly twenty-two thousand Uitlanders petitioned the Crown for the restitution of their rights as British subjects. Their appeal could not be ignored. "The spectacle," wrote Sir Alfred Milner, the high commissioner for South Africa,

> of thousands of British subjects kept permanently in the position of helots, constantly chafing under undoubted grievances and calling vainly to Her Majesty's government for redress, does steadily undermine the influence and reputation of Great Britain and the respect for the British Government within the Queen's Dominions.[1]

Milner opened negotiations with President Kruger at Blomfontein on May 31. There were varying expectations of what could be achieved. R. C. K. Ensor, who lived long enough to modify his pro-Boer judgments, nonetheless persisted in the view that Milner, at Blomfontein, was temperamentally unsuited to deal with "the Arcadian president; and after five days," notwithstanding contrary instructions from the home government, "he broke off the talks."[2]

The failure at the conference table galvanized Liberal back-benchers, publicists, and Nonconformist clergymen, who feared the imminence of war. On June 12, the Transvaal Committee was founded

> for the purpose of spreading accurate information by means of Lectures, Meetings, and circulation of Literature, &c., on the matters at issue between the two Governments, and to show that there was no question affecting the honour or interests of the Empire which called for War.

The chairman of the group was J. Passmore Edwards, a seventy-six-year-old former M.P. who had supported the Chartists, the anti-Corn Law campaign, and the agitation against the Crimean War; more recently, he had devoted his energies to the Anti-Gambling League and the Peace Society. The secretary, P. W. Clayden, was a veteran Radical journalist who was four years Edwards's junior. The treasurer was Dr. G. B. Clark, Liberal M.P. for Caithness.

1. Cd. 9345, no. 78.
2. *England, 1870–1914* (Oxford, 1963), p. 248.

The Transvaal Committee
Report of Six Months' Work   February 1, 1900

At a meeting of the Executive Committee of the Liberal Forwards, held at the Liberal Forwards Club on the 12th of June, 1899, a resolution was passed forming a Transvaal Committee "to watch the proceedings of the Colonial Office and to rouse public opinion to prevent a war between the British Empire and the Transvaal."

Mr. George W. E. Russell was appointed Chairman of the Committee, and Mr. Clayden and Mr. F. G. Thomas were authorised to address a circular to the Four Hundred members of the General Committee of the Liberal Forwards inviting them "to co-operate with the Committee to prevent a most wicked abuse of our national authority and power." The Executive Committee met again on the 13th of June, and determined that a meeting should be held in St. Martin's Hall, with Mr. Russell in the Chair "to protest against an aggressive policy in respect of the Transvaal." Meetings of the Committee were held on the 14th and 15th of June, at which a letter to the papers was drafted, pointing out that the policy of Mr. Chamberlain and Sir Alfred Milner was, even then, going straight to war, and appealing to the people of Great Britain "for such an unmistakeable expression of their will as shall render such a criminal policy impossible." The letter was signed by Mr. P. W. Clayden as Honorary Secretary of the Liberal Forwards, and was published in the leading newspapers all over the country. On the 21st of June a meeting of members of the Liberal Forwards Club was held after the House Dinner, under the chairmanship of Mr. C. P. Scott, M.P., "to consider the question of the Transvaal," and a resolution in favour of the Committee was adopted by a large majority.

The first Public Meeting was held in St. Martin's Hall on the 10th of July, Mr. George Russell in the Chair, "to protest against reckless threats of war with the Transvaal," at which

4

letters were read from many influential sympathisers, and which was addressed by Dr. Clark, M.P., Dr. Clifford, Mr. Molteno, Mr. Conybeare, Mr. H. J. Wilson, M.P., and Mr. W. M. Crook. The following resolution was passed:

> That this meeting, while desirous of obtaining for the Outlanders redress of their grievances by all legitimate means, condemns the reckless and mischievous attempts of a section of the Press and certain members of the British Government to force this country into war with the Transvaal.

The report of this meeting was issued as a pamphlet and very widely circulated. Meanwhile adhesions had come in so rapidly that a preliminary list of members of the Committee, containing more than 120 names, was affixed to the Report.

The success of the first meeting led to the holding of a large number of meetings in various parts of the country. At Manchester an independent Committee was formed which has carried on the Peace Movement with great industry and success in the whole North of England. In London the holding of a meeting in conjunction with the Bermondsey Labour League in Trafalgar Square was made the opportunity of organizing violent opposition, and the example was set of breaking up our meetings by organised violence. In spite, however, of the most unscrupulous misrepresentation in the Press and rowdyism in the street, a large number of meetings were held. Dr. Clark spoke in all parts of the country from Scotland to Devonshire, and at the invitation of the members of political clubs and other democratic organizations, lectures have been delivered, discussions conducted, and resolutions passed. . . .

An immense correspondence has been conducted. Letters are constantly received from sympathisers in various parts asking for information on special points, such as the taxation of the Uitlanders, the Native Question, the alleged Boer conspiracy and other subjects on which so much misrepresentation exists. The Committee in thus acting as an information bureau, has been able to afford valuable assistance to speakers and others, and indirectly to stimulate local efforts to further the cause of Peace.

The pro-Boer agitation was begun to champion the Boer cause at the conference table, not on the battlefield. The agitators were by no means inspired by the same motives: some wished to avoid war at all cost; others were more concerned with keeping public attention focused upon social problems at home; not least of all, there were those who sought to make political capital out of the government's predicament. These differences of emphasis, which were to work to the detriment of the pro-Boer movement, came to light at an early stage.

The Transvaal Committee
Report of a Public Meeting
in London, at St. Martin's Town Hall   July 10, 1899

. . . The Chairman, Mr. George W. E. Russell, said: We have been told by some of our sincere well-wishers that this meeting was out of date, and that by the time it was held all danger of war would be over. God grant that that may be the case. (Cheers.) As far as our present knowledge goes it will not do to reckon too confidently on that possibility. I remember very well that when the present Government was being formed, one of the most experienced politicians then in the House of Commons, who was leaving it and looking back over a long Parliamentary life, made to me this prediction: "I expect that this Government will go on pretty quietly for three or four years, and then at the end of that time, when they find their popularity waning, they will stir up a war in one part of the world or another." I have anticipated the fulfilment of that prediction during the last six months with great dread. There is no doubt that with regard to one member of the Cabinet that prophecy has come true, and that there is in the breast of a certain notorious politician an earnest desire to force matters in South Africa to what I may call advisedly a desperate conclusion. But, happily, we have no reason to suppose that this politician can lead his colleagues wheresoever he will. Lord Salisbury's love of peace, as his friends and admirers call it, or what I prefer to call Lord Salisbury's fear of a commotion, which made him so useless in the Græco-Turkish crisis, may possibly make him useful in the South African crisis. (Cheers.) It is to him and those in his Cabinet who adhere most closely to him that we must look for deliverance from the warlike machinations of those who have set their minds on a desperate solution of the matter. It is no part of my purpose to deny the existence of grievances that affect the Outlanders. I have not a sufficiently accurate and detailed knowledge of the life that is lived in the Transvaal to enable me to deny or to affirm that they labour under certain political disadvantages. At the same time, I would warn my friends against accepting unreservedly the heart-rending statements put forward in certain journals that are supposed to be under the influence of South African gold. Such statements must be taken with a grain of salt—with a good many grains of salt. Supposing, however, that the Outlanders labour under certain political disadvantages and difficulties, why are they there? They went to the Transvaal to please themselves. (Cheers.) They did not go with any commission from England, or in response to any invitation from the Government or the inhabitants of the Transvaal. They went—and nobody blamed them for so doing —to push their own fortunes and make money. And people who go to a foreign country simply to make money must expect to take the rough and the smooth together, and to accommodate themselves to the political conditions which they find in the home of their adoption. I dare say that the Polish Jews who come to make money in Whitechapel have good reason to complain of our Registration Laws. They have a perfect right to come. Yet it may take them several years to get on the Register. But if they were to invite the Czar to bombard London on that account, I think we should consider their action—to put it mildly—intemperate. I am far from saying the Outlanders have no right to protest or to agitate for political reform. (Hear, hear.) But I would have my hearers beware of the plausible appeals which have been made to democratic

7

sentiments and principles. These appeals, in respect of the
political hardships and grievances of our fellow-Englishmen
in the Transvaal, bear, in my opinion, a suspicious resem-
blance to the nauseous humbug about the peril of unprotected
women and children which was used to justify the infamous
and abortive Raid. (Cheers.) The advocates of war are pros-
tituting the sacred names of freedom and justice to glorify
money-getting and justify bloodshed. We protest against such
people monopolizing the name of patriot. We are the true
and real patriots. (Cheers.) We do not go swaggering about
the world like a company of mercenary swashbucklers, but we
are none the less patriotic on that account. Surely we have a
better claim to the title of patriots when we stand for the fair
fame of Christian England amongst the civilized nations of
the world. (Cheers.) Mr. Gladstone, speaking fifty years ago
on the subject of foreign policy, said: "When we are asking for
the maintenance of the rights which belong to our fellow-subjects resident abroad, let us do as we would be done by, and
let us pay that respect to a feeble State and to the infancy of
free institutions which we would desire and should exact from
others towards their maturity and their strength." Where Mr.
Gladstone stood in 1850 we stand now—for national faith and
honour against the frantic craving for unlimited extension
and against the yet more degraded and degrading lust of gold.
(Cheers.) In the face of our fellow-citizens we reaffirm our
unfaltering allegiance to those moral principles of political
action of which Mr. Bright once superbly said that "though
they were not given amid the thunders of Sinai they are not
less the commandments of God," nor less designed to promote
the happiness of the human family and the peace and welfare
of the world. (Loud cheers.) . . .

The Chairman: I now have pleasure in calling upon that
staunch friend of all good causes, Dr. [John] Clifford.

Dr. Clifford: . . . What is it that has created this crisis? First
of all it is asserted the Uitlanders have not got the franchise.
In a country like ours, is it necessary I should reply to that?
(No, no.) Half the people in this country have not got the
franchise. (Cheers.) And in my opinion the better half. (Loud

8

cheers.) Why don't we initiate an Amazonian fight—the fight of the women to get from men the franchise? (Loud cheers.) Instead of that you have your House of Lords voting against the admission of women to serve our city. I say this is a wrong to the city. (Cheers.) I do not put it on the ground of the rights of women, but I put it on the ground of the rights of the community. It is a crying wrong to reject good service from capable, cultured, trained, philanthropic, patriotic women. (Cheers.) For us to talk about starting a war for the Uitlanders while we keep women from the franchise in this country, is an absurdity complete and utter. (Cheers.) Then, again, who sent the Bishops and Archbishops to the House of Lords? Did you? (Cheers.) I had no share in it. (Cheers.) Lord Hugh Cecil suggests I should be made a peer. I do not want to be degraded. (Loud cheers and laughter.) If I went into a House of Parliament at all—(loud cheers)—I would enter it the elected representative of the people—(continued cheers)—and not because I was my father's son. Had you any part at all in sending Lord Salisbury to his present position? Who elected him to be practically king of this country? (A Voice: the Constitution.) Yes, the Constitution gave him his place in the House of Peers, but that House of Peers is not in the slightest degree representative of the people. It only speaks and acts for a fragment of them. It is a great grievance—the greatest grievance I have as a citizen. (Cheers.) If I wanted to get up a fight, it would be for the abolition straight away of the House of Lords. (Cheers.) It has been the patron of persecution. (Hear, hear.) It has been the nurse of intolerance, the mother of a thousand hindrances. I believe nothing has so much stood in the way of the real progress of the people as the House of Lords. (Loud cheers.) The Uitlanders' grievance is a mere flea bite to the grievance of having to bear with the obstinacy and stupidity of the House of Lords. (Hear, hear, and cheers.) Again, do you ever go through an election, any of you? What do you discover at such times? Man after man coming up to the Committee-room and saying, "Haven't I got a vote?" "Oh, no; you've changed your residence and lost it." Our registration laws are as great a grievance to the Britishers of this country, nay, a greater grievance than any the Uitlanders are suffering from. I am not airing this grievance for the sake of airing it, but for the sake of showing that the question in debate now is, whether this crisis in the Transvaal is to be settled by patience, by tact, by insight, by consideration, or by the brutal arbitrament of the sword. And I say, that if there is the slightest reason for using the sword on behalf of the Uitlanders, there is a thousand-fold more reason for using it on behalf of the Britishers. (Loud cheers.)

That there is a great deal of maladministration in the Transvaal, I have no doubt. I can imagine that the judiciary is not so effective as it should be— (hear, hear) —and that the police are open to bribes. (No.) But, the police of other towns —we will say nothing about London—did you ever hear anything about them. It really is too bad for these people to present these complaints as though they could only be dealt with by the sword; it is an indescribable wrong for Mr. Chamberlain to stir up ill-will by his menacing and irritating speeches: all that injustice ought to be got rid of in the Transvaal as we are getting rid of our injustices at home: by exposing each injustice, by debating it, and by bringing the people to see that the injustice is inimical to the entire welfare of the Empire. (A Voice: Republic, not Empire—the Transvaal.) This matter requires a great deal of patience. Patience is one thing that is wanted; consideration is the other. Look, for a moment, at the condition of things in the Transvaal during the last thirty or forty years. In Africa you have two races. You have more than two; but two in collision with one another—two civilizations in collision with one another. The Boer civilization has not yet reached the height of the nineteenth century civilization. You have, in addition to that, an inheritance of injustice, which is, I think, the greatest difficulty in connection with this problem. The Jameson Raid is spoken of by Mr. Chamberlain as having been atoned for; but you cannot atone for a wrong like that. Money won't do it. Diplomacy cannot remove it. Arbitration cannot extinguish it. (Hear, hear. A Voice: It was a mistake.) And supposing it was a mistake, the evil is done; you have created an injustice in

10

the Boer mind which will take centuries to wipe out. (Cheers.) What we have to do is to take care we solve the problem now in such a way that no sense of injustice shall be left behind. Then we shall have given stability to British power in South Africa; but if we inflict any injury in the process of solving this problem we shall imperil our own authority, and leave an evil which generations will not wipe out. What we ask for to-night, then, is patience and tact and justice to all interests concerned, so manifested by Her Majesty's Government that there shall not be left rankling in the hearts of the Boer people such a feeling of irritation as will make impossible the blending together of these two races, the harmonizing of these two peoples, already united by many bonds, and so they may march together in company with the rest of civilized peoples towards an era of justice, of liberty, of righteousness, and of universal well-being. (Loud cheers.)

[After further speeches, the resolution was put and carried unanimously "to protest against Reckless threats of War with the Transvaal." H. J. Wilson, M.P., and W. M. Crook, editor of the *Echo*, applauded the vote. Others were more qualified in their enthusiasm, articulating differences of opinion that were to divide the antiwar movement.]

Mr. Bourchier F. Hawkesley: I must apologise for rising at this late hour to address you on a motion which is always considered very much of a formality. I would like to say I came to this meeting, as my friend Mr. Crook came, to listen to the speakers at this meeting, which I understood from the notice was to protest against the threats of war. Such a protestation would have my most hearty support. I can only say that the last occasion on which I was in this hall was as one of the members of the Executive Committee of the International Crusade of Peace, and when I say this you will know I do not stand here as a Jingo. I listened to the speeches made in support of the resolution; but a very much wider meaning has been given to the meeting by the speeches we have heard from the introducer, and more especially the seconder, of what is usually a formal vote of thanks. I expected we should have

11

had other resolutions than the one which has taken up the whole of the time this evening. So far as that resolution is concerned it has my most hearty support; but I could not allow the report of a meeting which will be telegraphed to different parts of the world as a meeting of great influence held in the city of London, without explaining that the difficulty has arisen by the conduct of Her Majesty's Government. The Chairman and the speakers have admitted that there are grievances in the Transvaal, and I voted for the resolution; but we must not allow this meeting to conclude with the observations that were made, more particularly by my friend the editor of the *Echo*, who has gone very much further than the purpose for which this meeting was called. (Cries of "No!") I say he has. I repeat what I said just now—the difficulty does not arise from the troubles in the Transvaal, but from the conduct of Her Majesty's Ministers. We have no other means of dealing with a subject like this except by charging those persons who are responsible for the Government of this country. We are not brought to a crisis to-day because the Outlanders in the Transvaal presented a petition to Her Majesty. That was within their rights. But without warning of any kind we are suddenly plunged into a national crisis, because Her Majesty's Government has brought us into the difficulties we are in to-day. I have heard no single gentleman who has spoken to-night complain that our Ministers have allowed this thing to go on. That is where the trouble is. These despatches have been published over three weeks. That is where the trouble is. It would not be right—it would be unfair to those in the Transvaal who presented this petition if we closed this meeting without distinguishing, as we can do, between the trouble that has arisen and the merits of their case. At this late hour it is not for me to move a resolution, but I should like to support a strong vote of censure on Her Majesty's Government. During the last three weeks Mr. Chamberlain has explained. He went as far as man could go. He deliberately said that the proceeding of publishing these despatches was to press the matter on Her Majesty's Government.

It would then be a disastrous result if it were to go forth to South Africa that there had been a wholesale condemnation of the Outlanders' negotiation undistinguished from the action of Her Majesty's Government. We must not prejudice the rights of our citizens in the Transvaal. (Cheers.)

Mr. H. J. Wilson, M.P.: The original resolution carried unanimously by this meeting does condemn the reckless and mischievous attempts of certain Members of the British Government to force this country into a war with the Transvaal.

The Chairman: I do not think the proceeding is irregular. I know my friend Mr. Hawkesley too well to have expected a scathing accusation from his lips. Passing from this to the resolution, I will ask Mr. Crook to put it to the meeting.

The vote on being put was carried with acclamation.

The Chairman: I have only to thank you for that resolution, and for the speeches in which Mr. Wilson and Mr. Crook moved and seconded it in. I regard it as a high privilege to be allowed to preside over a meeting of this nature. We have been small in numbers, but enthusiastic in spirit. At any rate, if our meeting has done nothing else, it has given a great opportunity of registering a public protest against what we believe to be a moral abomination. (Cheers.) Mr. Crook was good enough to attribute to me what I hope is not a very uncommon quality among public men, that is, readiness to come forward in support of an unpopular cause. I hope I may lay claim to some share in that virtue, but I hope that I by no means monopolise it. I am surrounded by men on the platform who have fought for good and unpopular causes at home and abroad, many years before some of us attained man's estate. And now because I know one verse of a poet will linger in the mind of an audience long after prose remarks have died away into a well-deserved oblivion, I will give you a verse of Robert Browning:

Was it then all child's play, make-believe and mumming?
No, we battled it like men; not boylike sulked and whined:
Each of us heard clang God's "Come," and each was coming,
Soldiers all to forward face: not sneaks to lag behind.

13

During August and September, proposals and counterproposals proliferated. Any offer which seemed to promise a settlement was retracted, allowing each side to impute bad faith to the other. There was growing British opinion that force was the only remedy, to which John Morley replied in a speech to his constituents.

John Morley

Speech at Arbroath   September 5, 1899

You will have sown the seeds of division between the Dutch and the English in Cape Colony... [and] by the conflict between the two races of the whites . . . you will have—indeed some say you already have—stirred up a spirit of restlessness among the native population of South Africa, and, considering their vast superiority in number and the horrors of war between the white races and these Kaffirs, you cannot exaggerate the mischief of such a proceeding as that. . . .

Suppose you win in this conflict, you will have to set up a government which will be Ireland all over again, with what is called a loyal district, and outside of that an enormous territory . . . saturated with sullen disaffection. . . .

They will tell you tomorrow morning that I am pro-Boer. . . . I do not believe there can be greater difference in temperament, in pursuits, in tastes, in beliefs, than there are between the Boers and the very humble individual who is now addressing you. It is not for the sake of the Transvaal Republic alone, it is for the sake of South Africa, and it is for our own sake.

The Times, *September 6, 1899*

On September 8, Chamberlain made a last, conciliatory offer to Kruger. Although it was warmly received by leaders of the Cape Dutch, who served as intermediaries, it failed to impress the more truculent of the government's opponents at home. The National Administrative Council of the Independent Labour Party met at Blackburn the next day, and among those present were J. Keir Hardie, chairman, France Littlewood, J. Bruce Glasier, Philip Snowden, and J. Ramsay MacDonald. The following resolution was passed.

National Administrative Council
of the Independent Labour Party
Resolution adopted at Blackburn   September 9, 1899

The National Administrative Council of the I.L.P. protests against the manner in which the Government, by the tenor of their dispatches and their warlike preparations, have made a peaceful settlement difficult with the Transvaal Republic.

The policy of the Government can be explained only on the supposition that their intention has been to provoke a war of conquest to secure complete control in the interests of unscrupulous exploiters.

A war of aggression is, under any circumstances, an outrage on the moral sense of a civilised community and in the present instance particularly so, considering the sordid character of the real objects aimed at.

It is especially humiliating to the democratic instincts of this country that an ulterior and unworthy motive should be hidden under the pretence of broadening the political grievances of the Uitlanders. Even if the admitted grievances of the Uitlanders were the real reason of the threatened hostilities, war would be an extreme course quite uncalled for.

We also protest against the action of the press and the bulk of the leading politicians in strengthening the criminal conduct of the Government by misleading the public and rousing the passion for war, and we express the hope that it may not yet be too late for the manhood of the nation to prevent this outrage upon the conscience of our common humanity.

Quoted in William Stewart, J. Keir Hardie
(London, 1925), pp. 150–51

Morley, having broken his silence to address his constituents on the fifth, was as yet unwilling to associate himself formally with the gathering pro-Boer forces. For much of the previous year, he had been sequestered at the Red House on the Gladstone estate at Hawarden, where he was writing a mammoth biography of his old chief. F. W. Hirst, his young research assistant, urged him to accept an invitation from the Transvaal Committee to speak at a Manchester rally, but Morley distrusted C. P. Scott and L. T. Hobhouse, who organized the meeting, "as impractical and too fanatical."[1] Morley eventually acceded to the request, and provided an "epistolary version" of his impressions, including a snatch from his peroration.

John Morley

Transvaal Committee rally
at Manchester   **September 15, 1899**

We reached Manchester towards five. Friends met us, not less uneasy than I was, for the very different reason of apprehension lest the enemy should insist that any words the Lord might put into my mouth should not come out therefrom. The war party had publicly advertised and encouraged attempts to smash the meeting, and young men were earnestly exhorted in patriotic prints at least for one night to sacrifice their billiards and tobacco, for the honour of their native land. The huge St. James's Hall was packed as it never had been packed before. Aggressive music of various kinds was loud. The Chairman was Bright's eldest son, but not a word was he allowed to utter by an audience of between eight and ten thousand people. Then my turn came, and for ten minutes more I had to face the same severe ordeal. At length they allowed me for an instant to launch the single, wholly indisputable truth in my whole budget, namely, that I was a Lancashire man. This talisman proved my salvation. After an hour of a judicious mixture of moderation, breadth, good temper, with a slight guarded Lancastrian undertone of defiance, which they rather liked than resented, I sat down amid universal enthusiasm. The grand potent monosyllable with which I wound up was not to be resisted. "You may carry fire and sword into the midst of peace and industry: it will be wrong. A war of the strongest government in the world with untold

1. For Hirst's strenuous exertions and his account of the Manchester proceedings, see his diary entries for September 8, 11, 14, and 15, 1899, quoted in *In the Golden Days* (London, 1947), pp. 179–80, 183–84.

wealth and inexhaustible reserves against this little republic will bring you no glory: it will be wrong. You may make thousands of women widows, and thousands of children fatherless: it will be wrong. It may add a new province to your empire: it will still be wrong. You may give buoyancy to the African stock and share market: it will still be wrong," etc. etc. Courtney, who was only a Cornishman, came next, and made up for his sadly defective place of origin by a strong dish of sound arguments, spiced with the designation of Milner as "a lost mind."

The audience slowly poured itself away—both sections much mystified, one because they had been ruefully prepared for the wicked triumph of physical force, and lo! physical force was on their side as well as moral, and even oratorical force; the other because they had found a wholly unexpected quietus. Well may Carlyle talk of the unspeakable importance of man to man, though he spoils it by the qualification that the cry of a million voices is nothing; it is the response of the individual soul gives force and encouragement. True, true, but if, unlike Carlyle, you have something definite to get done, the cry of the million voices is by no means nothing. We had a railway journey to Chester, then in a slow horse-drive in sousing rain to our Red House at Hawarden, where we found a welcome meal. And so to bed at 1 A.M. with a really clear conscience.

Morley, Recollections *(New York, 1917), 2: 86–87*

Despite his reluctance to grace public platforms, Morley was as vehement as any pro-Boer in his private correspondence. "The guilty man is Milner, who has flung himself, before Kruger's very eyes, into the arms of the British jingoes at the Cape," he wrote to Lord Spencer.[1] Perhaps Morley's most emphatic, if least direct, contribution to the pro-Boer agitation was W. T. Stead, whom he had brought to the metropolis in 1880 as assistant editor of the *Pall Mall Gazette*. In 1890, Stead inaugurated his *Review of Reviews*,

1. Morley to Spencer, September 18, 1899, Earl Spencer Papers, Althorp.

an idiosyncratic blend of reporting and commentary. A complex personality, he boasted many improbable friendships, Cecil Rhodes and the Czar of Russia among them. With violent rhetoric that often stung his friends as much as his enemies, he championed a wide range of unpopular causes before he drowned in the *Titanic* disaster of 1912.

Shall I Slay My Brother Boer?
An Appeal to the Conscience of Britain
Preface

I have returned from a prolonged sojourn at the Hague, where the representatives of all the Powers were busily engaged in making provision for the preservation of the World's Peace.

I find my own country ringing from end to end with preparations for War.

I ask—Why?

For answer I am confronted with a weltering chaos of despatches, and my ears are deafened by the familiar bray of Jingo journalism.

But I have sought in vain for any statement, clear, precise, and universally accessible, setting forth soberly and seriously within the compass of a readable pamphlet, of the case either for or against an appeal to the *ultima ratio* of Nations.

As no one has yet produced such a pamphlet, I have perforce set my hand to the work.

This *brochure* is the result.

I am painfully conscious of its defects, but I venture to believe that it does at least bring into strong relief some of the considerations which should dominate the decision of a Nation suddenly called upon to confront the supreme issue of Peace or War.

September 21st, 1899   WILLIAM T. STEAD

•   •   •   •

Chapter II
A BRITISH DREYFUS CASE

The conscience of the whole civilised world has cried out in indignant unison against the travesty of justice which has just been witnessed at Rennes.

But the case of Dreyfus is but as the parable of the ewe-lamb, by which the prophet Nathan brought home to the Hebrew monarch a sense of his far more exceeding guilt.

"Thou art the man!" cried the ancient prophet to King David. "Thou art the man!" the accusing voice of Humanity will thunder in the ears of John Bull, if he should carry out, what seems his present intention, of making war on the Transvaal on pretexts compared with which those of the Court-martial at Rennes were respectable.

Dreyfus, like the Boer, belonged to an unpopular race. Personally, he appears to have been somewhat bumptious. Like the Transvaal, he was tried by a tribunal strongly prejudiced against him, and his conviction was obtained by the same unblushing appeals to national passion and self-interest which are relied upon in our press for hounding this nation into war.

In Mr. Chamberlain we have the General Mercier of the situation.

The verdict at Rennes condemned an innocent individual to save the honour of the French army.

If we go to war with the Transvaal, we condemn to death a State to save the prestige of the Jingoes who degrade the cause of British Imperialism by their savage determination to avenge Majuba.

The Court-martial at Rennes was not the first Court that tried Dreyfus. Neither is the present crisis the first attempt on the Transvaal.

The first attempt on the Transvaal was made three years ago, when Mr. Rhodes, with the full cognizance of Mr. Chamberlain, aided and abetted the conspiracy to overthrow the Boer Republic. This, like the first Court-martial which condemned Dreyfus, was a comparatively venial mistake, an error of judgment for which much excuse may be made.

In the ridiculous farce of the hushing-up committee at Westminster we had the counterpart of the Zola trial, which, although it concluded in a false verdict, nevertheless enlightened the world as to the complicity of Mr. Chamberlain and the Colonial Office in the attempt on the Transvaal.

The whole civilised world with unanimity execrated the miscarriage of justice which led to the condemnation of M. Zola.

But there was almost as universal a howl of execration from the press outside Great Britain at the way in which the South African Committee conspired to suppress evidence and to whitewash Mr. Chamberlain. The conscience of the civilised world was revolted by such a travesty of "investigation."

The verdict at Rennes of guilty with extenuating circumstances had its exact counterpart in the censure pronounced by the South African Committee on Mr. Rhodes, qualified by the extraordinary speech by Mr. Chamberlain in defence of the man whom, as member of the Committee, he had just condemned.

The refusal to take the evidence of Colonel Schwarzkoppen and Colonel Panizzardi is paralleled by the refusal to produce the incriminating cables, and the astounding and scandalous refusal to allow Mr. Hawkesley to give evidence which would have exposed the whole conspiracy.

Then in the fulness of time, the Transvaal has been again arraigned, and is being led forth for execution by no impartial tribunal, but by the very man, our own General Mercier, whom every Boer believes—not without reason—to have been privy to the conspiracy of 1895, and who has the strongest personal reasons for wishing to settle old scores with President Kruger.

Lying, perjury, and all the hideous offences against justice which we have been denouncing when they occurred in France, were rife before the South African Committee.

And the proposed war on the Transvaal is but the sequel to that disastrous and scandalous episode in our South African history.

Those who do not know or have forgotten the facts will howl at this plain statement of the analogy between the case of Dreyfus and that of the Transvaal. But the fact that outside the British Empire its justice will be universally admitted, should at least give the most heedless pause, and suggest grounds for a very careful examination of the facts of the case on which we are being rushed into war. Let us remember that the judgment of foreigners often anticipates the judgment of posterity.

It may be hoped that, inasmuch as the first Dreyfus case was brought to a close after a long series of scandalous miscarriages of justice by the full, free and unsolicited pardon of the innocent accused, so we may anticipate that, even at the eleventh hour, the conscience of this country may awake, and the Prime Minister of the Queen will remove from the national escutcheon a stain as foul as that by which the Dreyfus case sullied the fair fame of France.

On behalf of the Transvaal Committee, F. Reginald Statham wrote pamphlets and delivered public lectures. The author of several books on South Africa, where he had made his home, he was well equipped to describe conditions there. Selling for a penny, his *Truth About the Transvaal* ran through three editions before the outbreak of war. On September 25, he spoke at Newport in Monmouthshire.

F. Reginald Statham
Lecture at the Temperance Hall,
Newport, Monmouthshire   **September 25, 1899**

My object is to show you the way in which South Africa, which Mr. Gladstone's policy left peaceful, prosperous, and fairly on the road towards political union, has, by successive steps, . . . been made the prey of as wicked and corrupt a conspiracy as ever disgraced—or let us rather say came nearer to disgracing—the history of an Empire. . . . Mr. Alfred Beit and Mr. Cecil Rhodes were in search of new worlds to conquer. What they aimed at, what they are still aiming at, was the complete control of South Africa, including, of course, those Transvaal goldfields which, in 1888, were revealing their value. The Transvaal, however, could not be attacked all at once. The first step was to obtain a political footing in South Africa by getting hold of the interior. . . . Backed by the Rothschilds, Messrs. Beit and Rhodes went to the Government of the day

—it was a Tory Government—with a request to have handed over to them the whole interior of South Africa that lay within the British 'sphere of influence.' Their request, astonishing as the thing will seem to future historians, was granted. The whole 'hinterland' of South Africa was made over to Messrs. Beit and Rhodes, the only stipulation being that, presumably to reconcile English opinion to the step, two or three Dukes were to be thrown in as ornamental directors. Just consider for a moment the extraordinary nature of the step taken in the granting of the Charter to the British South Africa Company. . . . By a stroke of the pen, and with the assistance of two or three ornamental Dukes, this hinterland was absolutely given away to a brace of speculators, one of whom was at the time not even a British subject. Is it possible to imagine a more abject piece of folly, a more outrageous violation of all the principles of statesmanship and common sense? . . .

Here, then, was Mr. Rhodes, the political partner in the great conspiracy, placed in the position of a South African dictator. Look at the enormous strength of his position. As Premier of the Cape Colony he controlled the acts of the Governor. As Premier of the Cape Colony, and through the same Governor, acting in his capacity of High Commissioner, he controlled the policy of the Imperial Government. . . . For the very best man in the world such a position as this would be dangerous. How dangerous, then, when filled by an ambitious and scheming millionaire—a millionaire whose complete political failure, or even disgrace, would still leave him completely at liberty to enjoy all the advantages of a luxurious personal existence.

Reprinted as South Africa and the Transvaal
(London: The Transvaal Committee, 1900)

The *Manchester Guardian*, itself a staunch opponent of government policy, dutifully kept its readers informed of public statements and resolutions on the subject of the South African crisis. The listing for September 28, perhaps weighted on the antiwar side, typically reflected the divisions that had begun to crystallize during that week.

Manchester Guardian   **September 28, 1899**

The Master of Balliol has written a letter to Mr. Stead to acknowledge the receipt of his pamphlet "Shall I Slay My Brother Boer?" in which he says: "I cordially sympathise with you in the object of your efforts, for while I think we should be careful not to underestimate the wrongs of the Outlanders or to relax efforts for their redress, I believe that such a war would [be] both a crime and a blunder."

At a meeting yesterday of the executive of the Liverpool Evangelical Free Church Council the following resolution was passed: "That whilst desiring redress of the grievances of British residents in the Transvaal, the Council believes that the causes of discontent are all capable of being adjusted by pacific means, and are of a character that afford no justification for war. The Council is also of opinion that for two Christian nations to resort, under such circumstances, to hostilities would be a scandal upon Christianity, a deep and widespread injury to religion, and a source of enduring racial bitterness and animosity. The Council therefore strongly and most earnestly appeals to Her Majesty's Government to employ every method which negotiation and arbitration can devise to prevent the nations being plunged unto war, that must inevitably be calamitous and patricidal to both the contending Powers." The resolution, which is signed by Mr. Thomas Snape, president, and Mr. H. T. Spencer, honorary secretary, has been forwarded to Lord Salisbury, Mr. Balfour, and Mr. Chamberlain.

At a Council Meeting of the Manchester and District Liberal Unionist Association, held yesterday at the Memorial Hall, in this city, the following resolution was adopted: "That the Council of the Manchester and District Liberal Unionist Association desire to express their hearty approval of the wise and patient efforts of Her Majesty's Government to obtain by peaceful means the redress of the grievances of our fellow countrymen and others in the Transvaal. That in the opinion of the Council the action of the self-styled 'Peace party' can only result in misleading the Boers into the belief that the

Government is not supported by an overwhelming majority in this country, and thus make it increasingly difficult to obtain a speedy, complete, lasting, and peaceful solution of the present intolerable situation. That the Council desire further to assure Her Majesty's Government of their unabated confidence and continued support in whatever steps may be found necessary to finally remedy the long-standing differences with the Transvaal Government."

Mr. Edward Nicholls, the prospective Conservative candidate for the Accrington division, addressed a Primrose League meeting at Accrington last evening. Referring to the Transvaal crisis, he declared that if war ensued between us and the Boers the responsibility would lie not with the British Government but with the Boers, who had undoubtedly been totally misled as to the feeling in this country by remarks from unpatriotic statesmen, such as Sir W. Harcourt and Mr. John Morley, who by no means represented the sentiment of the vast bulk of the people of this country. No true patriot could doubt the righteousness of the attitude of this country.

The following resolution has been passed by the executive of the Halifax Liberal Association: "That this executive of the Liberal Association of Halifax condemns the manner in which the present Government is dealing with the Transvaal difficulty, believing that the difficulties existing between the two countries could be settled by arbitration, thereby avoiding war, for which they consider there is not sufficient justification."

One of the constant objectives of pro-Boer propaganda was to dispel the popular impression of the Boers as a nation of shrewd manipulators, determined to hoard their fantastic wealth. The real enemy was to be found not in the Boer settlements, where thrift and hard work were the rule, but in Johannesburg, that mecca for all the sins of modernity, where iniquity and corruption were rife. "Monte Carlo

24

superimposed upon Sodom and Gomorrah" was how one Cape politician pungently put it.[1]

J. A. Hobson, soon to establish his reputation with a classic treatise on *Imperialism* (1902), went to South Africa as special correspondent for the *Manchester Guardian*. His dispatches, which foreshadowed his subsequent theories, were distinguished by literary merit, comparatively restrained in their anti-semitic sentiments, but otherwise typical of the view that was taken.

Johannesburg Today

Manchester Guardian   September 28, 1899

After one has been travelling for a thousand miles through a bare and desolate country in which no single human settlement, with the solitary exception of Bloemfontein, the Free State capital, can even pretend to be a town, Johannesburg, the golden city of Africa, with its 80 miles of streets and its hundred thousand inhabitants, makes a powerful impression. It offers a weird mixture of civilisation and savagedom. Laid out in leisurely fashion, with broad and ample streets, where a handsome stone building breaks occasionally the meagre and ugly effect of hastily improved shop fronts and boarding houses, it has the potentiality of a splendid modern city of the Paris or Vienna order. There is plenty of room in Africa, and no inducement to overcrowding. In fact Johannesburg covers an immense area, reaching out its tentacles on every side and wearing the long gold reef, the Witwatersrand, with its mining villages, as a sort of long flapping tail. The entire city is the product of thirteen years' growth, and the amount of energy put into this little stretch of thirty miles of gold reef has been prodigious. Even at the present moment of slackness and depression, when gloom and terror hang over the place, all business is suspended, and the gaiety and social licence of the

1. Quoted in Sir William Butler, *An Autobiography* (London, 1913), p. 415.

town suffer a total eclipse, the outward signs of multifarious enterprise cannot fail to strike a stranger. Here, seven thousand miles from England, in the heart of a Republic of rude farmers of Dutch descent, grows up in a single decade a great city which, so far as the language and habits of the white population is concerned, is almost absolutely English. In Johannesburg the Boer population is a mere handful of officials and their families, some five thousand of the population; the rest is about evenly divided between white settlers, mostly from Great Britain, and the Kaffirs, who are everywhere in White Man's Africa the hewers of wood and drawers of water. The town is in some respects dominantly and even aggressively British, but British with a difference which it takes some little time to understand. That difference is mostly due to the Jewish factor. If one takes the recent figures of the census, there appears to be less than seven thousand Jews in Johannesburg; but the experience of the streets rapidly exposes this fallacy of figures. The shop fronts and business houses, the market place, the saloons, the "stoops" of the smart suburban houses are sufficient to convince one of the large presence of the chosen people. If any doubt remains, a walk outside the Exchange, where in the streets, "between the chains," the financial side of the gold business is transacted, will dispel it. So far as wealth and power and even numbers are concerned Johannesburg is essentially a Jewish town. Most of these Jews figure as British subjects, though many are in fact German and Russian Jews who have come to Africa after a brief sojourn in England. The rich, rigorous, and energetic financial and commercial families are chiefly English Jews, not a few of whom here, as elsewhere, have Anglicised their names after true parasitic fashion. I lay stress upon this fact because, though everyone knows the Jews are strong, their real strength here is much underestimated. Though figures are so misleading, it is worth while to mention that the directory of Johannesburg shows 68 Cowens against 21 Joneses and 53 Browns. The Jews take little active part in the Outlander agitation; they let others do that sort of work. But since half of the land and nine-tenths of the wealth of the Transvaal claimed for the

Outlander are chiefly theirs, they will be chief gainers by any settlement advantageous to the Outlander.

In ordinary times Johannesburg is a strong type of modern cosmopolitan civilisation, with some of its good and all its bad features. Of its extraordinary wealth and reckless luxury signs exist everywhere. Saloons, gambling halls, and other dens of vice abound, while only two years ago the prize ring of Johannesburg was the most famous in the world and had a virtual monopoly of the best talent. That the best society is very mixed it is needless to add when one remembers that a very few years has drawn from all quarters of the globe adventurous men and women in search of gold. That there are many sound and solid business men and their families, especially among the engineering and professional classes, men of grit and force of character as well as of business capacity, may well be admitted. But the strange taint of gold lust—*auri sacra fames*—everywhere pervades the atmosphere and dominates the life even of the shopkeeping and professional classes. Gambling in mining shares is well-nigh universal. I am assured that half the Cornish miners are always dabbling in them, seeking to make their thrift as profitable as they can by watching the market. Lotteries, horse-racing, and gambling of every sort are prevalent and absorbing pastimes. These, of course, are generally statements which are applicable to many places; but there can be no manner of doubt that the conditions under which this golden city has arisen have made it one of the most terrible haunts of greed, gambling, and every form of depravity which the world has ever seen. There are of course qualities which balance, screen, and in some eyes perhaps redeem the character of such a place. Never have I been so struck with the intellect and the audacious enterprise and foresight of great business men as here. Nor are these qualities confined to the Beits and Rudds and the other great capitalists: the town bristles and throbs with industrial and commercial energy: the bracing physical atmosphere (Johannesburg stands 6,000 feet above the sea) has marvellous tonic influences to evoke and stimulate mental energy. Everyone seems alert and tense, eager to grasp the skirts of some happy chance and raise himself, as he has seen some scores of others no better than himself raised to sudden affluence. The utter dependance upon financial "booms" and "slumps" conjoined with the strain and kaleidoscopic changes of the political situation, have bred by selection and by education a type of man and of society which is as different from that of Manchester as the latter is from the life of Hankow or Buenos Ayres.

All this stands on an external basis of picturesque savagery. The essentially serf civilisation of South Africa is represented by the prevalence of Kaffir or Zulu servants: all the hard manual labour is done by them, and strange flashes of savagedom give piquancy to the street life: as, for instance, the habit of Kaffirs, grotesquely painted and decorated, dashing through the streets harnessed to light rickshaws, carrying daintily dressed English ladies to evening parties. Ordinary street life is indeed a babel of races and tongues, not only the European languages, but the voices of Hindoos, Chinamen, Malays chime in with the various Kaffir dialects. The Boer, who is supposed in some obscure way to be the proprietor of the country, makes very little show. He is officially represented by the policeman or zarp (a word-composition of the initial letters of the Dutch words for "South African Republic police"), an innocent lump of stolidity who stands at the street corner. If you want to see the real Boer you have to get up early and visit the market. There you find him *in propria persona*, often with his family, and always with his waggon and team of oxen, with which he has brought his farm produce to market: often travelling a hundred miles and taking several days and nights on his patient journey, sleeping by night in a sort of upper loft of his waggon, by day tramping along with his team or smoking on the waggon seat while his Kaffir boy leads the oxen. Many scores of these Boers you can see any morning as the auctioneer is wheeled round the market and stops before each waggon to sell the produce. There is no mistake about the physical prowess of these men: almost to a man they are tall, strong limbed, and vigorous, with strong, calm, enduring faces, men difficult to dislodge from any position they have taken in bargain or in battle. These are the sons of the country: their fathers con-

28

quered and brought the land under rude cultivation and control: yet almost their only real connection with this treasure-centre of their land is these brief early morning visits to the market where they sell their farm produce to the horde of foreigners who are living in luxury upon the natural wealth they extract (through Kaffir labour) from the strip of land on which they settle. They take no part whatever either as capitalists, miners, professional men, or shopkeepers, in this curious scramble, but only pay these early morning calls with their oxen and drive back again.

Leonard Courtney, who had shared the platform with Morley at Manchester, was one of those anomalies who contributed to the richness of late Victorian political life. Along with Joseph Chamberlain and others, he had quit the Liberal Party when Gladstone took up the cause of Home Rule for Ireland; but, unlike most Liberal Unionists, he remained firmly wedded to traditional Liberal tenets.

That Courtney was a Liberal Unionist, a member of Chamberlain's own party, only enhanced his stature among the pro-Boers, who were overwhelmingly Liberals and Home Rulers. C. P. Scott, editor of the *Manchester Guardian* and member for Leigh, had helped to organize the meeting at Manchester on the fifteenth, and valued Courtney's participation.

C. P. Scott to Leonard Courtney   **October 6, 1899**

You seek nothing, you want nothing, but to help your country, and in the House and in the Country, everybody trusts your great knowledge as well as experience, and you are one of the rare men whose motives are never doubted. Am I not right in calling that a unique position?

Courtney Papers

Unfortunately, Courtney's Liberal Unionism worked to his distinct disadvantage among his Cornish constituents at Liskeard, the vast majority of whom were puzzled to see him consorting with his former political allies and allegedly betraying Chamberlain, the Liberal Unionist leader. Courtney journeyed to Liskeard on October 11 for a prearranged speech the next day that was intended to allay feeling against him. His task was made more difficult, if not impossible, by the publication that morning of Kruger's ultimatum, couched in the strongest language, which signaled the outbreak of war.

Courtney's wife, Kate, accompanied him to Liskeard. Like her sister, Mrs. Sidney Webb, she kept a diary. "What a moment to make a speech!" she recorded on the eleventh. The next day, she witnessed the chilly reception given her husband by his constituents.

Mrs. Leonard ("Kate") Courtney's diary   October 12, 1899

L. speaks for an hour and a half without recourse to a note, full of argument, reason, passion, and pathos. Impressed but did not turn his hearers, I think. He had refused to accept a simple vote of confidence, to be followed by a resolution in support of the war. The Resolution of confidence and regret at war was lost. L. made a touching little speech acknowledging the gravity of a vote against him at Liskeard, and the meeting broke up with no signs of exultation. Our nearest friends were much distressed; but though mortified I have great thankfulness that he was able to stand up so grandly for right at this moment when others are throwing up the sponge. And I must admit to feeling relief that the Conservatives have broken from him.

> *Quoted in G. P. Gooch,* Life of Lord Courtney
> *(London, 1920), pp. 381, 383*

If nothing else, Courtney had the sympathy of other pro-Boers, but few of them risked their reputations or their seats as he did.

F. A. Channing, M.P., to Leonard Courtney   October, 1899

You have behaved nobly and your constituents will recognise it soon. Do not hastily—even if worse things befall—give up your seat. In these wishy-washy times, when every timid timeserver has a sponge in hand to wipe off the truth if inconvenient, men of conscience and character who are in the House must stop there. No Liberal vote anyhow should ever be cast against a man like you.

Quoted in G. P. Gooch, Life of Lord Courtney
(London, 1920), p. 383

2:Partisans and Publicists

The dissenters on the Government benches were few and no threat to their nominal leaders. The situation was far different among the Liberals, who were savagely divided on matters of basic policy. The Liberal Imperialists, followers of Lord Rosebery, dismissed the pro-Boers within their party as inconsequential. R. B. Haldane cautioned Lord Milner not to "think that because of Harcourt's and Morley's speeches it is to be taken that Liberals as a whole have misunderstood your policy. On the contrary I am satisfied that four-fifths of our people really follow and assent to it."[1]

The *Westminster Gazette* took a moderate Liberal Imperialist line. Its editor was J. A. Spender, who, like H. H. Asquith and Sir Edward Grey, was a product of Balliol College, Oxford. Milner, too, was educated there.

Westminster Gazette (leader)   **October 12, 1899**

For the moment, the Boer ultimatum has salved uneasy consciences and rendered the discussion of alternative courses futile. Liberals, no more than Conservatives, need quarrel among themselves about what might have been. The momentary duty is to support the Government in making the inevitable expedition as prompt and effective as possible.

Spender's tempered injunctions could not be expected to register an effect upon W. T. Stead, the antithesis of what was popularly regarded as "the Balliol mind."

W. T. Stead
Speech at Westminster Chapel   **October 15, 1899**

The real root question which underlies everything, and of which this present trouble in the Transvaal is but a symptom, is the question whether or not we believe that there is a God who judgeth in the earth, who loves righteousness, and who abhors a lie. The whole of our trouble in the Transvaal springs out of the deliberate conviction, frankly expressed and un-

1. Haldane to Milner, Milner Papers, Bodleian Library, Oxford.

hesitatingly acted upon, that this is not true, and that it is sometimes good policy to tell a lie and stick to it. Knowing that we are going forth to battle with a lie in our right hand, I tremble as to the result.... I know that in this matter I am as a voice crying in the wilderness. I know that in the present moment of passion and fury, when passion is excited, and the streets ring with the cheers for the soldiers going to fight in this unholy quarrel, my voice will hardly be heard. But mark my words; if I am right we shall not have long to wait before we shall find that God is not dead, neither is He asleep; and if, as I believe, He loves this England of His, and this people of His, although but a small remnant are still faithful to Him, then, as upon Israel of old when they sinned and went in opposition to the Divine will, will descend disaster after disaster, until we turn from lying and all these evil ways into the paths of justice and truth.

> *Quoted in Stead*, Joseph Chamberlain:.
> Conspirator or Statesman?
> *(London, 1899), p. 3*

Nor could Spender have expected his words to be heeded by Irish Nationalist M.P.'s, who, despite their fierce differences, promptly identified themselves with the Boers as common victims of Anglo-Saxon oppression. Michael Davitt, who flaunted a reputation for extremism, put his case to a preponderantly hostile House of Commons.

Michael Davitt
Speech in the House of Commons   **October 17, 1899**

.... In conclusion, Mr. Speaker, I have spoken amidst some interruption, but I make no complaint. I recognise I am speaking in an alien assembly. I am called a traitor by the hon. Member for West Belfast who is not in his place, and by the London *Times*, because my sympathy goes out to a small nation of your own blood and faith, whom you intend to rob of its independence; because I side with a people less in number than the population of Birmingham, in a contest forced upon them by the Member for Birmingham [Chamberlain] in the name ... of the British Empire. Very well, if that is to be a traitor, then I feel more honoured in the title than if I were called the Colonial Secretary of a Government who will have the blood of a brave race and of your own soldiers upon his head. I have not, however, a monopoly of the title "traitor." The honour can be shared by no less a person than the central figure in this war tragedy, the Secretary of State for the Colonies, whom his present nominal chief, the Prime Minister, once termed a Jack Cade. This historic personage was both a traitor and a reputed robber, and yet the statesman whom the Marquess of Salisbury likened to Jack Cade is now the jingo hero of the hour. I find myself, therefore, in most distinguished company. It is only the other day that a present Prime Minister of the Queen was referred to as follows by the *Sun* newspaper, owned, I believe, by an hon. Member opposite:

> Mr. Schreiner, Cape Premier and Boer Agent, will be lucky if he does not hang from a Cape Town lamp-post before long. That would be a justifiable form of elevation for him, one which he has fairly earned.

I am in distinguished company. Mr. Gladstone was once called a traitor by the same class of Englishmen. So it has been with other men who have raised a voice against aggression and injustice. Washington was called a traitor in his day, so was O'Connell, and so, too, was the late Charles Stewart Parnell. Therefore I feel honoured in a special sense in being singled out for this distinction. For myself, when I die I aspire to have no better epitaph than this:

> Here lies a man who from his cradle to his grave was considered by his foes to be a traitor to alien rule and oppression in Ireland and in every land outside her shores.

Parliamentary Debates, *4th series, LXXVII, cols. 128–29*

Henry du Pré Labouchere, born in 1831, was among the last of the old-style Radicals. His pugnacity, which undoubtedly contributed to his failure to advance to the Liberal front bench, could at times be endearing. In his early career, he had distinguished himself as a crusading journalist, and he continued to own and edit *Truth,* an outspoken weekly devoted to uncovering abuses and protecting the underdog. It was in this spirit that he came to the defense of the Boers.

Henry Labouchere

Speech in the House of Commons   **October 17, 1899**

At present we are at war, and that war, we are told, is the act of the Boers; in fact, it is declared, the Transvaal have declared war upon us and not we on the Transvaal. I am not going into the origin of this dispute, nor am I going to follow all the phases of the diplomacy of the Colonial Secretary. I will only go so far back as I think will enable me to show that it is an entire error to suppose that the Transvaal Republic is responsible for the war. I say that we are responsible for it, and that it was the absolute act of the Colonial Secretary himself. On August 12, the Boers offered a scheme of arrangement which included a five years naturalisation law and franchise, and there were to be a greater number of members elected by the Uitlanders to the Volksraad than even was proposed by the Colonial Secretary or Sir Alfred Milner. The Boers agreed further, should any dispute arise as to the scope of the law, that there should be a consultation with Her Majesty's representative, and that Her Majesty's representative should be aided by a legal adviser. All the other issues were to be submitted for arbitration provided that the question of the suzerainty was dropped and that we agreed not to interfere with the internal affairs of the Transvaal. Sir, this proposal was refused by the right hon. Gentleman, and it was refused on account of the conditions attached to it. The Transvaal Government were under the impression that if they made this proposal, it would be acceded to by the Imperial Government. Certainly, I think, no one can read the despatches of Mr. Conyngham Greene without seeing that he himself was under the impression that Her Majesty's Government would assent to this proposal, and conveyed that impression to the Boer Government. When the terms were sent over to the Colonial Secretary, the right hon. Gentleman replied that if they were embodied in a scheme the Government would consider it upon its merits. If the Colonial Secretary intended to refuse to accept the scheme, he ought to have said so at once. The statement that he would consider it on its merits, coupled with the assurances of Mr. Greene, would lead the Transvaal Government to suppose that it would be accepted. I do not blame Mr. Greene for a moment; I only say that the circumstance was unfortunate, and tended to a great extent to increase the distrust the Boers evidently felt in regard to the action of the Colonial Secretary. Well, after further negotiations, which were not of a very conciliatory character, on the part of the Colonial Secretary and Sir Alfred Milner, a despatch was sent to the Transvaal on the 25th September, which was practically an ultimatum to that Government. That despatch said that it was useless to further pursue a discussion on the lines hitherto followed, and Her Majesty's Government were consequently prepared to consider the circumstances afresh and to formulate their own proposals for a final settlement of the issues which had been created in South Africa by the policy constantly followed for many years by the South African Republic, and they would communicate to them the result of their deliberations in a later despatch. On the 9th October no despatch had been received indicating those views, although on the 3rd or 4th President Kruger urged that he should know what were the terms to which he was asked to assent. But while no despatch was sent, the Reserves were called out at home, Parliament was called together, and additional troops, although there were already large numbers surrounding the Transvaal, were sent hurriedly to Natal. The Boers, therefore, were in this position—drastic demands had been made to alter entirely the relations which existed between that Government and ourselves. Meanwhile it was openly asserted in our newspapers—I suppose this will not be denied by the Colonial Secretary—that it was intended to enclose the Boer territory in a circle of iron, and that terms would be submitted to them when the Colonial Secretary chose—that is to say, when this chain of iron had been forged, and when it was perfectly obvious to everybody that they must either accept our terms or go to war. They had the choice between war and surrender at discretion. But although the Boers may be our enemies at the present time, let us be fair to them. If they had deemed this an attack on their independence, and had determined to fight rather than surrender, they would be utter fools if they had waited until the right hon. Gentleman's troops had arrived in overwhelming numbers and occupied the passes into their country. It is not fair to say that the situation has been changed by the Boers declaring war on us. I assert that the Colonial Secretary practically declared war on the Boers by sending them an ultimatum, the terms of which they were not prepared to accept, and therefore they were justified in anticipating events and in doing their best to occupy the passes leading to their country. It is perfectly true that the Colonial Secretary guaranteed the independence of the Transvaal, but there may be differences of opinion as to what that independence was. The complaint of the Boers was that the Colonial Secretary was attacking their independence. If the Colonial Secretary had angled for an opportunity to throw the odium of the actual outbreak of hostilities upon the Boers in order to get up public opinion in favour of this war, he could not have chosen a better mode than he did on this occasion. I do not blame the Boers for an instant; and I see the right hon. Gentleman the Member for Bodmin [Mr. Courtney] has said that he could not blame them. We really cannot in common fairness blame the Boers or throw upon them the responsibility of actual hostilities. But what was the Boers' reply to the Colonial Secretary's despatch? They replied to the proposal by offering arbitration, and they declared that unless this were accepted, or in the interval, pending receipt of conditions, more troops were massed, they would consider themselves at war with us on account of the ultimatum that had been sent to them. It is the common practice of countries who are inclined to go to war to throw the odium of actual hostilities upon each other. The House will remember that it was the habit of Prince Bismarck. He did so in the case of the German-Austrian war. He did it in the case of the French war, actually boasting that he had induced the world to believe that that was the case, and that a prejudice had been created against France in consequence. As the Leader of the Opposition truly says, the important fact at the present moment is that war now exists. And the practical question is, How are we to end it?

Parliamentary Debates, 4th series, LXXVII, cols. 101 ff.

In defiance of his party superiors, Philip Stanhope (later Baron Weardale) moved in the 1897 Parliament to censure the South Africa Committee for its inconclusive report on the circumstances of the Jameson Raid. Although the motion received only fifty-five Liberal votes, it marked "the first public division in the parliamentary party on a South African issue, and it was more serious than a revolt by a few Radicals on some issue of foreign policy. On the contrary," one historian has convincingly argued, "it was a precursor of the demonstrations of disunity which became so frequent during the South African War."[1]

It was therefore appropriate that Stanhope should rise in the House, two years later, to move to amend the Answer to the Queen's Speech by adding the following words:

> But we humbly represent to your Majesty our strong disapproval of the conduct of the negotiations with the Government of the Transvaal which have involved us in hostilities with the two South African Republics.

A more sweeping condemnation of government policy, moved by John Dillon, had failed to garner much support beyond the Irish benches.

The Stanhope Amendment
Speech in the House of Commons October 18, 1899

In the debate which took place yesterday on the Amendment of my hon. friend the Member for East Mayo, a distinct issue

1. Jeffrey Butler, *The Liberal Party and the Jameson Raid* (Oxford, 1968), p. 204.

was raised. He had my entire sympathy in the proposal he made for the submission of our difficulties with the Transvaal Republic to arbitration. But there is another aspect of the case which seems to me to require very special treatment, and that is the serious examination of the conduct of the negotiations by the Colonial Office, and the general course of events in connection with those negotiations which have led to our present hostilities with the South African Republic. There is a certain class of politicians who say that this country being at war it is undesirable to raise questions of this character. In the first place I may venture to point out that there are numerous precedents for raising issues of this description after war had actually commenced. The last one I think was in 1878, when upon the outbreak of the Afghan War the Liberal party took the occasion of the Queen's Speech, as we are taking it now, for the purpose of raising a distinct issue upon that war. An Amendment was moved in their name by a very respected Member of this House, Mr. Whitbread, and it received the almost unanimous support of the Liberal Party. It is true there is some distinction between the Afghan War and that in which we are now engaged. It is true that we began the Afghan War, and that in this case hostilities have been commenced by the invasion of British Colonies by the forces of the Transvaal. I am quite willing to admit the difference, but all the same I say that, while we must all be willing under the circumstances of the case to grant those supplies which are necessary for the defence of our Colonies, our mouths must not be closed upon the negotiations which have led up to this disastrous position, and resulted in a state of warfare between ourselves and the Governments of the Transvaal and the Orange Free State. Perhaps it may be convenient, in order to trace this matter to its source, that I should refer, first of all, to the year 1886, when the discovery of the goldfields imported an entirely new element into the affairs of the Transvaal and produced that combination of circumstances which have led to our present position. But although a very nondescript and not altogether British community was established at Johannesburg, I, for one, entirely acquiesce in

39

the view that those Uitlanders, particularly those of British extraction, have a claim to our protection and our assistance;
they have a claim to be supported in their desire for greater
political rights than they at present possess in the Transvaal.
The only point, and that is the grave point which I am to
raise, is that, admitting, if you like, that those political rights
ought to have been gained for them, we have gone the wrong
way to work to obtain them, and that in any case we ought
never to have found ourselves in the position of warfare in
which we find ourselves today. . . . Nobody who has studied the
history of this question doubted that if only patience, and,
above all, if abstention from illegal acts had been maintained,
we should have obtained those concessions for the Uitlander
population which we desired, and rightly desired, and none
of these difficulties would have arisen. In 1895 there was a
change of Government, and the Unionist party came into
power. They found themselves in a position of very great
difficulty, for they had to provide not only for their ordinary
friends, but also for the friends of the accommodating gentleman from Birmingham. The gentleman from Birmingham
had to be given an office in which his talents—which everybody will recognise—would have full display; but, at the same
time, it was hoped that he would not interfere too much with
the ordinary course of Conservative legislation. They thought
if he had a little preserve of his own in the Colonies he would
enjoy himself there, and would not be able to find time to
inconvenience the Conservative Party in their general course
of legislation. For a time all went well with the Unionist
party and with the Minister for the Colonies, who showed
enormous activity, and this was not contested by his colleagues,
who were glad to feel that the Colonial Secretary had enough
to do in his own Department, and consequently could not
interfere with theirs. But a moment arrived which disturbed
the equanimity of the Unionist party. The news arrived of the
Jameson raid—a designedly infamous transaction, which was
reprobated, but not sufficiently reprobated, by the House of
Commons, and the authors of which never received, as they
ought to have received, the punishment which they deserved.

The Committee which sat to investigate this matter presented a Report, and some of its conclusions gave satisfaction to the universal sentiment; but still, in my judgment, that Committee did not fulfil entirely either their task or the expectations which had been formed from the position occupied by the members of that Committee. At the end of the Session of 1897 I had thrown upon me the duty of making a motion in this House with regard to the Report of the South African Committee desiring that we should have more light, that they should produce more Papers, and that we should go really into the whole of these transactions, and clear the British name and credit from the motives which had been put upon these acts. The right hon. Gentleman the Colonial Secretary spoke late in the debate. I had asked him, in the course of my remarks, to be good enough to produce a certain letter—a letter addressed by him to Mr. Hawkesley, and conveying certain telegrams which were never published, but which it was very desirable should be published at the moment, and I asked him whether there was any objection to that letter, and the one to which it was a reply, being produced. I ask him that question again now. All I can say is that he absolutely ignored my former question and passed it by. And why? One knows perfectly well why, for it was because he could not respond. Will the right hon. Gentleman now produce those letters? Not only was there no response, but the right hon. Gentleman seized the opportunity offered by the debate on the Report of the South African Committee—which was charged with the duty of examining into a transaction which the whole public opinion of the world and the British Empire reprobated—the right hon. Gentleman got up at the last moment in that debate, and from his place in Parliament whitewashed the principal instigator of that Raid, and, in a sense, entirely did away with any of the good, or any of the advantage which might have been derived from the Report of the South African Committee. I am not going to enter more fully into the particulars of the exact personal responsibility of the right hon. Gentleman in regard to the Jameson Raid. But I have received to-day a book. I have had nothing whatever to do

41

with the drawing up of that book, but I have read it with some interest. It is called, "Are We in the Right? An Appeal to Honest Men," by Mr. W. T. Stead. [Ministerial laughter.] I noticed that the Leader of the House laughed when I read the title of the book. I would invite the right hon. Gentleman to read the book, and he will see in it a series of charges made without the smallest circumlocution against the Colonial Secretary. I neither wish to support them nor in any way to deal with them, but I do say that the dissemination of a book like that containing a series of charges against a public man of such a character cannot be, in the eyes of the public, passed by in silence by the right hon. Gentleman and his colleagues, and can only be dealt with in a manner which will clear entirely the right hon. Gentleman of those charges. I desire to pass from that particular subject of the responsibility of the right hon. Gentleman to the more immediate question of the effect of the right hon. Gentleman's actions. The effect of the right hon. Gentleman's actions was necessarily to throw all the progressive party in the Transvaal into the arms of the reactionary party. I ask any Englishman who found himself an inhabitant of the Transvaal, and who was a witness of all that occurred with regard to this matter, whether he would not from that moment have said, "Well, I have perhaps some mistrust of British Government, but so long as the British Government is in this matter represented by the present Colonial Secretary that mistrust will be so profound that I shall never be able to come to any reasonable settlement." That was the frame of mind of the people of the Transvaal, as a very natural consequence of the Jameson raid, and of the actions of the right hon. Gentleman. But I am bound to say that at that moment, or immediately subsequent to the Jameson raid, the right hon. Gentleman used language in this House which was satisfactory. I remember that, in answer to a speech of the right hon. Gentleman the Member for Sheffield, he distinctly repudiated any desire to interfere with the internal arrangements of the Transvaal, and he said that the suggestion of the right hon. Gentleman would involve the expenditure of £10,000,000, £20,000,000, or £30,000,000 for the sending out of a large army for the commission of a crime which he thought this country ought not to permit. Now what has happened to cause the right hon. Gentleman to so completely change his views? I am afraid that it is because the right hon. Gentleman has fallen under influences of a different kind to those which animated him at that time, because when Mr. Cecil Rhodes, the principal instigator of this Raid, went back to South Africa and found that he no longer received the support of the majority of the people of Cape Colony, when in the general election which ensued his adversaries were returned and Mr. Rhodes himself was displaced from power, what happened then? Why Mr. Rhodes said to himself, "What we cannot get by fair and constitutional means we will get by foul and hidden means. We cannot any longer do any good by constitutional agitation, so we will found an insidious league, and we will supply it with money." Accordingly, the South African League was formed, and Mr. Rhodes and his associates—generally of the German Jew extraction—found money in thousands for its propaganda. By this league in South Africa and here they have poisoned the wells of public knowledge. Money has been lavished in the London world and in the press, and the result has been that little by little public opinion has been wrought up and inflamed, and now, instead of finding the English people dealing with this matter in a truly English spirit, we are dealing with it in a spirit which generations to come will condemn, and which I believe within a few months of this time the electorate of this country will finally and absolutely repudiate. . . .

Parliamentary Debates, *4th series, LXXVII, cols. 181 ff.*

Stanhope's motion, carefully drafted, provided the occasion for a full-scale debate on the origins of the war. Liberal critics of the government received welcome support from Sir Edward Clarke, the Conservative member for Plymouth, who had served as solicitor-general in Lord Salisbury's previous administration. His skillful cross-examination of Chamberlain elicited the admission that the Boers had proved more than willing to offer accommodations. Mrs. Courtney heard the debate from the visitors' gallery.

Mrs. Leonard ("Kate") Courtney's diary   October 19, 1899

One of the most dramatic incidents I have seen in the House. The Conservative benches were silent. I do do not think that Sir Edward [Clarke] himself was at all prepared for such a statement, and his tone was full of surprised and almost painful emotion. I said to Lady Harcourt, who is near us, Chamberlain is a beaten man, morally at any rate. No one will forget the scene. . .—Clarke's pained earnestness, Chamberlain's hunted look, the dead silence on the Conservative side, and the repressed excitement of the Liberals.

> *Quoted in G. P. Gooch,* Life of Lord Courtney,
> *(London, 1920), p. 385*

As one of the signatories of the majority report of the South Africa Committee (Labouchere had issued a report of his own), J. E. Ellis had good reason to resent Philip Stanhope. But the venerable Liberal backbencher, a strong Quaker, gave his enthusiastic support to Stanhope's latest motion.

J. E. Ellis's diary   October, 1899

October 16. London. Went up with a distinct resolve to vote for the best form of words I could find expressive of condemnation of the diplomacy and negotiations which have landed us in war with South African Republic. To House, meeting P. Stanhope, who had shaped a most satisfactory amendment. Began to work for it. Rather depressed at so much coolness.

October 18. P. Stanhope moved amendment. S. Evans seconded in excellent speech. Harcourt followed about 4 p.m. in one of the best speeches I ever heard from him. Saw him after and was glad to find him wavering as to whether he should not support amendment.

Oct. 19. One of the most striking evenings I ever spent in the House. J. C[hamberlain] rose about 4 and spoke two hours and 40 minutes. Too personal and bitter at first. Called to order by Speaker. Gave the go-by very adroitly to Harcourt's scathing attack on the Blue Books and rallied the Government side during the last hour by appealing to "Patriotism," etc. Sir E. Clarke followed in delicate rapier-like dissection of C.'s speech, extracting one most damaging admission, of which he availed himself with supreme art. A. J. B[alfour] in last two minutes exhibiting great skill of appeal. Con. 2, Irish 43, Lib. 93, for Amendment, a very remarkable result considering how lukewarm our party was at the beginning of the week.

Quoted in A. T. Bassett,
The Life of the Rt. Hon. John Edward Ellis, M.P.
(London, 1914), pp. 168–69

Although it did not carry, the Stanhope amendment made a profound impression by the number and prominence of its adherents. Neither Campbell-Bannerman nor (predictably) the Liberal Imperialists supported it; but Harcourt voted in its favor, as did no fewer than eight future Liberal cabinet ministers.

In retrospect, the vote acquired a further significance as a kind of litmus paper test: in the general election of 1900, it was cited, perhaps more often than any other single factor, as the ultimate proof of pro-Boer sentiments.

Division List
**Stanhope amendment to the Answer
to the Queen's Speech**   **October 19, 1899**

Question put accordingly, "That those words be there added." The House divided:—Ayes, 135; Noes, 362. (Division List No. 5.)

AYES.

Abraham, William (Cork, N.E.)
Abraham, William (Rhondda)
Allan, William (Gateshead)
Allen, W. (Newc. under Lyme)
Ambrose, Robert

Ashton, Thomas Gair
Atherley-Jones, L.
Austin, M. (Limerick, W.)
Bainbridge, Emerson
Barlow, John Emmott
Barry, E. (Cork, S.)

Bayley, Thomas (Derbyshire)
Billson, Alfred
Birrell, Augustine
Blake, Edward
Brunner, Sir John Tomlinson
Bryce, Rt. Hon. James

Buchanan, Thomas
Ryburn
Burns, John
Burt, Thomas
Cameron, Sir Chas.
(Glasgow)
Cameron, Robert
(Durham)
Carvill, Patrick G.
Hamilton
Cawley, Frederick
Channing, Francis
Allston
Clark, Dr. G. B.
(Caithness-sh.)
Commins, Andrew
Courtney, Rt. Hon.
Leonard H.
Crilly, Daniel
Curran, Thomas B.
(Donegal)
Curran, Thomas
(Sligo, S.)
Daly, James
Dalziel, James
Henry
Davies, M. Vaughan-
(Cardigan)
Davitt, Michael
Dewar, Arthur
Dilke, Rt. Hon. Sir
Charles
Dillon, John
Donelan, Captain A.
Doogan, P. C.
Duckworth, James
Edwards, Owen
Morgan
Ellis, John Edward
Farquharson, Dr.
Robert

Fenwick, Charles
Field, William
(Dublin)
Flavin, Michael
Joseph
Fox, Dr. Joseph
Francis
Gibney, James
Gilhooly, James
Gurdon, Sir Wm.
Brampton
Harcourt, Rt. Hon.
Sir Wm.
Hayden, John
Patrick
Hayne, Rt. Hon.
Chas. Seale-
Healy, Maurice
(Cork)
Hedderwic',
Thomas C. H.
Hemphill, Rt. Hon.
Charles H.
Horniman,
Frederick John
Humphreys-Owen,
Arthur C.
Jacoby, James
Alfred
Jones, Wm.
(Carnarvonshire)
Jordan, Jeremiah
Kinloch, Sir John
Geo. Smyth
Labouchere, Henry
Langley, Batty
Lawson, Sir Wilfrid
(Cum'land)
Leuty, Thomas
Richmond
Lewis, John Herbert

Lloyd-George, David
Logan, John
William
Lough, Thomas
Macaleese, Daniel
MacDonnell, Dr.
M. A. (Qu's C)
Maclean, James
Mackenzie
MacNeill, John
Gordon Swift
M'Crae, George
M'Dermott, Patrick
M'Ewan, William
M'Ghee, Richard
M'Hugh, Patrick A.
(Leitrim)
M'Kenna, Reginald
M'Laren, Charles
Benjamin
M'Leod, John
Maddison, Fred
Maden, John Henry
Morley, Charles
(Breconshire)
Morley, Rt. Hon. J.
(Montrose)
Moulton, John
Fletcher
Norton, Capt. Cecil
William
Nussey, Thomas
Willans
O'Brien, Patrick
(Kilkenny)
O'Connor, Arthur
(Donegal)
O'Connor, Jas.
(Wicklow, W.)
O'Connor, T. P.
(Liverpool)

46

O'Malley, William
Pease, Alfred E.
  (Cleveland)
Pease, Joseph A.
  (Northum.)
Pickard, Benjamin
Pickersgill, Edward
  Hare
Pirie, Duncan V.
Power, Patrick
  Joseph
Price, Robert John
Priestley, Briggs
  (Yorks)
Randell, David
Redmond, William
  (Clare)
Reid, Sir Robert
  Threshie
Richardson, J.
  (Durham, S.E.)
Roberts, John Bryn
  (Eifion)
Roberts, John H.
  (Denbighs)

Samuel, J.
  (Stockton-on-Tees)
Schwann, Charles E.
Scott, Chas.
  Prestwich (Leigh)
Shaw, Thomas
  (Hawick B.)
Sinclair, Capt. John
  (Forfarsh.)
Soames, Arthur
  Wellesley
Souttar, Robinson
Steadman, William
  Charles
Stuart, James
  (Shoreditch)
Sullivan, Donal
  (Westmeath)
Sullivan, T. D.
  (Donegal, W.)
Tanner, Charles
  Kearns
Thomas, David A.
  (Merthyr)
Tuite, James

Wedderburn, Sir
  William
Weir, James
  Galloway
Whittaker, Thomas
  Palmer
Williams, John
  Carvell (Notts.)
Wilson, Frederick
  W. (Norfolk)
Wilson, H. J. (York,
  W. R.)
Wilson, John
  (Durham, Mid.)
Wilson, John
  (Govan)
Woodhouse, Sir
  J. T. (H'fl'd.)
Woods, Samuel
Young, Samuel
  (Cavan, East)
Yoxall, James Henry
Tellers for the
  Ayes—Mr. Philip
  Stanhope and Mr.
  Samuel Evans

Parliamentary Debates, *4th series, LXXVII, cols. 367–68*

W. T. Stead, with the presses of the *Review of Reviews* at his disposal, let loose a barrage of pamphlets. Highly personal in tone, they sometimes had the adverse effect of clouding the issues: many thought, for example, that his attempt to distinguish between the Jameson *Raid* and the Jameson *plan* gratuitously exculpated Chamberlain. Stead's impassioned rhetoric made his charges easy to dismiss. Questioned in the Commons about Stead's *Are We in the Right?*, A. J. Balfour replied that he had not read it, but "it appears to be a somewhat scurrilous document, which I think need not

disturb the honourable gentleman [Chamberlain] at all."[1]
J. E. Ellis told Campbell-Bannerman that Stead had sent him
two copies of the same pamphlet "and accosted me as the
'wicked Mr. Ellis' apropos of the S. A. Cttee.," hardly a way
to win a friend. "My view of the pamphlet is simple," Ellis
declared. "It does not contain a single *new fact* not even a
particle of one. . . . Of course Stead's object is to direct
the scent from Rhodes to Chamberlain. He says as much. I
don't think the pamphlet either has or will 'catch on.' "[2]

Joseph Chamberlain
Conspirator or Statesman?

Preface to the First Edition

The time has come when it is necessary to set forth in plain
words, which the plain man can understand, a narrative of
Mr. Chamberlain's complicity in the conspiracy to overthrow
the Government of the South African Republic in 1895.

Let me, at the beginning, emphasize the importance of distinguishing between the conspiracy to bring about a revolution
in the Transvaal with a British force on the Border in support,
which was the Jameson Plan, and the Jameson Raid. The two
things are almost always confounded by the indiscriminating
public. So far from being identical, the Jameson Raid cut the
throat of the conspiracy. Dr. Jameson acted, no doubt, with
the best intentions in the world, but, as a matter of fact, he
not only upset Mr. Rhodes's applecart, but from excessive
zeal caused the miscarriage of an enterprise which, however
indefensible it may have been from the point of view of constitutional law, would, if it had succeeded, have delivered us
from all our present troubles. If, therefore, any person should
say that Mr. Chamberlain was privy to the Raid, or that Mr.
Chamberlain had anything whatever to do with the Raid,
either that he knew about it beforehand, or that he sanctioned
it, or that he was in any way whatever responsible for it, such
person would say that which is not true. The Raid was Dr.

1. *Parliamentary Debates*, 4th series, LXXVII, col. 549 (October
25, 1899).
2. Ellis to Campbell-Bannerman, November 3, 1899, quoted in
Butler, *The Liberal Party and the Jameson Raid*, pp. 235–36.

Jameson's own act, and it spoiled everything. The Jameson Plan was that to which Mr. Chamberlain was privy.

I have never made any charge, or accusation, or complaint against Mr. Chamberlain for the support which he gave to the conspiracy against the Government of Paul Kruger. Neither do I at this moment lay any stress upon that side of the question. Others, no doubt, take a very serious view of the matter. They may be right, and I may be wrong. All that I wish to point out is that, so far from being animated, as many ignorantly declare, by a persistent and vindictive animosity against Mr. Chamberlain, I have from first to last endeavoured to make every conceivable excuse for his action in the autumn of 1895. If since I have been driven to criticize his action, it has been due, not to anything that he did in 1895, but to the manner in which he persisted, in the face of all warnings and protests, in adopting a policy of concealing the truth, denying facts and making both parties in the House of Commons unwilling accomplices in a conspiracy to deceive the nation, which is, I believe, without parallel in the history of Parliamentary Government. It is this offence which is rank, an offence committed in the full light of day, after careful and long deliberation, and with the distinct purpose and object of concealing the truth and giving official Parliamentary currency to a lie.

If any one blames me for this publication, I have only to say that I have been so vehemently assailed, alike by friends and foes, for saying that the scandal of the South African Committee was far more serious than that of the Raid, that a plain straightforward narrative compiled from the official record is necessary to show that I have not spoken without book.

W. T. STEAD

Oct. 25th, 1899

Published by the Review of Reviews

Are We in the Right? An Appeal to Honest Men
W. T. Stead   Second edition, January 9, 1900

Chapter I
THE APPEAL TO HONEST MEN

I appeal to honest men, because it is only an honest man who will admit that the question whether we are in the right or wrong in this war is not in the least affected by the fact that the immediate cause of the rupture was the Boers' Ultimatum.

To those professors of unctuous rectitude who pretend that there can be no question as to the justice of this war, because, as the *Standard* actually declared, "we are fighting in self-defence," it is idle to address any appeal based either on reason, conscience, or common-sense. But there are many who are incapable of deluding themselves by such cant, and to them I appeal.

Are we in the right in this war? It is a question worth considering. It is not settled by waving the Union Jack—not even by chanting "Rule Britannia." The attempt to silence its consideration by brutal violence and rowdy clamour is well calculated to give pause to all reflecting men. The Jewish mob which cried out "Crucify Him! Crucify Him!" imagined that they had effectually carried their point. They gained their immediate end no doubt. Not even the pleading voice of the Roman judge could be heard above the din. They got their way and secured the Crucifixion. But it brought them an immortality of infamy, and afforded us the supreme example of the murderous results which are apt to follow when the stormy clamour of an excited mob is allowed to silence the still small voice of reason and justice.

What is the first condition of just judgment? Is it not ability to put ourselves in our brother's place, to consider what we should do if we were standing in his shoes, and then when we have, with a sympathetic imagination, examined the facts, to judge him as we should wish ourselves to be judged?

Put yourself in President Kruger's place, and ask whether you would not do exactly as President Kruger has done—only more so—so far as relates to the Ultimatum. The case is clear as daylight. There is fortunately no dispute as to the facts. Which side is right or which is wrong in the controversy may for the moment be ignored, for the intrinsic merits of the dispute do not affect the simple question which must first be disposed of.

The Boers, rightly or wrongly, believe, and are prepared to die rather than abandon their belief, that the Convention of 1884 did, in the words of successive English statesmen, from Lord Derby to Mr. Chamberlain, guarantee them an absolute right of internal self-government, which forbade any interference by Great Britain in their affairs.

The British Government, rightly or wrongly, believes that —despite Mr. Chamberlain's explicit repudiation of any right to interfere to force upon the Transvaal reforms in the internal affairs of the State—the time has come when it must for the protection of its subjects interfere directly in the internal affairs of the Transvaal, and finding its interference resented proceeds to enforce its demands by the despatch of horse, foot, and artillery for the avowed purpose of compelling the Boers to submit.

Every additional soldier sent to South Africa since the Bloemfontein Conference was sent out admittedly and avowedly as a menace to President Kruger, in order to induce him by the display of armed force to permit us to dictate our own terms as to the way in which his country should be governed. It is not generally known in this country that as long ago as last August the Boers were plainly told by the British Agent at Pretoria that we should make war upon them if they refused to concede the five years' franchise. The fact, however, stands on record in Mr. Conyngham Greene's telegram of 15th August, which is found in Blue Book, C. 9521, page 45. After describing how the State-Attorney came to see him about the franchise, he says:—

> I spoke to him very seriously. I explained that I had no idea whether Her Majesty's Government would consent not to press their demand (for the joint inquiry); but that the situation was most critical, and that Her Majesty's Government, who had given pledges to the Uitlanders, *would be bound to assert their demands, and, if necessary, to press them by force.* I said that the only chance for the South African Republic Government was an immediate surrender to the Bloemfontein minimum.

Thus we see that the Transvaal Government is strictly accurate when in its Manifesto it declares:—

> Great Britain has offered two alternatives—a Five Years' franchise or War.

Whether the Boers or the British were right in their original contention, no one questions the fact that the despatch of thousands of armed men from the inexhaustible store of our Imperial resources to the frontiers of the Transvaal was a menace of war. "Do what we tell you, or it will be worse for you! If you don't give in we shall send thousands and ever more thousands of soldiers to surround you, to throttle you, and to compel you to submit." That was our policy. A glance at any of our war-organs will prove the matter beyond doubt. The Boers bore it patiently for a time. But at last they were driven, first to remonstrate, and then to declare that the despatch of any more troops, or a refusal to withdraw those already sent to overawe them, must be regarded as a Declaration of War. And because they did this, we are told that they began the war, and we are fighting in self-defence!

Put ourselves in their place. Imagine that the French had a difference of opinion with us, say as to the evacuation of Egypt.

Our declarations and our pledges on that subject were quite as explicit and as precise—to say the very least—as anything the Boers ever promised about the Outlanders. Suppose that the French intimated that in their judgment the time had come for us to fulfil our obligations, to keep our word, and to clear out of the Nile Valley. We should, of course, object. Suppose, then, that France began despatching ironclad after ironclad to lie off the Suez Canal; suppose that she avowed her intention and had the means to send a fleet twice as strong as any we could muster to Alexandria, with an army large enough to sweep Egypt from the Mediterranean to Omdurman, how long should we be in discovering that such action on the part of France made her the aggressor, and justified us in stopping it by an immediate challenge and ultimatum? No State in the world would consider itself bound to wait until its neighbour brought up overpowering forces with the avowed object of coercion.

If a highwayman presents a pistol at your head, you do not become the aggressor if you throw up his hand.

Hence I address my Appeal to men honest enough to admit that the Boers' Ultimatum in no way affects the question as to the right or wrong of this war.

If we had been in President Kruger's place we should with one consent have been declaring that the Ultimatum was forced from us by the deliberate and calculated aggression of a State determined to destroy our independence. This is so obvious that argument is wasted upon those who have not sufficient tincture of the elementary virtue of honesty to admit it at once without reserve.

To those honest men and to those alone I address myself. As for the others, who in the vein of Mr. Pecksniff are protesting that they are reluctantly driven to make war in self-defence, we might as well discuss the Ten Commandments with a pirate, or discourse to a burglar upon the Sermon on the Mount.

The merits of a policy leading to war, and of a policy which has, unfortunately, culminated in war, are no more affected by the question as to which party first took the responsibility of challenging the intentions of the other, than the merits of the dispute between the American colonists and George III were affected by the question as to which fired the first shot in the Revolutionary War.

Having thus disposed of the controversy as to the Ultimatum, without more delay I proceed to discuss the question "Are we in the right in this war?"

Socialists and the War

Publicists for the I. L. P. echoed the Radical argument that the war was a venture for capitalist gain; not only had economic conditions pitted nation against nation, but also man against man. Each week in the *Labour Leader*, published

at London and Glasgow under J. Keir Hardie's editorship,
the Boers were envied, not for their mineral wealth, but for
having retained the social virtues that Britain allegedly lost
at the time of industrialization.

A Capitalist's War
J. Keir Hardie   **The Labour Leader, January 6, 1900**

. . . Whatever the result of this war may be, the Socialist movement in England stands to benefit. With very few exceptions,
the movement is solid against the war and for peace. . . .

The war is a capitalists' war, begotten by capitalists' money,
lied into being by a perjured mercenary capitalist press, and
fathered by unscrupulous politicians, themselves the merest
tools of the capitalists. As a pastoral people the Boers doubtless have all the failings of the fine qualities which pertain to
that mode of life; but whatever these failings might have been
they are virtues compared to the turbid pollution and refined
cruelty which is inseparable from the operation of capitalism.
As Socialists, our sympathies are bound to be with the Boers.
Their Republican form of Government bespeaks freedom, and
is thus hateful to tyrants, whilst their methods of production
for use are much nearer our ideal than any form of exploitation for profit.

A translation of an article supplied to
l'Humanité Nouvelle

Those socialists who opposed the war invariably differed in
the points they chose to emphasize. Edward Carpenter, one
of the most eccentric of them (the causes he championed
included spiritualism and homosexual love) published a
pamphlet on New Year's Day, 1900, for the Labour Press,
Manchester. Copies sold for 9d. per hundred, or six shillings
per thousand ("carriage paid"), thereby insuring wide
distribution.

Boer and Briton
Edward Carpenter

. . . Just think for a moment of the situation. Think of these
Dutch *bauers* or *boers* (farmers) who emigrated to South

Africa in the 17th century; and of the French Huguenots who followed—some of the best people in Europe. They settled at the Cape; but the English coming there a hundred years ago, soon began to crowd them out. And so, in 1836, occurred the Great Trek. Harnessing their bullocks to their wagons, and putting their wives, their families and all their possessions on board, they tracked a thousand miles up into the interior, and made for themselves a home afar from the English, in an arid unfertile land where before the wild beasts had been. If ever a people on earth made good their right to their land these people did. They loved it passionately—it was the Promised land of their wanderings—and they love it still. (Perhaps *our* people who have no land, cannot understand that!) *And they will fight for it to the end.*

They may have their faults. They have been hard on the Kaffirs and other natives, barbarous at times, but I doubt whether they have been so *systematically* cruel as the English. They may be narrowminded and old-fashioned in their ideas, but so far in the present war they seem to have acted more humanely than our professional troops. Religious, almost puritanical (for they descend from much the same puritan sources as we do), simple in their lives, loving their land, their cattle, their homes—they have only asked to be left alone in their own country.

Well, think of this people so living; and then think again of Johannesburg since gold was found there, since the gold fever set in—a hell full of Jews, financiers, greedy speculators, adventurers, prostitutes, bars, banks, gaming saloons, and every invention of the devil. Think of this people, these peasant farmers, not only witnessing with utmost disgust this open sore of commercial corruption, but seeing the covetous eyes of Rhodes and his crew fixed upon them for their undoing, and the certainty that ere long their land would be completely overrun.

You see, if the Boers had chosen to pack off the whole crew they would have had a perfect right to do so. (Think for a moment, if Liverpool were to be overrun by 100,000 Chinese, smothering our civilisation, and introducing their hated cus-

toms and ways—what should we do?) They would have had a
perfect right to pack them off, according to the very ideas of
independence and freedom which the name of England has
always stood for. . . .

Commercial Capitalism has been rampant in South Africa
for years. Capitalism, the bloodless soulless rule of Companies,
is bad enough here in England; but in Africa it is far worse.
There is no public opinion to restrain it there; the Kaffirs and
even the white wage-workers are at its mercy. Terrible have
been the cruelties perpetrated in the Diamond Fields of Kimberley, and in the Gold-mines of Rhodesia. Kimberley itself,
about which there is a good deal of sentiment just now, has
been of late years uninhabitable except by minions of the De
Beers Syndicate. A commercial tyranny reigns there, exceeding
anything we know in England. Conditions in Johannesburg
were rapidly drifting in the same direction. The financiers
have been looking forward to complete control of the labor-
conditions there. "Wages would be cut down, dividends would
be increased," said Mr. Hammond to the *South African Goldfields Co.*, "by two million sterling per annum" as soon as the
English obtained control. The Stock Exchange shouted itself
hoarse with fiendish delight when war was declared. Rhodesian
stock went up; the Chartered Company's shares rose from 2⅝
to 4¼. Lies were circulated by a corrupt Press; and a wave of
silly Jingo-Imperialism swept over our land. And so in obedi-
ence to this money-mongering Capitalism—our Princes, our
Government, our official classes being all more or less en-
tangled in it—we are fighting an inglorious war—a war to which
there can be no satisfactory end, since with it the flames of disaffection spread faster than they can be extinguished.

I have said a wave of Jingo-Imperialism swept over our
country. When that wave retires there will be left an odd-
looking mud-bank behind—and on it the word "Conscription"!
How will the great British Public like that? O, great B.P., to
have the blood of your sons spilt like water, and to be fooled
in this way by a few millionaires and gold-grubbers working
for their own ends, and making a Catspaw of you!

Turn the page. For what might not England do?

56

What might not England do? Think of this great land which in its beginnings has stood for so much that is noble down the centuries. With our marvellous command of materials, our resource, tradition, our splendid organising capacity, think what a real empire we might build in the hearts of the lesser races of the world—a real empire of Humanity. I have in India seen the affection which the millions there are ready to feel for any Englishman who treats them in a friendly spirit. It is the same in Africa—the Dutch are bound to us by ties of affection, common tradition, intermarriage. It is the same in Egypt and other lands. What a kingdom we might establish, if in our great power we could only come among all these peoples in a spirit of understanding and sympathy—to heal race-divisions, to build an empire in their hearts, the greatest the world has ever seen! But now we are but digging our own graves.

For the Money interest for its own ends sows the seeds of hatred—lust of gold, lust of territory, lying words and lust of domination. And our official classes, fine though they are in some respects—manly, brave, practical, and excellent organisers —are alas! too dull-headed, too dull-hearted, to rise to an understanding of the situation. Our generals suffer from beef in the brain, and our politicians from the dross of gold in the heart. None of these classes have any ideal but a commercial one; and half the time they are being led by the nose by the Jews, and have actually not the sense to see that they are being so led.

If only England *could* understand her true mission to the world—her true Patriotism, so far more glorious than the shoddy article that is marketed in the Music-halls,—her mission of love and healing to the lesser races of the Earth—she might indeed face the 20th century with a new hope. The men of our official classes cannot, as it seems, understand it; the Church, that might preach it, has sold its soul to Mammon; will the Workmen and the Women of England rise and show the way?

Mrs. Webb, a socialist of yet another hue, mused privately in the pages of her diary. Earlier, she had identified her husband and herself as occupants of a "middle position"

57

within the Fabian Society, less enthusiastic about the war than Graham Wallas or Bernard Shaw, while less "desperately against it" than J. Ramsay MacDonald or Sydney Oliver.

Beatrice Webb's diary

Torquay, January 31st [1900]—The last six months, and especially the last month at Plymouth, have been darkened by the nightmare of war. The horrible consciousness that we have, as a nation, shown ourselves to be unscrupulous in methods, vulgar in manners as well as inefficient, is an unpleasant background to one's personal life—a background always present, when one wakes in the night and in the intervals of leisure during the day. The Boers are, man for man, our superiors in dignity, devotion and capacity—yes, *in capacity*. That, to a ruling race, is the hardest hit of all. It may be that war was inevitable: I am inclined to think it was: but that it should come about through muddy intrigues and capitalist pressure and that we should have proved so incapable alike in statesmanship and in generalship is humiliating. I sometimes wonder whether we could take a beating and be the better for it? This would be the real test of the heart and intellect of the British race: much more so than if we succeed after a long and costly conflict. If we win, we shall soon forget the lessons of the war. Once again we shall have "muddled through." Pecuniary self-interest will be again rehabilitated as an Empire-building principle. Once again the English gentleman, with his so-called habit of command, will have proved to be the equal of the foreign expert with his scientific knowledge. Once again our politicians and staff officers will bask in the smiles of London "society," and will chatter bad metaphysics and worse economics in country house parties, imagining themselves to be men of the world because they have neither the knowledge nor the industry to be professional administrators and skilled soldiers.

To us public affairs seem gloomy; the middle-classes are materialistic, and the working-class stupid, and in large sections sottish, with no interest except in racing odds, whilst the Government of the country is firmly in the hands of little cliques of landlords and great capitalists, and their hangers-on.

The social enthusiasm that inspired the intellectual proletariat of ten years ago has died down and given place to a wave of scepticism about the desirability, or possibility, of any substantial change in society as we know it. There may be the beginnings of intellectual curiosity, but it is still a flicker and not a flame. And, meanwhile, the rich are rolling in wealth and every class, except the sweated worker, has more than its accustomed livelihood. Pleasure and ease are desired by all men and women: science, literature and art, even social ambition and party politics, have given way to the love of mental excitement and physical enjoyment. If we found ourselves faced with real disaster, should we as a nation have the nerve and persistency to stand up against it? That is the question that haunts me.

Quoted in Beatrice Webb, Our Partnership, *ed. B. Drake and M. I. Cole (New York, 1948), pp 194–95*

British socialists, when they spoke about the working classes of South Africa, tended to ignore the nonwhite population. On the other hand, apologists for the war often identified themselves as protectors of the Kaffirs against Boer inhumanity. This claim was disputed by Radical pro-Boers, who considered their countrymen unfit to point an accusing finger at the Boers.

The Case of the Natives
The Morning Leader   **January 6, 1900**

Mr. Rhodes once complained with exceeding bitterness that "they think more of one native at home than of the whole of South Africa." In those days the Churches were ranged against him. But the times have changed, and Mr. Hugh Price Hughes comes forward to plead in one breath for Mr. Rhodes and the "niggers" who were once such a thorn in his side. The *Methodist Times* has discovered yet another pretext for destroying the independence of the Transvaal.

Some apologists hold that we are waging war to rescue the "helots" of Johannesburg from intolerable oppression, while Mr. Hays Hammond of the Consolidated Goldfields, has told us that it is to dower them with two millions and a quarter in increased dividends. Some will have it that we are but repelling Boer aggression, while others think that our armies are now busied in asserting British prestige and Paramountcy. Mr. Hughes has an entirely novel theory. He assures us that "England is now fighting against the slavery of the African race as truly as the Northern States fought against it in the Civil War." Whether we know it or not, we are avenging the wrongs of the Kaffirs whom the Dutch have so long oppressed —for Mr. Hughes can hardly suppose that actual slavery prevails in the Transvaal. It is a comfortable theory, though we doubt whether it would justify the diplomatic provocations and the campaign of lies that brought the war about. But is it true? Will the natives be the gainers when the Union Jack floats over the Rand?

Before we consider the case of the Transvaal it may be well to take a summary glance at the present position of things in our own colonies and possessions:

1. In the strip of East African coast—a British Protectorate —which faces Zanzibar, the full "legal status of slavery" is maintained, and fugitive slaves have even been handed back to their owners by British officials.

2. In Zanzibar and Pemba the manumission of slaves, presided over by Sir Arthur Hardinge, is proceeding slowly, and many thousands are still in bondage.

3. In Natal the corvee system prevails, and all natives not employed by whites may be impressed to labor for six months of the year on the roads.

4. In Bechuanaland, after a recent minor rebellion, natives were parcelled out among the Cape farmers and indentured to them as virtual slaves for a term of years.

5. Under the Chartered Company in Rhodesia the chiefs are required, under compulsion, to furnish batches of young natives to work in the mines, and the ingenious plan of taxing the Kaffir in money rather than in kind has been adopted so that he may be forced to earn the pittance which the prospectors are willing to pay him.

6. In Kimberley what is known as the "compound" system

prevails. All natives who work in the diamond fields are required to "reside" under lock and key, day and night, in certain compounds, which resemble spacious prisons. So stringent
is the system that even the sick are treated only within the
prison yard. On no pretext whatever is a native allowed to
leave his compound.

After all, the hands of the Northern States were a little
cleaner than our own when they championed the cause of the
slave.

It would be easy to make an *ex parte* defence of the Dutch,
but we prefer instead to accept the deliberate judgment of the
only impartial writer on South Africa known to us—Mr. Bryce.
He tells us that the laws of the Boer Republics are indeed
harsher than those of the English colonies—though of course
they in no way sanction slavery—but, on the other hand, "one
often hears that the Dutch get on better with their black servants than the English do." The attitude of *both* races to the
blacks he describes as "contemptuous, unfriendly, and even
suspicious," and elsewhere he speaks of the "deep and widespread aversion to the colored people."

... We agree, therefore, with Mr. Hughes in deploring the
Boer treatment of the native for the same reason that we condemn the behaviour of our own colonists. But to his contention that the blacks will gain by the substitution of British
for Boer rule there is a clearer answer.

The Rand financiers have told us very plainly what they
mean to do when, at the price of gallant lives and broken
hearts, they rule as absolutely in Johannesburg as they do in
Kimberley. At a meeting of the Consolidated Goldfields Company of South Africa held in the City on 14 Nov., the consult-
ing engineer boldly announced that under English rule he
hoped to be able to cut down the wages of the Kaffirs by one
half, and a director who followed him declared that they
would *compel* the natives to work for them. Here are some
passages from their speeches:

Mr. Hays Hammond was tolerably frank:

> There are, said Mr. Hammond, in South Africa mil-
> lions of Kaffirs, and it does seem preposterous that we

are not able to obtain 70,000 or 80,000 Kaffirs to work
upon the mines. . . . With good government there should
be an abundance of labor, and with an abundance of
labor *there will be no difficulty in cutting down wages,*
because it is preposterous to pay a Kaffir the present
wages. He would be quite as well satisfied—*in fact, he
would work longer—if you gave him half the amount.*
(Laughter.) His wages are altogether disproportionate to
his requirements. (Renewed laughter.)

But the voice of the philanthropist spoke even more clearly
through Mr. Rudd:

If they could only get one-half the natives to work
three months of the year it would work wonders. He was
not pleading for the mines, or urging the views of capitalists, but from the point of view of progress, agriculture,
public works, mines, and the general prosperity of the
country. *They should try some cogent form of inducement or practically compel the native,* through taxation
or in some other way, to contribute his quota to the good
of the community, and to a certain extent he would then
have to work.

. . . As a study in complicated cant this would be difficult to
beat. In St. James's Hall Mr. Hughes preaches a crusade against
slavery. In the City Mr. Rudd chuckles at the prospect of
forced native labour won by the statesmanship of Mr. Rhodes
and Sir Alfred Milner. Yet Mr. Rudd and Mr. Hughes are
both defending the same war.

Reprinted as Morning Leader *Leaflet No. 2*

Both sides in the Boer War debate appealed to history to
justify their stands. To an extent, this was *pro forma*:
the Victorian mind tended to regard history and politics
as inseparable. But rarely was Clio conscripted for such active
duty. Various accounts traced the causes of the struggle
back beyond the Jameson Raid to the British seizure of
Cape Town during the Napoleonic wars, to the constitutional
settlements of the 1850s, to the annexation of the Transvaal
in 1877, to the 1881 Boer victory at Majuba Hill, or to the
discovery of gold five years later. Supporters of the war

indicted Gladstone for betraying imperial interests during his second government; opponents retorted that the present situation had been created by the failure of British statesmen to act in a Gladstonian spirit.

Frederic Harrison, whose literary criticism and Radical politics were tinged with a Comptean historicism, delivered public lectures on December 7, 1899, and January 31, 1900. The texts were published in the press and, shortly thereafter, in pamphlet form by the South Africa Conciliation Committee.

The Boer Republics

Frederic Harrison   **SAAC Pamphlet No. 21**

... We now come to the Great Trek—one of the most extraordinary stories in the history of the Empire. Smarting under their grievances, and despairing of living under British rule, Dutch farmers put their families and moveables into wagons and crossed the Orange River to the Northern veldt to seek a new home in the wilderness, where they could be free from what they regarded as intolerable oppression. Our judicious guide insists that no single event—least of all emancipation—brought on this emigration, but causes of disaffection which had been accumulating since 1811 for 25 years. He adopts the language of the wise and brave Peter Retief, that they were driven forth by the license given to Hottentot vagrants, by the ruin caused by the emancipation scheme and its mal-administration, by the incessant invasion of Kaffir savages, that they might find in the desert new homes, free from the oppression of the British Government.

Some eight or ten thousand souls went forth in the years 1836–8, in small parties of a few hundred each; for the veldt would not suffice for more than a score or two of wagons in one place. The Government found it could not stop them, but it claimed them as subjects, and had them searched for arms and powder. They trekked slowly on, month after month, into the wilderness, meeting wild beasts and wandering tribes of blacks, cut to pieces by hordes of savages, by famine, by drought, by fever, or again in ambushes, or losing their way in the arid veldt. One party pushed up some 800 miles to the Northern part of the Transvaal; another party were slaughtered and exterminated—men, women, and children; one party trekked on till a feeble remnant, stricken with fever, at last reached the coast of Delagoa Bay. Now and then they met and vanquished terrible impis of Zulus and Matabeles, under Dingaan and Moselekatze. Peter Retief and all his comrades were treacherously massacred by Dingaan in Natal. But in spite of ferocious Zulus and cunning Basutos, in spite of famine, and disease, and exhaustion, the indomitable Boer Trek went on. In one of these parties was a little boy of ten, just old enough to drag his musket—Paul Kruger, now President of the Transvaal. In another party was Pieter Joubert, father of the Boer Commander-in-Chief, himself fourth in descent from the old Huguenot of 1689.

It might be a new sensation to turn to the story of some of these desperate combats of the Boers with the natives fifty and sixty years ago. It is a thrilling story how one party of trek-farmers drove back the terrible Moselekatze across the Limpopo, how another took a fearful revenge on the treacherous Dingaan at the Blood River, a little north-east of Dundee. These Zulu and Matabele armies of 8,000 or 10,000 strong were, at least, as brave and as well-disciplined as the warriors whom Lobengula and Cetewayo, their descendants, led in recent years against us. The Boer farmers were but a few hundred in each commando, armed with old flintlocks; they had to beat back these terrible savages by sheer point-blank fighting. Their victories are amongst the most famous records in African history, and justify their celebration of December 16th as Dingaan's Day, when they cleared Natal of the ferocious Zulu chief.

Having driven the Matabele chief, Moselekatze, north of the Limpopo, and having driven the Zulu chief, Dingaan, into Zululand, the Boers settled down in the Orange State, in the Transvaal, and in Natal, all three lands which had been practically cleared of native inhabitants by these two desolating chiefs. In Natal, the Boers now founded townships, Petermaritzburg, named after two of their leaders, Weenen and

other villages, and started an independent Republic of
Natalia. But Great Britain does not love independent Republics on her frontier, especially if they are weak; least of all,
if they have access to the sea coast. The Imperial Government
never recognised Natalia; and, as it held on to the port of
Durban, it sent up a force by sea, drove the Dutch back west-
ward, and extinguished the young Dutch Republic of Natalia
(after six years of life), and in 1845 founded the British Colony
of Natal. Thereupon, the majority of the Boer farmers resumed their long Trek, sullenly recrossed the Drakensberg
chain, and settled down in the Orange State, and partly passed
again into the Transvaal.

The state of things now was somewhat anomalous. Boers,
numbering in all about 15,000, were loosely scattered about
in the vast area of veldt, 600 to 700 miles across, between the
Orange and the Limpopo Rivers. There were about 4,000
adult males, spread over 160,000 square miles, in vast detached
grazing farms. There was no general government. The British
Government did not interfere with them; gave them no protection; neither police, nor soldiers, nor magistrates. But it
obstinately claimed them as British subjects, under the antique rule of law that no subject of the Crown could put off
his allegiance. This claim the Boers, who had been wandering
and settling outside the actual British frontier for nearly
twenty years, as obstinately refused to admit.

... This is not the place or time to rehearse the trite story of
Outlander grievances and Boer misrule. I have come here to
state historic facts, not to plead the Boer case or to excuse or
justify Boer policy. I am quite willing to believe that much of
it was unjust as well as unwise. I do not doubt that the railway and mining and dynamite monopolies were oppressive,
that their Protective tariff almost outdid that of President Mc-
Kinley; that the education of English children was neglected,
as indeed it is in France; that the municipal government of
the Rand was as bad as it is in Spain; that the Chamber was
open to bribes, as it is said to be in the United States. All this
and more may be true, but, as Mr. Bryce justly insists, it gave
no legitimate ground for war.

And on the top of this race antipathy, of these bitter memories, of these incessant menaces, of these well-grounded fears, came the Raid; organised by the Prime Minister of a great British colony, carried out by the armed forces raised under Royal Charter, and led by men of rank in the Queen's service. Of this Raid, wherein, as Mr. Lecky says, a Privy Councillor and servant of the Crown organised a conspiracy to overthrow the Government of a friendly State, deceiving the High Commissioner, his own colleagues in the Ministry, and the great companies for which he was the principal trustee, I will not here speak. The Colonial Secretary told Parliament that all this was "a mistake," but that the author of it "had done nothing dishonourable." Mr. Rhodes admitted that he had upset the apple-cart; and gracefully retired from the scene uncondemned.

He ceased to be Prime Minister, but he continued to build Empire, to menace the independence of the Boers, to labour for colouring South Africa pink in spite of Boer, in spite of a Parliamentary majority in Cape Colony, at the cost of our good name and welfare in the United Kingdom. Mr. Cecil Rhodes is, after all, only one, no doubt the greatest, but the type of groups of keen, ambitious, reckless men who have forced us into war—a war wherein the whole Empire is now being strained to its roots in order to crush some 50,000 herdsmen, whose ancestors for a whole century have struggled to be free from British grip. If I felt free to speak my whole mind, I should speak of it as a new Imperial Raid, carried out in the name of our Queen, under the instigation of a combination of trading syndicates. It would take us too far to consider the justice or morality of these raids, whether Chartered of Imperial, and we might be told that all this was "unctuous rectitude." Rectitude of any kind, it seems, has gone out of fashion. But I am old-fashioned enough to prefer it to unctuous turpitude. And I prefer the name of a just, peaceful, and righteous England to that of an Empire scrambling for half a continent at the bidding and in the interest of cosmopolitan gamblers and speculative companies, in search of bigger dividends and higher premiums.

3:The Committees

The Stop the War Committee

Many pro-Boers were soon distressed by the incoherence of their movement and by their own failure to coordinate propaganda. Silas K. Hocking, a prolific and immensely popular late Victorian novelist who had by then "drifted out of the Methodist ministry,"[1] decided to take things in hand. On Christmas eve, he wrote an open letter calling upon men of peace and good will to band together.

Silas K. Hocking

Letter to the Press   **December 24, 1899**

Sir,—There are many people who think, with myself, that the time has come when some organised attempt should be made by those who believe in the New Testament to put a stop to the inhuman slaughter that is going on in South Africa—a slaughter that is not only a disgrace to civilisation, but which brings our Christianity into utter contempt. Surely sufficient blood has been shed. No one can any longer doubt the courage or the skill of either of the combatants, but why prolong the strife? Cannot we in the name of the Prince of Peace cry "Halt!" and seek some peaceful settlement of the questions in dispute? As the greater, and as we think the more Christian, nation we should cover ourselves with honour in asking for an armistice and seeking a settlement by peaceful means. We can win no honour by fighting, whatever the issues may be. In order to test the extent of the feeling to which I have given expression and with a view to holding a conference in London at an early date, I shall be willing to receive the names of any who may be willing to co-operate.

Quoted in William Stewart, J. Keir Hardie
(London, 1925), pp. 155–56

Hocking's appeal led directly to the formation of the Stop the War Committee, the most vociferous—and therefore the most infamous—of the pro-Boer agencies. W. T. Stead, a member of its executive committee, promptly established

1. Hocking, *My Book of Memory* (London, 1923), p. 177; also, *Dictionary of National Biography, 1931–1940*, p. 436.

himself as a moving force in the organization. W. M. Crook, whose pro-Boer activities cost him the editorship of the *Echo*, described the Committee's inception to Stead's biographer.

W. M. Crook to Frederic Whyte

I protested strongly against the name, as I considered it unnecessarily provocative and irritating, but Stead insisted that it was the name most descriptive of what we were out to accomplish and, as the majority of our associates agreed with him, I bowed to their decision. Stead was Treasurer and found most of the money for carrying out our operations. I believe he would have bankrupted himself but for Mr. Stout, his manager, who with friendly guile concealed from him some of the profits of the *Review of Reviews* (already beginning to dwindle) and banked them separately for the benefit of the Stead household!

Quoted in Whyte, W. T. Stead (*London, 1925*), *2:172*

In addition to Crook and Stead, each of whom pledged their journals to the committee and its work, the officers included Harold Rylett and Alfred Marks, joint editors of the *New Age*. The committee could also depend upon favorable publicity from *Truth*, the *Manchester Guardian*, the *Morning Leader*, the *Speaker*, and the *Star*. A network of provincial committees was set up to disseminate antiwar literature and provide platforms for speakers, who were sent on tour. Within three months, however, the committee abandoned its lecture programs for fear of inciting violence. At the end of a year's operations, a report and statement of accounts was issued.

Stop the War Committee
Report and Statement of Accounts
(January 11 to December 31, 1900)   January 21, 1901

The Stop-the-War Committee was established at a Conference of Friends of Peace summoned by Rev. Silas K. Hocking in Exeter Hall, on January 11, 1900. Its mandate was contained in the following resolutions:

That in the opinion of this Conference the present war between the Christian States in South Africa is a scandal to Christendom and a disgrace to civilisation, which it is the duty of all Christians to endeavour to stop.

That while to provoke an unnecessary war is a crime against humanity, the continuation for the sake of Imperial prestige is a grievous addition to the national guilt.

Therefore, we appeal to the Governments of the Empire and of the Republics to arrest the present purposeless effusion of blood in order that for the first time we may be informed what it is that each is fighting for, and so pave the way for an honourable agreement to be arrived at either by direct negotiation or by the mediation of some friendly neutral in accordance with the principles of the Hague Conference.

That this Conference is of opinion that the present war was brought about by the circulation of statements for which there is no foundation in truth, and by the overbearing diplomacy of the Colonial Secretary. It declares its profound conviction that all our difficulties originate in the well-founded distrust entertained by the Burghers of Mr. Chamberlain, whose share in the Rhodes-Jameson conspiracy was rendered all the more conspicuous by the attempt to hoodwink the Select Committee of the House of Commons.

It denounces as dishonest his attempt to revive the suzerainty of 1881, which was abandoned in 1884. It condemns as an act of distinct bad faith the repudiation of his own offer of a Joint Committee of Enquiry into the seven years' franchise the moment it was accepted by President Kruger, and it regards with horror and indignation his cynical admission that this bloody and disastrous war was due to his failure to write an intelligible despatch in reply to the offer of a five years' franchise.

This Conference further repudiates as a disingenuous afterthought the myth of a great Dutch conspiracy, and brands as untrue the statement that the armaments of the Burghers began before 1895, or had any other origin than the legitimate desire to protect themselves against a

renewal of the conspiracy. It deplores the persistent refusal of our Government to accept President Kruger's
earnest and oft-repeated entreaties to allow all differences
between us to be settled by arbitration, and finally this
Conference expresses its solemn conviction that there is
no possibility of restoring peace to South Africa until
Mr. Chamberlain is removed from the Colonial Office
and is no longer permitted to occupy a position of trust
which he has abused by wrecking the peace of the Empire and besmirching the fair fame of our country.

That this Conference, believing that all lawful means
should be used to arrest the continuance of this unjust
and unnecessary war, appoints a Committee and in-
structs it to do whatever it can to give effect to the Resolutions, either by means of the Press, the pulpit, the
platform, or by appealing to the Constituencies whenever
bye-elections take place.

The Committee was constituted as follows:

President: THE REV. JOHN CLIFFORD, D.D.
Chairman of Executive: REV. SILAS K. HOCKING
Hon. Treasurer: MR. ALFRED MARKS
Hon. Secretary: MR. W. M. CROOK
Members of Executive:

MR. G. H. PERRIS	MRS. SHELDON AMOS
MR. HAROLD RYLETT	MRS. COBDEN UNWIN
MR. FRANK SMITH	MISS BARNICOAT
MR. W. T. STEAD	
REV. W. URWICK	

The first step taken by the Committee was to issue the
following placard, which set forth the reasons why it appealed
to the nation to stop the war.

STOP THE WAR!
AN APPEAL TO THE PEOPLE

To Our Fellow Countrymen:

WE APPEAL TO YOU TO STOP THE WAR.

It is an unjust War which ought never to have been pro-
voked.

It is a War in which we have nothing to gain, everything to lose.

To "put it through" merely because we are in it, is to add crime to crime.

AND ALL FOR WHAT?

Why are our sons and brothers killing and being killed in South Africa?

Why are happy homes made desolate, wives widowed, and children left fatherless?

LET US FACE THE FACTS!

There would have been no War if we had consented to Arbitration, which President Kruger begged for, but which we haughtily refused.

There would have been no War if the Government had counted the cost.

There would have been no War if the capitalists at the goldfields had not hoped it would reduce wages and increase dividends.

There would have been no War but for the campaign of lies undertaken to make men mad against the Boers.

AND WHO ARE THE BOERS?

The Boers are the Dutch of South Africa, white men, and Protestant Christians like ourselves.

They read the same Bible, keep the same Sabbath, and pray to the same God as ourselves.

They believe that they are fighting for Freedom and Fatherland, with the unanimous support of Europe excepting Turkey.

WHAT ARE WE FIGHTING FOR?

We have been at War for three months, thousands have been killed and wounded, but to this day neither side knows what the other is fighting for.

Each side asserts that the other is fighting for something which the other denies that it wants.

WHY NOT CALL A TRUCE?

We might then get to know for the first time what is the real difference between us.

And when we had in black and white what each side wants we should then be able to see what could be done to arrange matters.

If we could not agree on a Settlement, then we ought to refer the difference to Arbitration.

IF WE "PUT IT THROUGH" WHAT DOES IT MEAN?
The sacrifice of the lives of 20,000 of our brave sons.
The slaughter of at least as many brave Boers.
Hard times for the poor at home.
Dislocation of Trade.
The Increase of Taxation.
The waste of £100,000,000 of our hard-earned money.
And in the end,
CONSCRIPTION.

IS THE GAME WORTH THE CANDLE?
If we wade through blood to hoist the Union Jack at Pretoria our difficulties will then only have begun.
We shall have conquered a people we cannot govern.
We can never govern them with their consent.
If we try to govern them against their will we shall have to keep 50,000 soldiers in their country.

WE DO NOT WANT ANOTHER IRELAND IN SOUTH AFRICA.
Therefore we appeal to you to

STOP THE WAR AND STOP IT NOW!

. . . The Committee feels that as it accurately diagnosed the future more than twelve months ago it may appeal with some confidence to its supporters. Its policy in the future as in the past is one of uncompromising opposition to the war. The formula "Stop the War and Stop it Now," is as sound to-day as it was when the Committee was constituted, and the war can be stopped only in one of two ways. Either the Dutch must be exterminated, or we must complete our evacuation of the two Republics, and concede that demand for arbitration which the Boers have made from the first. . . .

The Committee, therefore, appeals with confidence for a renewal of subscriptions to enable it to keep up a *mitraille* of pamphlets, broadsheets, and leaflets for the purpose of driving conviction into the public mind as to the insanity and criminality of this war. The time is not one which calls for mealy-mouthed utterances. The Committee believes that this war, which from its beginning was a crime without justification or excuse, has now degenerated into a campaign of extermination, carried out by a policy of systematic devastation, the like of which for atrocity can only be paralleled in our time by the operations of the Turks in Armenia and Bulgaria. Never before has the British nation attempted the extermination of an entire nationality. Never before have we waged unrelenting war upon the women and children of brave men whom we are unable to subdue in battle. This professedly Christian nation is now proceeding in a policy of murder, wholesale and retail, which renders our religion a hollow farce, and exposes us to the contempt and execration even of the heathen world.

Face to face with such a phenomenon of unprecedented crime there is only one thing for us to do, and that is to Stop the War and Stop it at once, and stop it in the only way in which it can be stopped—by ceasing to murder and to steal, by retiring within our own possessions, and making such amends as we can to the people whose homesteads we have burnt, and whose country we have converted into a blackened wilderness.

SILAS K. HOCKING,
Chairman

ALFRED MARKS,
Hon. Treasurer

HAROLD RYLETT,
Hon. Secretary

4, CLOCK HOUSE,
 ARUNDEL STREET, STRAND,
  W.C.

"STOP-THE-WAR" COMMITTEE

BALANCE SHEET from January 11 to December 31, 1900

RECEIPTS	£	s.	d.	EXPENDITURE	£	s.	d.
Subscriptions	2,586	3	6	Rent of Offices	94	14	5
Sums collected at				Salaries	168	0	6
meetings	45	18	9	Expenses of			
Sums received for				meetings	218	4	3
publications	88	11	7	Printing, advertising, purchase			
				of books, etc.	1,263	16	9
				Postage and carriage of			
				parcels	615	19	8
				Office expenses and sundries	165	17	10
				Outstanding accounts (printing)	101	18	9
				Balance on December 31	92	1	8
	£2,720	13	10		£2,720	13	10

ALFRED MARKS, *Hon. Treas.*
Audited and found correct,
VICTOR BAUER, Chartered Accountant,
January 9, 1901 166, Adelaide Road, London, N.W.

It was as a clearing house for pro-Boer pamphlets (a sample packet was available free upon request) that the Stop the War Committee was most active. These consisted largely of reprints of journal articles (information was considered all the more incriminating if it first appeared in the press, especially the Tory press), parliamentary and other speeches, and occasional manifestos that wielded history as a weapon. Rarely did these publications exceed four pages in length: many were only two pages long, and set in bold type. Cheaply priced, they were designed to pass quickly from hand

to hand, leaving those who scanned them with an impression
of a few essential points: the immorality and extravagance
of the war; the bravery and charity of the enemy; the
duplicity of British statesmanship; and, not least of all, the
avarice of the Government's supporters.

The War Blight on Social Reforms
STW Committee Pamphlet No. 13

The Feeding of the Underfed Scholars

We are spending £100,000,000 in slaughter, in order to
soothe the offended pride of Englishmen in the Transvaal
who were making millions if they were capitalists, and earning
£1 a-day if they were workmen; meanwhile, 55,000 children
are driven every day hungry and underfed into the public
schools of London. *Punch* has done good service in the cause
of sanity and humanity by publishing the following verse:

Fire eaters of the Music Halls, in vain ye take my name,
   When your patriotic ballads rise and swell;
I am not all for glory and for military fame
   And the thunder of the cannon and the shell.
I am not merely Amazon, with bloody sword and spear,
   And death is not the harvest I would reap,
I am a woman, I am a mother, and I still have ears to hear
   The wailing of my children when they weep.
    Hark! I hear them; they are crying;
    'Tis of hunger they are dying—
See this hollow cheek and weary sunken head!
    Lo, they perish of starvation,
    And you give them—education!
Ah! before you teach, for God's sake, give them bread!

The Housing of the People

Speaking at Manchester in October, Sir H. Campbell-Bannerman referred as follows to the Bitter Cry of those who have
"No Room to Live":

    Here is a grievance to which the complaints of the
Transvaal Uitlanders are a mere empty cry. (Loud and

continued cheering.) Here is a peril at our own doors—
(hear, hear) —greater than we can fear from any Boer
aggression. Here are destruction and misery exceeding
that of War— (cheers) —working and waxing in the
houses of our own people. The necessary cures may be
drastic. We may have to touch the Land Laws. (Cheers.)
The rights of property may not be safe from us, and
great public expenditure may be required, but a remedy
must be found. (Cheers.)

But the money that might have rehoused a nation has been
spent in slaughtering our Brother Boer in South Africa.

Old Age Pensions

Mr. Chamberlain is now free to evade all pretence of fulfilling his election pledges.

To provide a pension for the worn-out veterans of British
industry would require millions.

But so many millions have been spent in South African War
that all hope of Old Age Pensions must be abandoned.

To add 2½ millions to the annual dividends of the Consolidated Gold Fields Co. we spend £100,000,000. But to save
the working man from the Workhouse by providing him a
pension in his Old Age—Not a Penny!

And Mr. Chaplin now tells us that the improvement of our
Workhouses must be abandoned because the Government has
no money to spare.

Why?

Because they have spent it in Slaughter!

Death to the Republics! DEATH!
The New War and Its War Cry!
A Protest and an Appeal
STW Committee Pamphlet No. 17

When the Stop the War Committee was formed the first
resolution passed at the Conference in Exeter Hall called
upon both parties to say plainly what they were fighting for,
in order that, if possible, some peaceful solution might be
arrived at.

We have now the response to that appeal from both camps. It simplifies the situation, but it does not bring us nearer Peace. For while the Presidents state that they are fighting to secure and safeguard the incontestable independence of both Republics, Lord Salisbury throws off the mask, and declares War to the knife against the independence either of the South African Republic or of the Orange Free State.

The War, therefore, will go on. But it is at least a comfort to know what we are fighting for. There is no longer any nonsense about paramountcy or franchise or any of the other subterfuges which were used "with intent to deceive." We are fighting for conquest, invading the territory of States whose independence we have repeatedly recognised in order to destroy that independence.

"Death to the Republics! Death!" is the new battle cry of the Empire.

But are we going to stand silent by when this crime is being perpetrated in our name?

Some of us at least dare not accept any such responsibility. Hence the Executive Committee of the "Stop the War" movement unanimously passed the following resolution:

> That as the reply of the Prime Minister to the appeal of Presidents Kruger and Steyn tears off the mask and reveals for the first time the truth so long denied that this War is being waged for the destruction of the independence of the Dutch Commonwealths of South Africa, this Committee declares that the time has now come for all who are opposed to carrying on a War of extermination to unite in making solemn protest by all means still left available to the free citizens of this country against a cause which involves the repudiation of solemn national pledges, and commits this country to a crime against the principle of nationality unparalleled since the partition of Poland.

Copies of this resolution have been sent to all Ministers, Members of Parliament, and others interested in public affairs. It was also decided to hold another Conference at an early date in Exeter Hall for the purpose of submitting the above resolution to a full meeting of the General Committee.

The Reply of the Republics to Lord Salisbury

On March 13th Mr. State Secretary Reitz published the official reply of the Republics to Lord Salisbury's despatch refusing to treat for Peace. He says:

> In reference to Lord Salisbury's assertion that the Ultimatum of the Republic was the first step towards hostilities, the real truth is that a continuous threat was made on the part of the British Government ever since the Bloemfontein Conference to bring about changes in the internal government of the South African Republic, although this was totally opposed to the rights guaranteed by existing Conventions. At the same time an abnormal number of British troops was concentrating in the neighbourhood of the Republican borders, and an intimation was subsequently conveyed from Sir Alfred Milner to President Steyn that the concentration of these troops had reference only to the Transvaal, and was not directed against the Orange Free State.
>
> Negotiations were then suddenly broken off, with a threat that the British Government would take its own steps to remove the grievances of its subjects in the South African Republic. The Governments of the Republics waited two weeks, during which time Mr. Chamberlain made constant bellicose speeches. Sir Alfred Milner refused Mr. Steyn an explanation of the warlike preparations, an Army Corps was shipped to South Africa, and the British Military Reserves were called up. All these facts indicated belligerent intentions on the part of the British Government.
>
> Then only was a firm communication—denominated an Ultimatum by the British people—addressed to Her Majesty's Government, demanding the removal of the troops on the borders and the settlement of all differences by means of impartial Arbitration.
>
> That was not necessarily intended as a message of War.

Concerning the armaments, Mr. Reitz says:—

> These were bought openly in England and Europe, and the High Commissioner boasted full knowledge of

them at Bloemfontein; and also full descriptions of these armaments were found among officers' papers at Dundee.

Both the arming and the Ultimatum were protective measures, subsequent to the Raid and to the discovery through concealed cables that British Cabinet Ministers were implicated in an attempt to filch away the independence of the Republics.

Now all doubt is removed by Lord Salisbury's telegram. The burghers must fight for their national existence, trusting that God will defend the right.

The above, which has been published throughout the Republics, will not be forwarded to Lord Salisbury.

Our Brave Brother Boer. The Verdict of Tommy Atkins! STW Committee Pamphlet No. 42

The special War correspondent of *The Daily News,* who was made prisoner by the Boers in the reconnaissance at Rensburg, has contributed to his paper (Monday, April 2) a very interesting account of his treatment at the hands of his captors:

> For a day and a-half I lay at that laager whilst our wounded men were brought in, and here I should like to say a word to the people of England. Our men when wounded are treated by the Boers with manly gentleness and kindly consideration. When we left the laager in an open trolly, we, some half-dozen Australians and about as many Boers, all wounded, were driven for some hours to a small hospital, the name of which I do not know. It was simply a farmhouse turned into a place for the wounded. On the road thither we called at many farms, and at every one, men, women, and children came out to see us. Not one taunting word was uttered in our hearing, not one braggart sentence passed their lips. Men brought us cooling drinks, or moved us into more comfortable positions on the trolly. Women, with gentle fingers, shifted bandages, or washed wounds, or gave us little dainties that come so pleasant in such a time; whilst the little children crowded round us with tears running down their cheeks as they looked upon the bloodstained

khaki clothing of the wounded British. Let no man or woman in all the British Empire whose son or husband lies wounded in the hands of the Boers fear for his welfare, for it is foul slander to say that the Boers do not treat their wounded well. England does not treat her own men better than the Boers treat the wounded British, and I am writing of that which I have seen and know beyond the shadow of a doubt.

From the little farmhouse hospital I was sent on in an ambulance train to the hospital at Springfontein, where all the nurses and medical staff are foreigners, all of them trained and skilful. I only had a day or two here, and then I was sent by train in an ambulance carriage to the capital of the Orange Free State, and here I am at the time of writing in Bloemfontein Hospital.

I have made it my business to go about amongst the private soldiers, to question them concerning the treatment they have received since the moment the Mauser rifles tumbled them over, and I say emphatically that in every solitary instance, without one single exception, our countrymen declare that they have been grandly treated. Not by the hospital nurses only, not by the officials alone, but by the very men whom they were fighting. Our "Tommies" are not the men to waste praise on any men, unless it is well deserved, but this is just about how "Tommy" sums up the situation:

"The Boer is a rough-looking beggar in the field, 'e don't wear no uniform, 'nd 'e don't know enough about soldiers' drill to keep himself warm, but 'e can fight in 'is own blooming style, which ain't our style. If 'ed come out on the veldt 'nd fight us our way, we'd lick 'im every time; but when it comes to fightin' in the kopjes, why, the Boer is a dandy, 'nd if the rest of Europe don't think so, only let 'em have a try at 'im 'nd see. But when 'e has shot you 'e acts like a blessed Christian, 'nd bears no malice. 'E's like a bloomin' South Sea Cocoanut, not much to look at outside, but white 'nd sweet inside when yer know 'im, 'nd it's when your wounded 'nd a prisoner that you get a chance to know 'im, see." And "Tommy" is about right in his judgment.

A Rochdale soldier, writing after Spion Kop, about the feeling in camp about Mr. Chamberlain, says:—

> Poor old Joe! He does fairly get it. The troops curse him from morn till night.

That curse causeless does not come.

The South Africa Conciliation Committee

Many critics of the war kept their distance from the Stop the War Committee either because they disdained its solecisms, or because they considered its tactics unnecessarily provocative, or because, as M.P.'s, they feared possible electoral repercussions.

Four days after Hocking convened his conference, it was announced that yet another antiwar organization had been founded, the South Africa Conciliation Committee. Although its sponsors tactfully avoided saying as much, the new committee was conceived as a direct response to the previous one, which threatened to pull too far to the Left. Its avowed purpose was not to demand peace at any price, but to prepare British opinion for a just settlement at the earliest appropriate opportunity. Leonard Courtney was president, and he brought with him many of his associates from the old Transvaal Committee, which continued to function although its objectives were now sadly out-of-date.

The charter members of the SACC, too numerous to catalogue, formed a general committee: they included an array of Liberal journalists (Massingham, Brailsford, Lehmann, Gooch, Clayden, Hammond, and even J. A. Spender), several prosperous businessmen (Sir John Brunner, Alfred Mond, George Cadbury, and a couple of Rowntrees), prominent intellectuals (Frederic Harrison and other high priests of Positivism, Herbert Spencer, W. M. Rosetti), clergymen (the Bishop of Hereford, the Dean of Lincoln, the Dean of Winchester, Canon Barnett of Toynbee Hall, and Dr. Clifford), assorted academics (including Gilbert Murray, the Oxford classicist), and the usual complement of M.P.'s.

More judicious in its statements than the Stop the War Committee, the SACC produced a shower of leaflets which consisted largely of letters and articles excerpted from the quality journals. "Published in the Interests of Truth," these included on-the-spot reports from South Africa "by a lady," gracious tributes to "Boer humanity," and gleanings from the writings and speeches of Edmund Burke, from whom the spokesmen for the SACC claimed ideological descent. A sampling is provided below, including Pamphlet No. 15, which reprinted the circular letter that brought the committee to life.

The Committee's Manifesto as Issued to the Public Press on 15th January, 1900
SACC Pamphlet No. 15

SIR,—The deplorable expenditure of blood and money which has already taken place in South Africa, bringing with it misery to our Colonies at the Cape and grave peril to the Empire, has suggested to many besides ourselves the formation of a Committee for the dissemination of accurate information on the whole dispute, and for the consideration, as soon as a proper opportunity arises, of some peaceable settlement of the great conflict between this country and the Boer Republics.

We have known now for a long time that such a settlement was within our grasp when the Government of the Transvaal made the proposals contained in their Despatch of August 22nd last, and that the reply of the British Government on August 28th was intended—though not so understood by President Kruger—to be an acceptance of nine-tenths of those proposals.

Quite recently we have learned that the armaments of the Transvaal, which have been widely regarded as a direct menace to this country, were recognised by the British Government as being so far the result of the Raid as to preclude that Government from any right of protest against them. It appears, therefore, that the theory of the so-called Dutch conspiracy to oust British power from South Africa rests on the most shadowy foundation, and that the war was entered into under misapprehensions on the part of both this country and the Transvaal.

In view of the now recognised facts of the past, we think it to be not less contrary to reason than abhorrent to humanity to wage war for aggressive purposes beyond the point which may be necessary either for the protection of the Queen's subjects or for the preservation of the integrity of her dominions. We therefore invite all sympathisers with us to join in the furtherance of the following objects:

1. To watch South African affairs with a view to issuing accurate intelligence, and taking such other steps as may be necessary for enabling the public to form a just estimate of the political questions affecting the Colonies and the States of South Africa.

2. To advocate the paramount importance of a policy, the object of which shall be to re-establish goodwill between the British and Dutch races in South Africa by a full recognition of the just claims of both, and to urge a pacific settlement upon these principles of the deplorable conflict between this country and the two Republics at the earliest moment when such a settlement is practicable.

And we request those who think with us to send their names, either as Members or Associates, to the Secretary of the South Africa Conciliation Committee, Talbot House, Arundel Street, Strand.

> We are, Sir,
> Your obedient Servants,
> (*Signed*)
>
> LEONARD H. COURTNEY,
> *President*
>
> F. C. SELOUS,
> *Vice-President*
>
> FREDERIC MACKARNESS,
> *Chairman*

January 15th

The South Africa Conciliation Committee
Aims and Methods
SACC Pamphlet No. 18

Aims

1. To urge upon the people of Great Britain and Ireland a peaceable settlement of the great conflict between this country and the two Boer Republics at the earliest moment when such a settlement is possible.

2. To advocate the paramount importance of making that settlement one which will establish goodwill between the British and Dutch races in South Africa by a full recognition of the just claims of both.

Methods of Work

Those who are in sympathy with these objects are invited to assist the Committee, and to watch South African news with a view to forming a just estimate, and leading others to form a just estimate, of political questions affecting the Colonies and States of South Africa.

All, whether men or women, who are deeply impressed with the calamity and folly of this war can and should help—some with money, some with active work for an honourable peace—some with both—all who *care* sufficiently will find some way of working.

To those who can give active help the Committee would say: Consider yourself what you can do.

Can you form, or assist in forming, a Local Branch?

Can you speak at Village or Ward Meetings, or Workmen's Clubs?

If you are not prepared to speak can you organise such gatherings or Drawing-room Meetings to which a Speaker might be sent by the Committee?

You can watch the local paper in your neighbourhood and, perhaps, write occasionally a careful letter to it.

If you can do none of these things, you can at least distribute literature supplied by the Committee, and when you have influence add a private word of your own.

And you can strengthen the hands of those who are fighting
the battle for the real honour and safety of their country
by giving them your countenance and your sympathy
whenever and wherever they appear in public. Do not
stay away because you are now in the minority.

It behooves us, though the minority, to press the truth as
we see it with zeal and courage but without temper or exaggeration; remembering that most of those who differ from us
have had scanty opportunity of knowing the truth and are as
high-minded and anxious to judge rightly as ourselves.

GOD SAVE OUR QUEEN AND COUNTRY.

An Incident at Ladysmith
SACC Pamphlet No. 20

The following is an Extract from a Letter dated Ladysmith,
January 7th, from a Royal Army Medical Corps Officer:

> One of the Boer medical officers rode in to us under a
> Red Cross flag, and asked us to go and bury our dead,
> which, of course, we did. But the sight of those poor
> fellows lying on the hill, some of them dreadfully riddled
> with bullets, I can never forget. The Boers were very
> good; in fact, one would hardly have thought they were
> enemies. They talked to us quite freely, and helped us
> to dig the graves, and to carry our dead. There was one
> very touching incident. After our Major had read the
> Burial Service, one of the Boers stepped out and said a
> short prayer, hoping the war would soon end, and while
> we stood with heads uncovered, they sang a hymn in
> Dutch. It cut our fellows up very much indeed; in fact,
> we could hardly speak for some time.

The Treatment of the Natives in South Africa
SACC Pamphlet No. 41

To anyone who has studied the complex problems of South
African life it must be evident that native administration, and
not the antagonism between the white races must before long

become the most urgent and vital of all South African questions, and the most fraught with peril, unless it be dealt with systematically, and not spasmodically as it has been in the past.

Here in Great Britain the *danger* of it is commonly overlooked, but in South Africa it is an ever present apprehension. . . .

The imminence of the peril, even in time of peace, arising from their immense and ever increasing numerical superiority, ought surely to be a sufficient proof of the inexpediency, of the folly, to put it on no higher ground, of arming the natives against the Boers as the British Government has announced they contemplate doing; apart from the shame of the thing, they may kindle a flame they may find it impossible to control. For the natives are no longer the unthinking savages they were a few years ago: they are beginning to have aspirations, to feel the quickening impulse of a national sentiment. . . .

There are not many of these highly-educated natives, but one might arise at any moment to act as a deliverer of his race, who might obtain sufficient power over the ignorant and inflammable masses of his countrymen to raise a revolt extending from one end of his country to the other. The situation is not pleasant to contemplate; and it is becoming more difficult every day, and the need for some settled native policy more imperative.

We are apt to expect too much from the natives, and if they do not always come up to our standard to grow impatient and out of temper with them, which is a fatal mistake. They require firm and, indeed, rather severe treatment, but treatment which they can understand. They do not resent severity in the least; they respect it, but they keenly resent injustice, and that, alas! is what has been consistently meted out to them heretofore. Not, however, by the Dutch any more than by ourselves; we have both been equally to blame, although all the British Christian denominations—Church of England, Catholic and Wesleyan—have united in declaring that the war is in reality being waged to put a stop to the cruel treatment of the natives by the Dutch, and to inaugurate a better state of affairs under our own rule. Unfortunately, history shows that we are seeking to extract the mote from our neighbour's eye regardless of the beam that is within our own. The Dutch have not treated the natives well, far from it, but the net result of our rule has, on the whole, been more injurious to the native races than has theirs. . . .

The truth of the matter is that native ill-usage is due, not to the different temperaments of the English and Dutch, but to a disturbed frontier, a rough class of settlers, outrages and thefts on both sides, and consequent brutal and vindictive reprisals. . . .

The two races, it should be explained, start with entirely different conceptions of the natives. The British assert theoretically that all men are equal, blacks and whites alike; but this theory has not prevented the perpetration under their rule of abominable cruelties and oppression, although it has also enabled some few individuals to rise to a higher level than they would have been able to do under a Dutch government.

The Dutch, on the other hand, declare quite frankly that the natives are inferior beings, who must not on any account be admitted to equality; but this conception of their status, although it has oftentimes led to the committal of dreadful barbarities, has yet on the whole not been found incompatible with humane and kindly treatment, even in the old slave days. "The testimony of everyone competent to form an opinion," says Dr. Theal, "concurred that in no other part of the world was bondage so light."

It is laid down as a fundamental principle in the Transvaal Grondwet that there is no equality of rights between white men and black, and President Kruger once made a speech in which he said that it was contrary to the Scriptures to assert that they could ever be equal, and that he would never be a party to so unchristian a doctrine; but in the same speech he dwelt most strongly on the duty of using the blacks kindly, and of bettering their condition, as much as possible. . . .

Mr. Chamberlain, who does not lose an opportunity to malign the Boers, stated recently in Parliament that "the great trek was caused because the Boers wanted to be free to wallop their own niggers." He also said (on the 19th October, 1899), "the treatment of the natives of the Transvaal has been disgraceful; it has been brutal; it has been unworthy of a civilised power." Has our own treatment of them been any better? And is there much trustworthy evidence that the Dutch habitually ill-use the natives under their control? Most of the evidence is all the other way....

It cannot be insisted upon too often, or too strenuously, that we must deal with the native question with a full recognition of our own failings in the past, and that only harm can arise from a Pharisaical assumption of our philanthropic superiority to the Dutch. Nothing, indeed, has done more harm to the natives, or has aroused a bitterer feeling against ourselves than the spasms of compunction with which we have from time to time been visited. Instead of recognising that our administration has been faulty, we have salved our conscience with a flood of invective against the Dutch, and against the Colonists generally, for the barbarities of which they have been guilty, ignoring the fact that it is individuals that have been guilty of them and not races, and that these have been found amongst new arrivals from home quite as often as amongst the older settlers, and have been made possible by the defective administration of both the English and the Dutch states. Both races have, indeed, much to repair, much to make amends for; and they can best do that by the adoption of some settled common policy; for there is nothing that so unsettles the native mind as vacillation....

Lord Salisbury has given a pledge that when the time comes for settlement the interests of the natives shall not be forgotten, but care must be taken that this essential fact is not lost sight of, that it is the capitalists, not the Dutch, who are the natives' deadliest foes....

We shall have an opportunity when the war is over of making in conjunction with the Dutch a native South Africa at least as justly governed as India, but to do that we must deprive the Chartered Company of their powers, just as we put an end to the East India Company in 1857. If, instead, we are led by a section of the missionaries into a crusade against the Dutch, we shall be merely playing into the capitalists' hands, and diverting attention from their misdeeds. What is of far more urgent importance is that the charter of the British South Africa Company should be revoked, and a stop put to the opening up of Africa by any system of enforced labour, under whatever name it may be disguised.

War for Freedom and Justice!
SACC Pamphlet No. 46

Avowed Objects of the War.	Some Results of the War.
1. To establish genuine Self-Government in the Transvaal.	1. To establish military autocracy in the Republics, with the abridgment and possible withdrawal of self-government in Cape Colony.
2. To extend the Franchise to Britons.	2. To take the Franchise away from Boers and Britons.
3. To secure Freedom of the Press.	3. To prohibit the circulation of the chief Dutch and some English newspapers over large districts of Cape Colony and Natal.
4. To secure Freedom of Public Meeting.	4. To destroy the right of Free Meeting in England by ruffianism condoned by authority, and to abolish it by Martial Law in large districts of our Colonies.
5. To stop excessive Taxation and waste of Public Funds.	5. To tax the resources of the Transvaal (chiefly British) for a war indemnity, and to support a large standing army of British troops.

6. To secure Fair Administration of Justice.

6. To replace trial by jury both in the Republics and in parts of our Colonies by Martial Law under which military officials sentence civilians to long terms of imprisonment, and officials of the Capitalist League and other partisan politicians put into prison their private political opponents and confiscate and sell their property without any sort of trial.

4:The Liberal Response

Party Individualists

Whether they chose to affiliate with any of the antiwar groups or with none, parliamentary critics made their chief contribution, as one would expect, on the floor of the House of Commons. They too were divided between those who preferred to condemn the origins of the war and those who preferred to condemn its prosecution. Lord Edmond Fitzmaurice (the younger brother of Lord Lansdowne and a steadfast Liberal) made an unsuccessful attempt to reconcile the two factions, when, on January 30, he proposed an amendment that would "humbly express our regret at the want of knowledge, foresight, and judgment displayed by Your Majesty's advisers, alike in their conduct of South African affairs since 1895 and in their preparations for the war now proceeding."[1] The divergence continued, as evidenced by the following speeches by James Bryce (who had ties to the South Africa Conciliation Committee), John Burns (a Stop-the-War activist), and Sir Charles Dilke (a free agent).

Bryce, a respected party figure with sound Gladstonian credentials, seized upon A. J. Balfour's casual remark that, in his view, war had been inevitable.

James Bryce
Speech in the House of Commons   February 2, 1900

Very well; that is destiny. The right hon. Gentleman carries this theory still further. He says that not only was the war inevitable, but the ignorance of the Government was inevitable, and if the ignorance of the Government was inevitable the want of preparation was inevitable. I will carry the chain of fate one step further. Not only was the war inevitable, and not only was the unpreparedness inevitable, but the indignation of the country is inevitable, and a vote of censure such as this is the only course which can be followed when such diplomacy has been pursued and such deplorable results have followed. The right hon. Gentleman and the Prime Minister find

1. *Parliamentary Debates*, 4th series, LXXVIII, cols. 113 ff.

fate and the British constitution sufficient to explain all our misfortunes. As regards the British constitution I will say just one thing. There was a Roman maxim, worthy of Imperial Rome, and worthy to be remembered by Imperial England, that Empire is preserved by the same arts by which it has been acquired. If the British constitution was good enough to enable us to build up the gigantic Empire over which the Queen reigns, surely it is good enough to maintain that Empire. I have said nothing in these remarks about the morality of this war, nor about its justice. I have not touched upon those topics because I desired to keep the discussion on the ground of British interest alone, to look upon it simply as to what the true interest of this country is, and to show how gravely those interests have suffered. We are very often told that it is a question between Imperialists on the one hand and what are called "Little Englanders" on the other. My complaint against the Government is that they have struck a great and heavy blow at our Imperial interests. So far from complaining from the point of view of the man who does not value the connection of this country with her colonies and the possession of our transmarine dominions, I accuse the Government from the point of view of one who does value that connection. Our hold upon our self-governing colonies has rested for these many years past upon friendship and attachment. It is because we have given them self-government, and because we have endeavoured to keep them cordially attached to ourselves, and to make them value the Imperial connection, that we have been strong in their support. But I fear that at present we have destroyed those feelings—[Cries of dissent.] Hon. Gentlemen should let me finish my sentence—I fear that we have at present destroyed those feelings in the bulk of the population in South Africa. That is a serious matter. It is a serious matter to alienate the majority of the population of a great colony which is important not only from its wealth, its population, but also from its strategic position. In most wars we have at any rate this consolation, that although we may be hard pressed for the moment, we can look forward to and contemplate, after the war is ended, a better state of things for which sacrifices will have been made not in vain. But here, I am sorry to say, I see difficulties at the end of this war quite as great as the difficulties which surrounded us at the beginning. The clouds which hang about us now are dark enough, but the clouds which will hang about South Africa when the war has come to an end will be quite as dark and quite as hard to dispel. But, Sir, we must go on. It is one of the curses of the position into which we have got that we cannot stop. . . .But when the time comes for a settlement at the end of the war we must show a change of spirit in our policy. In endeavouring to settle the affairs of South Africa in the future we must show more wisdom, more judgment, more foresight than the Government has shown in the past. It is not merely our material strength; it is not merely our wealth and the unrivalled magnitude of our Navy that have given us our great position in the world and have extended our Empire, it has been the respect we have generally inspired for our sense of justice and for our respect for the rights of other nations. I do not say that even Britain has not sometimes been wanting in that feeling, but I venture to claim that on the whole her foreign and colonial policy shows that she has not only a love of freedom, but also a respect for the rights of other communities. It is by showing that respect and by the wise principles of the policy we have followed towards our colonies that we have attained our present strength and greatness. Latterly things have changed. ["No."] I am afraid they have. I am afraid that latterly we have begun to indulge in a haughty, changed spirit, and in a spirit which has sometimes not been regardful of the rights of other States, and of late years we have sometimes given cause to other countries to question our regard for international rights and the purity of our motives. I believe that in a return to those better traditions by which the British Empire has been won lies the best hope of recovering, so far as we can, the trust and the confidence of the Dutch in South Africa, and of establishing our dominion there as well as elsewhere upon the best and surest of foundations—the affection of our fellow sub-jects.

Parliamentary Debates, *4th series, LXXVIII, cols. 471–74*

John Burns, the notorious "man with the red flag" in the 1889 London dockers' strike, was soon to reveal himself a tame lion as president of the Local Government Board (1905–14). In the meantime, however, he continued to roar ferociously. His February 6 speech in the Commons was reprinted as a penny pamphlet by the Stop the War Committee (*The Trail of the Financial Serpent*), and issued by the South Africa Conciliation Committee as Pamphlet No. 19 (*The Views of a Labour Member on the Justice of the War*).

John Burns

Speech in the House of Commons   **February 6, 1900**

...I can remember reading, as a schoolboy, with pride and pleasure, how Old England, from King Alfred's time, has been the protector of liberty and freedom. That is the quality that differentiates us from all other countries in the world. Except Ireland, Britain has been through centuries the knight-errant of the smaller peoples. Who set Belgium on its legs, gave Greece it independence, helped united Italy, and stood by Switzerland from time to time? England. In this war England is not fulfilling her traditional task, the protector of the smaller nations, and the British Army, which used to be for all good causes the Sir Galahad of History, has become in Africa the janissary of the Jews.... I spent my Christmas holidays going through the books of the Chartered Company's shareholders, and I find that nearly every one who has spoken in this debate here, in the House of Lords, and in the country, has his patriotism strengthened and his speeches lengthened by the amount of his holding in the stock of the South Africa Company. It would be interesting if we could have a share list brought up-to-date to see who are the shareholders—the Duke of Fife, the Marquess of Lorne, three hundred and fifty generals and army officers, and newspaper proprietors by the yard. Then we find the shareholders in the books of the

Chartered Company are also the men who figured as the Johannesburg prisoners; four of whom alone owned £12,-000,000 of money, poor oppressed creatures; they were also the Jameson raiders; and we also find them directors of the Savage South African Show at Olympia. Why was that started? To acquaint the people on this side with the customs and idiosyncrasies of the natives of Africa? No, it is part of a scheme to inflame the minds of the people with regard to the war against their better conscience and their better knowledge. Then we come to the Rhodesian press, and we find all the newspapers were captured by the Rhodesian gang, and I am surprised and ashamed that a great paper like the *Times*, the greatest newspaper in the world, but the smallest organ for oppressed humanity, should have employed the Moneypennys and such people as correspondents. Wherever we go in this matter we see the same thing. Wherever we examine there is the financial Jew operating, directing, inspiring the agencies that have led to this war. They were supreme at the South African Committee in 1897. I thought I had landed myself in a synagogue when I went to hear the Commission; when I went to hear the trial of the Johannesburg prisoners before the Chief Justice I thought I had dropped into some place in Aldgate or Houndsditch; and when we see how the delay of the inquiry was brought about, and how the prisoners were allowed to escape with light punishment, and how exalted personages obtruded themselves into the Committee and smiled upon the chief culprits, we see the force which is moving this country on to war. And for all this intrigue on the part of smart society for money, the nation incurs the debt of war. The trail of the financial serpent is over this war from beginning to end. I consider it my duty to the labour constituency I represent to say that I have a right to protest against this war. The Highland Brigade with typical valour and character share the brunt of battle with Welsh, Irish, and Englishmen, of the most serious struggles which have ever been compressed into three or four months of hard fighting; those men have shown they were heroes, but it is heroism wasted for ignoble ends. You should have gone to the relief of the Armenians against the

Turk if you wanted war merely for war's sake. The crime of it all is that these brave lads from Inverness and Glasgow and the Rifle Brigade are fighting for an unrighteous cause, a cause which brings no military credit, will deprive a brave people of their freedom, and ultimately land us in conscription. The Highland Brigade, for example, who had so nobly done their duty by the side of men of other nationalities, were too good to waste on Mr. Rutherfoord Harris and Mr. Beit. I protest against the incompetency displayed in the arrangements for the war, the hollowness of its object, the immorality of its aim, the stupidity with which the negotiations were conducted, and above all the want of taste, tact, and temper too frequently shown by the Colonial Secretary, the result being that we have been dragged into a war that has besmirched the fair name of the country. (Cheers.)

Parliamentary Debates, *4th series, LXXVIII, cols. 795–97*

Sir Charles Dilke, who launched his parliamentary career in the 1870s, had distinguished himself from the start as a trenchant critic of Conservative policy in South Africa. His close friend and ally in these early years was "Radical Joe" Chamberlain, who had since strayed from the appointed path. Dilke was often tipped as Gladstone's successor, until he was named corespondent in a sensational divorce suit. Exiled to the backbenches, he nonetheless remained an authority on military and imperial issues, about which he wrote extensively.

Sir Charles Dilke
Speech in the House of Commons   **February 11, 1900**

In one of Shakespeare's plays, the first part of "Henry VI," a messenger comes in to the council and tells what is the state of things prevailing with regard to the British arms in France. He relates there a state of things which is very similar to that existing as regards our arms in South Africa now. I have no doubt that the messenger was not a popular person at the time he made that speech, and that the leading member of the council had the same view with regard to his statements of fact as the First Lord of the Treasury has with regard to this debate, namely, that the country takes no interest in it at all. But I cannot help thinking there have been, and will be, matters raised in this debate in which the country does take the very deepest interest. I certainly have become aware of such an interest by the ordinary means by which a Member of this House obtains information as to the opinions of his own constituents. We need hardly dwell upon the winter through which we have passed. There is hardly a Member of this House—I doubt if there is one—who has not relatives or dear friends either dead, wounded, prisoners at Pretoria, or dying of typhoid in one of those entrenched camps the history of which, as has been said by the greatest of military writers, is inextricably mixed up with the history of capitulations. The country has gone through an awful winter, and under our constitutional system there are persons responsible, and we have to examine the nature and character of that responsibility. Some Government speakers who during the recess have addressed the country have drawn certain comparisons between the occurrences in this war and those in the Crimean War. There is this great difference, that in the Crimean War the arms of this country met with no single check. We went even in that terrible autumn and winter from the victory of the Alma to the victory of Balaclava and on to that of Inkerman. Throughout the whole of the Crimean War the British arms never met with a check at all. ["Redan."] What occurred in that instance? The Town was taken, it was evacuated that night. There was a slight repulse, but the town was evacuated on the night of the great attack, and Sebastopol fell with losses, even in the final attack, which are small compared with the losses we have suffered in this campaign, and without a single prisoner being taken. I remember—I am sorry to say I am old enough—on the night of the fireworks of the peace illumination at the close of the war—I was a child in the crowd—I passed the residence of a Member of this House who had illuminated his house with a transparency, in which he said, "This is a mourning for a war disgracefully conducted." I confess that I believe the present war has been far more disgracefully conducted than the Crimean War had been, and that the mourning is far more applicable to this case. Now, with regard to the checks or reverses—that is the accepted phrase—we are really afraid in these days to talk about "disasters"—the First Lord of the Treasury at Manchester distinctly stated there had been "no disaster." There has been no single great engagement in which we have met with an absolute disaster, but for the first time in our military history there has been a succession of checks or reverses—unredeemed as they have been by a single great military success in the whole course of the war—in many of which we have left prisoners in the enemy's hands. . . .

Can any Member of this House deny that the net result of these proceedings has been disastrous to the belief of the world in our ability to conduct a war? Therefore, if there has been, as the right hon. Gentleman says, no one disaster, surely the result of the proceedings has been one disastrous to the credit of this country. There has been one immense redemption of that disaster, which is that all the Powers, however hostile, have very frankly acknowledged on these occasions the heroism of the officers and men. Our military reputation, which undoubtedly never stood lower in the eyes of the world than at the present moment, is redeemed in that respect, and the individual courage of officers and men never stood higher in the estimate of the world than it does now. It seems to me to be a patriotic duty of those who have in the past discussed in this House the question of Cabinet responsibility for military preparations to discuss the question now; to see who is responsible, whom I will not say we will hang, but whom we are to hold blameworthy in the highest degree for what has occurred.

Parliamentary Debates, *4th series, LXXVIII, cols. 296–98*

Pleading the excuse that he was too busy writing his life of Gladstone, Morley held aloof from the parliamentary agitation. "Mr. Morley is my leader," Lloyd George complained to Hirst, "but it is very distressing that he won't keep the field."[1]

1. Quoted in Hirst, *In the Golden Days* (London, 1947), p. 206.

John Morley to Leonard Courtney　　　　**April 5, 1900**

I cannot persuade myself that the moment requires parliamentary action, though I see nothing decisive to be said against it. The germs of misgiving about the whole vile policy are very visible. Every day of military suspense will tend to develope [sic] them. I believe that time will soon be much more ripe for effective protest and useful discussion than now. I enclose you the passage of Cobden to which I referred on Tuesday: "You might as well reason with mad dogs as with men when they have begun to spill each other's blood. I was so convinced during the Crimean war of the utter uselessness of raising one's voice in opposition to war when it has once begun, that I made up my mind that, so long as I was in public life, should a war again break out between England and a Great Power, I would never open my mouth on the subject from the time the first gun was fired until peace was made."

Quoted in G. P. Gooch, Life of Lord Courtney
(London, 1920), p. 404

Liberals in League

On February 14, Liberal M.P.'s and publicists (in some cases one and the same) gathered at the Westminster Palace Hotel, London, to devise some intrinsically Liberal form of opposition to the war. Some of the participants belonged to the Transvaal Committee or to the South Africa Conciliation Committee, neither of which were explicitly political in character; markedly few were involved in the Stop the War Committee.

The result was the creation of a League of Liberals Against Aggression and Militarism, which was intended on the one hand to stem the drift towards Rosebery within the party, and, on the other, to prepare for the approaching general election. An account of the February 14 proceedings appeared in the *Speaker*, a weekly journal of party opinion which, the previous October, had come under the editorship of J. L. Hammond.

The Liberal Response

The resolutions adopted by a gathering representative of every part of the country were direct, explicit, and vigorous. The first resolution condemned the war, and demanded a declaration from the Government of the objects for which it is being prosecuted. It was moved by Mr. [David] Lloyd George, fresh from his oratorical triumph in the House of Commons, and seconded by Mr. [Thomas] Burt, who said that of all the Northumberland miners who had returned from the Transvaal he had not found one who approved of the war. Mr. [Herbert] Paul, in moving a resolution calling for the publication of the suppressed correspondence relating to the Raid, exposed some of the calumnies by which the nation had been tricked into this war. The third resolution, protesting against increasing military expenditure, and proposals for conscription, was moved by Sir Brampton Gurdon, whose dislike of the word "Imperial" was very clearly shared by his audience. Mr. [F. A.] Channing in seconding it drew an instructive parallel from the career of Pitt whose talents, pledged to the cause of economical reform, were diverted and absorbed by the exigencies of an aggressive foreign policy. The fourth resolution was appropriately moved by Mr. George Russell. It reaffirmed the loyalty of the meeting to the principles for which Mr. Gladstone had fought his greatest campaigns, and the significance of Mr. Russell's allusion to those campaigns was quickly caught up by the meeting:

> The word Imperialism stood to them as a hissing and an execration and a laughing-stock. Some gentlemen who were his comrades and associates of that time were very clearly present to his mind, and he thought that they would agree with him that they would have had uncommonly little chance of entering the House of Commons—absolutely no chance at all of crossing the threshold of Downing Street—if in 1800 or between that year and 1885 they had shown the slightest vestige of those Imperial instincts of which they were now so proud.

Mr. [F.] Maddison in supporting the resolution repudiated the title of "Peace-at-any-Price," and indignantly protested against the hypocrisy which called a capitalists' war a war for freedom.

Sir John Brunner moved a resolution recommending that a permanent organisation should be formed to provide for a vigorous propaganda throughout the country. Sir John Brunner, who is nothing if not outspoken, recommended other Liberal members to follow his example and unravel the sinister history of the capitalist conspiracy which had led to the war. Mr. [C. P.] Scott argued that the chief value of the proposal was that it was no mere temporary expedient, but an attempt to provide for the permanent needs of Liberalism. One of the events of the afternoon was a speech in which Mr. Cronwright Schreiner described the despotism of DeBeers, and appealed to the English love of freedom to spare the two Republics. Several gentlemen were unable to be present, and wrote letters of sympathy.

The chairman of the league was R. C. ("Rudie") Lehmann, an accomplished journalist, who was soon temporarily installed as editor of the *Daily News*, and later elected to the 1906 Parliament. The treasurer, appropriately enough, was Sir John Brunner, cofounder of one of the nation's largest industrial empires (Brunner, Mond and Company, a parent firm of Imperial Chemical Industries), whom *The Times* blithely dubbed "the Chemical Croesus." There were thirty-one members of the executive committee, no fewer than thirteen of whom were M.P.'s. J. A. Bright and H. N. Gladstone were included for obvious reasons, Robert Spence Watson as president of the National Liberal Federation, and, among the journalists, there were J. A. Hobson, H. N. Brailsford, Hammond, and Hirst. An array of pamphlets was issued over the League imprint, not easily distinguishable from those of other groups which the League helped to distribute. There was also a statement of aims and a circular letter addressed to the Liberal rank and file.

Basis

As a result of the Liberal Conference held on Wednesday, February 14th [1900], at the Westminster Palace Hotel, London, a central organisation has been established to carry out the policy contained in the Resolutions then passed. Briefly the objects are:

(1) To combat, by vigorous propaganda, the growth of a spirit of Aggression and Militarism.
(2) As a consequence, to recommend to the Electorate a policy which shall promote peace and conciliation in dealing with foreign nations on the lines laid down by the Hague Conference, and shall respect and strengthen the rights of self-government enjoyed by our Colonies.
(3) To enforce a sane policy with respect to the alarming growth of armaments, and to urge retrenchment as a necessary prelude to social progress and political reform.
(4) To co-operate with those Associations which have for their object the spread of truthful information about the condition of South Africa and the causes and necessary consequences of the War, and to insist that no settlement will be permanently satisfactory which does not take into account the feelings of the Dutch, who form the majority of the white population in South Africa.

The League will work by means of a central organisation in London. It will issue literature, provide lecturers and speakers, and will from time to time organise meetings in different parts of the country. As these efforts will necessitate a large expenditure of money, donations and annual subscriptions are earnestly invited from those who wish well to the movement. A *minimum* subscription of *2s. 6d.* will qualify for membership of the League. Subscriptions should be sent to the Secretary at the above address. There will be an Annual Meeting of the League.

8 SERJEANTS' INN,
FLEET STREET, E.C.

Dear Sir,

The General Election cannot now be long delayed, even if the Government were to retain office for the full constitutional term. Sir M. Hicks Beach has indicated that if the war is finished successfully before that term expires, Parliament will be dissolved immediately, and the Government will appeal to the country on its policy for the settlement in South Africa.

If the peace is to be other than a "Roman peace," if the settlement is to be other than an armed occupation and a military despotism, and unless South Africa is to groan like Europe under the burden of armaments, it is essential that the Liberal Party should be able to enforce its traditional policy, which has played so important a part in the building up of the Empire. That policy, of which the greatest exponent was Mr. Gladstone, has always been to respect the rights of small nationalities, to allow our Colonies full liberty to manage their own affairs without dictation from the home Parliament, in which they are unrepresented, and to hold Peace one of the greatest glories of a nation.

It was the opposite policy which lost us the United States of America.

This League has been formed for the purpose of rousing the Liberal Party and the nation at large to a sense of the real danger, which lies not so much in the war as in the policy of which it is the most disastrous among many manifestations. During its five years of office this Government has exposed the country to a perpetual series of alarms—from the Raid and the Venezuelan affair to the Fashoda Crisis, the Indian Frontier War, the Chinese Imbroglio, and the present campaign. Our permanent expenditure on armaments had risen by more than 30 per cent. before the present war commenced. The immediate danger lies in the settlement which is to follow this war.

In our second pamphlet the future of South Africa is discussed, and the following suggestions are made as the basis of a practical settlement:

(1) That we recognise the autonomy of the Republics, provided

(2) that we can secure effective guarantees for permanent peace

    (a) by a compulsory disarmament which will relieve South Africa from militarism and the British taxpayer from its burdens, and (*b*) by recourse to arbitration for the adjustment of future differences.

This policy, we believe, has the assent of the great majority of Liberals in the country, but hitherto, for a variety of reasons, it has not received, in the press and on the platform, anything like an adequate expression. We do not seek to set up any rival organisation to those which already exist in the Liberal Party. Our purpose is to appeal to the present asssociations, to disseminate literature and information, and to send out capable and experienced speakers. To do this on any adequate scale funds are urgently required, and we have already an earnest that they will be forthcoming. We venture to appeal to you as a Liberal to support us in this work. A subscription list and form is enclosed, and the Secretary will be glad to give further information at any time. The Committee will also be glad to know if, and to what extent, they may count on your support and co-operation in carrying on the work of the League by speaking, or distributing literature, or by any other means.

Yours faithfully,
A. M. SCOTT,
Secretary

5:The Free-Speech Controversy

Pro-Boer M.P.'s suffered heckling and other traditional forms of harassment when they spoke in the House. But they took it all in their stride, and, being old hands at the parliamentary game, gave as good as they got. More serious were the systematic disruptions that occurred at pro-Boer public meetings. These were often apparently countenanced by local police, and tacitly condoned by government officials. Without any doubt, they were reported by the press in such a way as to encourage reoccurrences. "When pro-Boers . . . insult the living and the dead by extolling the nation's enemies," declared the *Yorkshire Post* (March 9, 1900), "they do what is not only foolish but wicked, and openly invite the ill-usage they afterwards receive."

The irony was noted that Englishmen, who professed to be fighting to safeguard the liberties of their fellow subjects in South Africa, denied their fellow subjects at home the right to exercise the same liberties. Late in the evening on March 2, the venerable Sir Wilfrid Lawson (an M.P. for forty years) rushed breathlessly into the House to describe a situation he had just witnessed.

Sir Wilfrid Lawson
Speech in the House of Commons　　　　　　　**March 2, 1900**

. . . I wish to call the attention of the Home Secretary to something which has occurred to-night, and to explain the circumstances. A meeting was announced to be held in Exeter Hall to-night, the object being to stop the war. It was quite an orderly meeting, but I suppose it will not stop the war. In consequence of the announcement that the meeting would be held, the following notice appeared in an evening paper, and I believe it was also published on placards. But I am not certain on that point. I think the House will see, however, that it is a distinct incitement to, I will not say riot, but to disorderly conduct.

> Pro-Boers in Exeter Hall. Stop the War meeting to-night. Ought not to be allowed to meet and thus publicly con-

demn the war. People who rejoiced exceedingly last night can maintain their enthusiasm by going to Exeter Hall to-night and showing the pro-Boers that their sentiments are not popular.

I believe that these sentiments are not popular with hon. Gentlemen opposite, but then they show it in a proper way, and they do not attack me. [An HON. MEMBER: We ought to do so.] We were all orderly at Exeter Hall. I was there. Soon after we had commenced the meeting, however, a tremendous noise was heard, the door was forced open, in spite of our attempts to keep it closed, and a number of men rushed into the room shouting and yelling and waving the Union Jack, an emblem which I, as a patriotic Englishman, am very sorry to see so often used as an implement of disorder. Well, this body of assailants was repulsed. I am happy to say we were strong enough to do that. The meeting again proceeded in an orderly manner for fifteen or twenty minutes, when news came up that there was a violent contest going on on the stairs, that it would not be safe to continue, and that the best way would be to conclude the meeting. We decided to do so, and the question then was how to get home. Just as we had decided to break up the meeting fresh news came that our forces had rallied and again repulsed the enemy. The result was that we managed to hold the meeting quite decently. It was a ticket meeting, paid for with our own money. After another interval we were again disturbed by hideous shouts and roars outside, but at the end of two hours we concluded our meeting. My hon. friends who were with me managed to get out by a side door, which was kindly opened for us; we got into a four-wheeled cab, and told the driver to take us by the most unfrequented ways to this House, which we reached in safety. I bring this before the House because I am informed that when a message was sent to the police they did not seem at all inclined to come and keep order. At all events they were very tardy in doing it. I believe they did come at last, and I really believe there would have been serious work if they had not come. What I want to do now is to call the attention of

106

the right hon. Gentleman the Home Secretary, who is the head of the police force, to the facts, and ask him to be good enough to give orders to the police that on future occasions like this they shall protect the people attending these meetings. However unpopular our opinions may be, I think we ought to be allowed to express them, and the more so because we are so small a minority. I appeal with confidence to the right hon. Gentleman to protect orderly people who are engaged in holding a perfectly legitimate meeting. As I understand it, one of the reasons advanced for this war in the Transvaal is that our fellow-subjects out there were not allowed free speech, and yet that is the very privilege it is sought to deprive us of.

Parliamentary Debates, *4th series, LXXIX, cols. 1624–26*

A month later, the *Manchester Guardian* continued to protest the incident, and the official disregard that had made it possible.

Manchester Guardian   **April 2, 1900**

It will be remembered that during the Peace Conference held at Exeter Hall on the evening of March 2 a determined attempt was made to break up the meeting. The attempt was unsuccessful, but several people were injured, and some damage was done to property. About a week before the meeting the promoters sent one of their number to Scotland Yard to ask that policemen should be posted in the building, and they offered to pay for their services. This gentleman had an interview with Sir Charles Howard, who, however, refused to permit the police to be on duty in the hall. The chairman of the meeting (Mr. Robinson Souttar, M.P.), the hon. secretary of the Stop-the-War Committee, and several of the stewards who were in the thick of the fight have since sworn affidavits, and Messrs. Charles Russell and Co. were instructed by the Committee to communicate with the Home Secretary. This that firm did in a letter of the 14th March, observing in the course of their letter, "These declarations, it is submitted, show that the police authorities, and particularly Sir Charles Howard, the Commissioner, have not performed their duty as they ought to have done, and the gentlemen making the declarations are desirous to bring this conduct to your notice, in the confident expectation that you will see that a proper reprimand is given, and that steps will be taken to ensure no repetition of it in the future." Fifteen days later the Home Secretary briefly replied that after full inquiry into the matter "he finds no sufficient ground for any action on his part." This, then, is the position. The friends of peace summon a purely private ticket meeting in the heart of the capital. Hearing that there was likely to be disturbance, they ask for police protection and offer to pay for it. This is refused at the head office. The meeting is attacked by an organised mob. The promoters of the meeting try to give some of the rioters into charge, but no police are available in the building. After several messages had been despatched to Bow-street—one of them, signed by the chairman of the meeting, stating that there might be bloodshed—the police tardily arrive. Though several people were bleeding and the staircase of the building was full of rioters the police do not make a single arrest. Apparently, in the opinion of the present Government, the mob now have the power of deciding what private meetings they will or will not break up, and the police refuse to protect a meeting till life is in danger. It is certain the matter will not be allowed to rest where it is. . . .

Irish M.P.'s, often depicted by their opponents as the elected representatives of a society of hooligans, were pleased to cite evidence that Irishmen had no monopoly on mob violence. They were joined by Liberal spokesmen, who pressed the government for assurances that order would be maintained.

March 15, 1900

MR. WILLIAM REDMOND: I beg to ask the Secretary of State for the Home Department if his attention has been called to the recent riots in Stratford-on-Avon, and to the statement of Mr. H. H. Bullard that his house was invaded by a mob, who broke the windows and damaged or completely destroyed his whole stock of old china and antique furniture; and what steps are being taken by the Government to protect peaceable citizens from such proceedings.

SIR M. WHITE RIDLEY [Home Secretary]: Yes, Sir, I have made inquiries, but as proceedings are being taken against two of the ringleaders, and as I am informed that Mr. Bullard is about to make a claim under the Riot (Damages) Act, 1886, it would not be proper for me to say more at present except that I hope the local authorities, on whom the responsibility lies, will everywhere exercise firmness in preventing such riotous proceedings.

MR. WILLIAM REDMOND: Perhaps the right hon. Gentleman will be good enough to say a word in answer to the concluding part of my question, with regard to the steps to be taken to prevent a recurrence of these disorders.

SIR M. WHITE RIDLEY: I thought my answer implied that I thought the Government could not do anything more at present. Proceedings are, as I explained, being taken against two of the ringleaders, and a claim for damages will be made. Under those circumstances it would be highly improper for me to say anything as to the circumstances attending these proceedings.

MR. WILLIAM REDMOND: Is the right hon. Gentleman aware that under similar circumstances in Ireland trial by jury would have been suspended under the Coercion Act?

[No Answer was given.]

MR. LOUGH (Islington, W.): I beg to ask the Secretary of State for the Home Department whether his attention has been called to a meeting near Highbury Corner, which was being conducted in a perfectly quiet manner, last Sunday, until broken up by the police on the ground that it was likely to become disorderly; whether this is a sufficient pretext for interfering with a peacefully conducted meeting; and whether he can promise that such gatherings shall be protected in future.

109

SIR M. WHITE RIDLEY: I have made enquiry into this matter. The police did not interfere until the meeting had in their judgment become disorderly and there was serious danger of a breach of the peace. I am of opinion that the police were entirely justified in the action they took.

MR. PATRICK O'BRIEN: I beg to ask Mr. Attorney General whether his attention has been called to the damage to property in Scarborough during recent riots, belonging to Mr. Woodhead, a late Member of this House, and other persons; and whether he can say from what source, if any, compensation can be claimed by those persons out of public funds.

THE ATTORNEY GENERAL (Sir Richard Webster, Isle of Wight): I have not seen any particulars of the incident to which the hon. Member refers, and it is, therefore, not possible for me to express any opinion as to whether any proceedings for compensation would be successful.

SIR H. CAMPBELL-BANNERMAN (Stirling Burghs): I beg to ask the First Lord of the Treasury whether, in view of the numerous recent instances of disturbance connected with meetings called for the discussion of South African affairs, or directed against the person and property of individuals owing to their supposed opinions about the present war, Her Majesty's Government will cause inquiry to be made how far and by whom these disturbances were organised; and will he consider what steps are necessary to prevent a repetition of such occurrences, and to punish the offenders.

MR. A. J. BALFOUR: Every case reported to my right hon. friend the Home Secretary has been carefully examined, and every such unhappy occurrence will be so examined. There is not the slightest evidence that there has been any organisation of these demonstrations, which appear to be absolutely spontaneous in their character as far as the evidence which has come before my right hon. friend goes to show. As the right hon. Gentleman is aware, it is the local authorities who are responsible both for the maintenance of order and for the punishment of transgressors, and any aid which can be given to them in carrying out those duties shall, of course, be readily afforded. Speaking for myself, I strongly deprecate these demonstrations, and I expect no good of them. I think that they are contrary to the best traditions of English life. For a large part of my political life I have belonged to a party which was unable to hold meetings in certain portions of the country, and, therefore, I am at least as anxious on this subject at the right hon. Gentleman, who has been more fortunately situated than I myself could possibly be. But I think that the responsibility rests not only upon the local authorities and upon those concerned in these unfortunate proceedings, but also upon those who called the meetings. It must be remembered that public feeling is necessarily deeply stirred at the present time. In every district of the country there are persons who have lost relatives or friends in the present war; and nine-tenths of the country—ninety-nine hundredths of the country—believe, rightly or wrongly, that these meetings are called for an object which, if it were effectual, would render the occurrence of these great calamities possible. They think that in no other country in the world, and least of all in the Transvaal itself, would such meetings be tolerated; and they are aware that the fact of such meetings being held is, by people who know little of our methods and traditions, used abroad as an indication of a divided country and a hesitating Government. In these circumstances, the tension of public opinion must necessarily be of a kind affording grave anxiety to those responsible for the public peace; and I venture to add that those who call these meetings ought to be careful lest they ask more of human nature than all history shows that human nature is capable of giving.

Parliamentary Debates, *4th series, LXXX, cols. 926–29*

Balfour's typically detached reply, and his attribution of blame to the pro-Boers themselves, infuriated Liberal opinion. Sir Robert T. Reid (who, as Lord Loreburn, was to become Lord Chancellor in 1905), boldly moved the adjournment of the House for the purpose of discussing "the recent serious disturbances in many parts of the country." His motion, not surprisingly, did not carry; but it received 120 votes (there were 229 "Noes"), and Asquith was among its supporters.[1]

Sir R. T. Reid
Speech in the House of Commons   March 15, 1900

It is not in the slightest degree my intention to misrepresent the right hon. Gentleman, but the House has heard the whole of his answer, and I am entitled to hold and to express the opinion that that answer was not such an answer as ought to have come from a Minister of the Crown under the grave circumstances in which the question was put. ["Oh, oh?"] I hope, however, that at all events right hon. and hon. Gentlemen will respect the right of free speech in this House. Even if they are not prepared to respect that right outside the House, we are determined to assert our rights here in the matter. I wish to advert to the nature of these meetings and the nature of the disturbances which have taken place. The right hon. Gentleman spoke, in the first place—or at least I understand him so—as if these meetings were public meetings, and, in the second place, as though the disturbances had been confined to places in which attempts had been made to hold meetings. Neither of those assumptions is accurate. Let me advert to some of these instances. There was a meeting broken up at Mile End, when an attack was made by some hundreds of persons; railings and staircases were broken, and several people cut and injured. There was another case at Thornbury, where a meeting was stopped by a mob of about 200 persons, who smashed the windows, and perpetrated various acts of violence. A local timber merchant sent a letter to the press giving his experience. He said that he was seized by about a dozen men, thrown violently to the ground, kicked and knocked insensible; that there was only one policeman on the spot; that he had about 1,400 yards to go through the main street to reach his residence, in traversing which distance he was knocked down twelve or thirteen times. There was another

1. *Parliamentary Debates,* LXXX, cols. 981 ff., division list no. 67.

case at Exeter Hall, in which a meeting was convoked by tickets, the public not being invited. My right hon. friend beside me reminds me that the Government are expressly responsible for peace in the metropolis. In regard to that meeting, notice was given beforehand to the police and assistance was requested in anticipation of some disturbance. While a Member of this House was addressing that meeting there was a most violent attack by hundreds of persons, and a free fight took place, lasting about twenty minutes, in which blows were exchanged, and there was very serious danger to the women as well as to the men at the meeting. There were thousands of people congregated in the Strand, many of whom were riotous and disorderly, and I am not aware that any steps have been taken to bring before the magistrates the persons responsible for this disgraceful scene. There was another case in Edinburgh, an account of which was given in the *Scotsman* newspaper. A crowd of about 2,000 people contrived to force an entry into the Queen Street Hall, and I am sorry to say that amongst the crowd that took part in the attack were some of the Yeomanry Sharpshooters. Mr. Cronwright Schreiner was present on that occasion—an Englishman from Cape Colony who married a German lady, and who came over to this country as a loyal British subject, with no desire except that of reasoning with the public in regard to the best methods of preserving the South African dominions to this country. He may be right or he may be wrong in his opinion; that has nothing whatever to do with the matter. He entertains honest opinions, which are shared by thousands of our fellow-countrymen in South Africa, and he is entitled to have—I will not say a hearing, because people are not bound to go and hear unless they think fit—but he is entitled to protection of life and limb while he is discharging the duty which is open to every citizen in a law-abiding country. This gentleman was roughly handled. He was chased to his hotel, where I am sorry to say the threats of force were so great that he was compelled to leave in order to prevent the hotel itself being attacked and seriously damaged. There are a number of other places—

113

LORD BALCARRES (Lancashire, Chorley) : How many?

SIR R. T. REID: There are quite a number of them. The list I have here is by no means complete, but these are some of the places contained in it—Paddington, Sheffield, York, West Bromwich, Canterbury, Ramsgate, Exeter Hall, Midhurst, Gloucester, Weston-super-Mare, Highbury, Northampton, New Cross, Peterhead, Redruth, Leicester, Brierly Hill, Dundee, Glasgow, Gateshead, Derby, Norwich, and Reading. ["Scarborough."] In Scarborough there was a reception—not a public meeting at all—in Messrs. Rowntree's cafe, a place known to everybody who has visited Scarborough. Every window in that cafe was smashed by an infuriated crowd, largely drunk, I believe, as most of these crowds are on these occasions. All the windows were smashed also at Messrs. Rowntree's grocery premises, and the riot continued until two o'clock in the morning, and damage was done, according to the *Westminster Gazette*, which was estimated to be considerably upwards of £1,000. At last the Riot Act was read at about two o'clock in the morning, and the military were called out. I have given so far the references to a number of other cases, but these are the cases in which meetings took place, most of them private meetings, where evidently, by some organised mob, a terror for life and limb was created, and apparently the police were unable to offer an adequate protection at the time. Let me turn to other cases in which there was no public meeting at all, and I will only give a couple of cases. There was the case of Midhurst. At that place there was no public meeting, and no such provocation as the right hon. Gentleman the Leader of the House suggests. There was a great deal of smashing of plate-glass windows, some women were injured, and there were placards published in the streets suggesting and inciting violence against persons who were called pro-Boers. [Ministerial cheers.] I do not know whether hon. Gentlemen opposite think that is the way to discourage violence in the different parts of this country. As a matter of fact, in most cases, the people who were attacked, whose windows were smashed, and whose wives and children were terrified, disclaimed entirely having any sympathy whatever with what are called pro-Boer views. They were persons who had been attacked sometimes in the newspaper press, and in other instances by the scurrilous falsehoods repeated about other men's opinions; but whatever their opinions may be, what possible right or justification is there for men or women in their own homes in this country being attacked by a riotous mob and being driven to fly for protection to other places outside the town?. . .

Parliamentary Debates, 4th series, LXXX, cols. 941–44

The issue of free speech allowed Campbell-Bannerman to support the pro-Boers without yet joining them in outright opposition to the war.

Campbell-Bannerman
Speech in the House of Commons   **March 15, 1900**

Property does not matter so much, and even a broken head does not so much matter; there is something behind and below it which is a much more serious question—it is the right of free opinion and the free expression of opinion. The breaking of plate glass windows is a disgraceful proceeding and it is to be regretted, but plate glass windows can be restored; but if you take away the right of free speech, which the people of this country have always enjoyed, you cannot readily restore that.

Parliamentary Debates, 4th series, LXXX, col. 980

As a ministerial organ, *The Times* was inclined to dismiss the controversy as a tempest in a teapot, and adhered to Balfour's view that "responsibility" rested with "the organizers of the demonstrations" who make "a deliberate attempt . . . to misrepresent the feelings of the vast majority of those who have suffered cruel losses in the war they believe to be both just and necessary" (March 16, 1900).

The pro-Boers, who adamantly rejected the politics of *The Times*, also rejected its logic. Waving the banner of free speech, they portrayed themselves as the spiritual heirs of

Peter Wentworth, Sir John Eliot, and John Pym. By deflecting attention to this subsidiary issue, they could speak as the proponents of a higher patriotism, and, at the same time, could provide the Liberal Opposition with a semblance of unity. The following pamphlet appeared in the wake of the March 15 free speech debate.

The Right of Free Speech

We are sacrificing thousands of lives and millions of treasure to secure the liberties and privileges of a handful of Outlanders in the South African Republic.

But at the same time we are allowing the fundamental rights of free-born Britons to be filched from us and trampled under foot by ruffianly mobs incited by scoundrelly newspapers whose exploits in the suppression of liberty are excused even when perfunctorily condemned by Ministers of the Crown.

The right of public meeting for the public discussion of public affairs is the basis of all our liberties. Parliamentary government itself sprang out of this fundamental right of a free people. Without the right of public meeting democratic government becomes impossible.

But what has become to-day of that indispensable foundation of all our liberties?

The Right of Public Meeting to discuss the supreme question of public interest at the present time has absolutely ceased to exist for all those who are not prepared to support a war of extermination in South Africa.

This right has been destroyed by the simple but effective process of organising a violent and lawless attack by a more or less intoxicated mob upon every public meeting held to discuss any subject connected with the war, either its genesis, its conduct, or the future settlement of Africa. A company of brawling ruffians introduced into any public hall can easily render discussion impossible by yelling and singing, and can compel the dissolution of the meeting by the summary process of a free fight. It is not necessary for such a demonstration of the power of the mob to be made more than once or twice.

116

A single tumult suffices to lead lessees and owners of public halls to refuse to let their premises for public meetings certain to be attacked, and instead of insisting upon defending this sacred right of a free people, cowardly and nerveless public authorities eagerly evade their responsibilities by urging the promoters of public meetings to abstain from "provoking attack." As a result, public meetings to advocate Peace, in our public halls in Britain to-day, have become impossible.

That would be serious enough. But it is but the beginning of the new despotism. The right of free speech has heretofore been regarded as the inalienable privilege of Englishmen. Whatever might be the case in other countries, ours was the land where man might say the thing he would. That has been the distinguishing pride and glory of our land. But the right of free speech is fast following the right of public meeting into limbo. Within the last three weeks we have seen successful attacks in all parts of the Kingdom directed against the exercise of the right of free speech in private. To challenge a public verdict in public halls to which the public is freely admitted might possibly be deprecated in times of great popular excitement. But the result has proved that the only effect of shrinking from the assertion of the right of public meeting is that private meetings in halls hired by private persons in order that specially invited companies of friends could be able to exchange their views and acquire information are immediately subjected to the same ruffianly attacks. To the passionate and drunken mob, the distinction between public and private meetings is as naught. The habit of mind, or rather the mood of temper, that leads men to break up assemblies of those from whom they dissent, does not discriminate. It is enough that in a hall, in a café, or even in a private house, two or three are met together to strengthen each other in their unpopular opinions—there the mob feels it must be in the midst of them to express its brutal will with clamour and with bludgeon.

That this is no exaggeration is proved by the outrageous riot at Scarborough, which necessitated the calling out of the military. The mob attacked a small party of friends meeting privately in a café. At Gateshead, if it had not been for the presence of a strong posse of police, a similar attack would have been made upon the private residence of Dr. Spence Watson. Within the last three weeks, private meetings summoned by invitation, admission being strictly confined to friends of Peace, have been violently attacked at Mile End, at Exeter Hall (where the assailants, although beaten off, made the Strand a pandemonium for three hours), at Edinburgh, at Dundee, at West Bromwich, at Leicester and at Paddington, where the assailants were successful. Meetings which were arranged at Gateshead and at Scarborough were rendered impossible by the assembling of tumultuous mobs which threatened violence. Under the influence of the terrorism thus established meetings which were arranged for were abandoned under the double pressure of the owners of public halls or of local authorities at Holborn, Leeds, Liverpool, Sheffield, York, Hastings, Croydon, New Cross, Weston-super-Mare, and Derby.

Where, then, is the right of Free Speech in Britain this day?

But, although the right of Free Speech has rapidly shared the fate of the right of Public Meeting, there is still a lower depth of degradation into which a nation may descend. That is when liberty of opinion itself is treated as an offence, to be punished by money fine and injury to the person. Into that abyss this once free England is sinking to-day. In all parts of the land inoffensive citizens have been subjected to violence in person and in goods, not because they have taken part in public or in private meetings, but because they were known to dissent from the opinions of the majority. Tradesmen's windows have been smashed and their property injured in the following places where no public or private meetings had been held: Canterbury, Margate, Midhurst, Weston-super-Mare, Peterhead, Redruth, Brierley Hill, Leighton Buzzard, Norwich, and Yarmouth.

This being the case, it is high time that all those who care for liberty should ask themselves what must be done to revindicate our imperilled rights. The debate in the House of Commons on Thursday, March 15, revealed only too plainly the malignant joy with which the majority in the House of Commons would welcome the gagging of all those who oppose the

War. While paying lip-service to the cause of liberty, they addressed themselves sedulously to pander to the passions of the mob by endeavouring to throw upon the holders of Peace meetings the responsibility for the criminal violence of those who endeavour to suppress them. Against this fatal doctrine that the right to hold public meetings depends in the slightest degree upon the popularity or unpopularity of those who summon them, it is necessary to register instant and solemn protest. Majorities and popular causes stand in little need of protection. They can very well protect themselves. But the more unpopular the cause, the smaller the minority that sustains it, the more imperative is the duty of the authorities, both local and Imperial, to protect its meetings from attack. Instead of alluding, with the Home Secretary, to the unpopularity of a citizen as if it condoned or justified the smashing of his windows, a Minister really devoted to law and order would recognise in the fact of such unpopularity a summons to double vigilance and increased severity of censure.

This is no new battle. It is one that has perpetually to be fought and won as each new issue comes before the public. The last great struggle for liberty was made by the Salvation Army, which, by sheer dint of suffering and patience, succeeded in compelling indolent and timid local authorities and unsympathetic Home Secretaries to recognise that the right of public procession and of open-air preaching was not to be sacrificed to the savage opposition of ginshops and their victims. Local authorities all over the country, backed up by the Home Office, tried to dissuade the Salvationists from holding processions in districts where acquiescence in their flaunting parade, to use Mr. Balfour's phrase, was asking more of human nature than human nature is capable of giving. They insisted upon the grave responsibility of those who ordered such processions, and they gave the Salvationists plainly to understand that they entirely sympathised with the ruffians who attacked the processionists rather than with the processionists. But General Booth was not to be intimidated. He was defending the legal liberties of the citizens. He went on undismayed by the warnings of Ministers and the savagery of the mob. There were

119

riots here and there. The military were occasionally called out. But after a time the magistrates and police discovered that it was not the line of least resistance to run over the liberties and rights of Englishmen, and so after a time the rowdies were summarily suppressed and the right of procession was established beyond all gainsaying.

If Stop the War people were to parade the Strand and the City with banners and bands, setting forth their abhorrence of the present War, they would be acting within their legal rights, and they would have a right to insist that the Government should protect them from molestation even if it were necessary to call out the last remaining battalions of our army in order to keep their would-be assailants at bay. But the friends of Peace have been most pacific. They have been most considerate of the difficulties of the authorities in a season of popular delirium. They have held no processions. They have, to a great extent, abstained from public meetings. And now, as their reward, they are lectured by Mr. Balfour and the Home Secretary as if they were the real criminals when they venture meekly to suggest that in free England private meetings ought not to be broken up by ruffianly mobs and that private citizens ought to be protected from being rabbled by Hooligans because of the unpopularity of their political opinions.

It becomes a serious question which must be gravely considered whether under these circumstances the Friends of Peace should not adopt a forward policy and see whether a stout resolve to hold Peace processions and public meetings would not open the eyes of Ministers to a truer sense of their responsibilities and their duties.

Mob violence, no laughing matter to its victims, nonetheless offered random moments of comic relief. Harold Spender reported in the *Manchester Guardian* (May 24, 1900) that, on the evening of May 19,

> the mob at Highgate went to wreck the windows of Mr. Silas Hocking, who has taken a prominent part in the

'Stop-the-War' campaign. They found only one house in the street without a Union Jack, and wrecked the windows. Unfortunately for them, it was the house of a strong Imperialist. One of Mr. Hocking's children had put out a flag!

That Hocking eventually contradicted the published report of this incident[1] is an indication that the pro-Boers sometimes exaggerated the reprisals they suffered. One of the most effective of the pro-Boer itinerant lecturers was S. C. Cronwright-Schreiner, husband of the celebrated novelist and brother-in-law of the South African statesman. Although his meetings frequently ended in riot, and he himself was assaulted, he was not daunted. His appearance at Penistone on April 21 passed without incident, proving that free speech was not impossible.

S. C. Cronwright-Schreiner
Speech to the Holmfirth Division
Liberal Association at Penistone   April 21, 1900

The Chairman, in opening the proceedings, said he...had an announcement to make. About a week previously their Member, Mr. [H. J.] Wilson, told the . . . secretary and himself that if they thought it desirable and if it would be agreeable to the Council Mr. Cronwright-Schreiner would be willing to attend the meeting and address the Council on the South African question. (Cheers.) They thought that the offer ought to be accepted. (Hear, hear.) It was only right, they thought, that the Council should have all the information it could get on the question, and especially from one who had lived in South Africa all his life and held a very important position there. . . . Of course there was this difficulty—that they had to observe a certain amount of secrecy. They knew of the disgraceful proceedings at Scarborough and Sheffield when Mr. Cronwright-Schreiner was going to address private meetings, and although they had no fear of any such "gentlemanly" behaviour in the Holmfirth division, they thought it best that the matter should be kept a secret, and they decided that be-

1. Hocking, *My Book of Memory* (London, 1923), pp. 185–86.

fore he arrived they would put it to the meeting whether they wished him to address them or not. He wished to say that Mr. Cronwright-Schreiner was a gentleman of pure English blood. His grandparents went from England to South Africa; he himself was a British subject, and had not any Dutch blood in his veins. Not that he would be any the worse for that, but certain newspapers were constantly insinuating that he was particularly favourable to Mr. Kruger's policy in the Transvaal. As a matter of fact, Mr. Cronwright-Schreiner was not favourable to that policy; he belonged to the progressive party, and was against the policy of the Afrikander Bond. The Chairman asked the meeting to signify its willingness or otherwise to hear Mr. Cronwright-Schreiner. There was a loud response of "Aye," and none to the contrary....

The Chairman said he had great pleasure in calling on Mr. Cronwright-Schreiner to address the meeting. In the name of that meeting he wished to say how strongly they condemned the abominable conduct that had been shown to him at previous meetings. (Hear, hear.) They hoped he would find that in the Holmfirth Division they were more gentlemanly and that there was one thing they prized—freedom of speech. (Applause.) They hoped when he went away from England he would forget that he had been abominably treated in the country that witnessed the birth of free speech....

Mr. Cronwright-Schreiner then addressed the meeting in a speech of nearly one hour's duration....

With regard to what the Chairman had said about his own efforts, he would like to say this, that he did not identify the mob with the nation, nor even with the town wherein it assembled and disgraced the name of Englishmen. (Hear, hear.) They found in every community a number of people who lacked manliness, gentlemanly behaviour, and bravery. Those were the people who assembled in mobs and who considered it brave to attack single individuals and hustle women, and who considered they were upholding the honour of England by breaking down what was an Englishman's greatest heritage, perhaps—free speech (cheers),—men who were clamouring for free speech for aliens in another country and refusing it to their fellow subjects in their own country. (Renewed cheers.) He found it was assumed that the moment they took what the war party called a pro-Boer attitude they identified themselves with the cause of the Boer, and appeared as the Boer's champions. Now his attitude was taken, and he assumed that of his audience was, because they held they were safeguarding the permanent interests of Great Britain and of the Empire; not only because they wanted to see justice done to another and a smaller people, but because they wanted to see their own people do the great, and the large, and the statesmanlike thing. If any section of a country was to be considered as its enemy it was that which arrogated to itself the title of Imperialist, the section which lost sight of the great issues which lay beyond the present moment, and concentrated its attention upon some false issue of the moment which obscured its sight. He held that in this matter he was looking to the permanent interests of the Empire, and he was as certain as that two and two made four that history would indorse the attitude of himself and friends towards this momentous question. (Hear, hear.) It seemed also to be assumed by people who did not think as they thought that the moment they took a hostile attitude to the war they vilified the soldier. Now, he was one of those who wished to see war cease in all parts of the world, just as duelling had ceased as a method of settling individual disputes, and he desired to see an international court of arbitration formed for settling international disputes; but he had a profound regard for any man who was prepared to sacrifice his life in the performance of his duty. That was what the British soldier was doing, and he honoured him for it. In his own mind the soldier was satisfied he was furthering the interests of Queen and country, and for that he was prepared, if need be, to die. If all of us were prepared, each according to his highest conception of what was right, to do our duty as unselfishly as a brave soldier, it would be well. (Hear, hear.). . .

It puzzled anyone to ascertain what the war was about. He could not get the same reply from two people. One would tell you it was about the franchise, losing sight of the fact that, whereas at Bloemfontien Sir Alfred Milner had demanded a five years' franchise, seven seats for the Gold Fields and one-fifth of the seats in the Raad for the Gold Fields as a minimum; losing sight also of the fact that there was now in the Transvaal a seven years' naturalisation and franchise law, which was actually more liberal in character and with less irritating restrictions than the franchise law in this country, because it carried with it not only the right to the franchise the moment one was naturalised, but gave a man the right to vote for both the Legislative Councils and for the President and Commandant-General. In this country when certain tortuous steps, which might occupy nearly seven years in getting over, had been taken, the enfranchised one could only vote for one Chamber, and all that the representatives of the people did in that Chamber might be neutralised or rejected by the hereditary Assembly. (Hear, hear.) Then it was said it was a question of securing equal rights for white people, while many who said this were clamouring for the disfranchisement of whole districts in Cape Colony in which a few people who had been goaded to more than they could endure had taken up arms against Great Britain, and their object in doing this was that they might be able to govern the country through a minority. Another would tell you it was a matter of taxation, losing sight of the fact that taxation in the Transvaal was less than that per head in Cape Colony, and that whereas under the Transvaal gold law the taxation ranged from 2½ perhaps to 5 per cent, in Rhodesia, which was British territory, the miners had petitioned that the Transvaal gold laws should be introduced there instead of those now in operation. And as for the talk of a tax being put upon foodstuffs, the Transvaal was the one State in South Africa where no special tax was laid on food. The consequence was that, although Johannesburg was a thousand miles inland, living was as cheap there (as regards food) to the plain livers at Kimberley. So that whatever the argument put forward for the war, he had always found an adequate answer was forthcoming. But when these so-called arguments had been exploded one after another, their opponents abandoned them altogether, and said the war was about something else. . . .

The Dutch were absolutely certain in the future to be in a much greater numerical superiority than at present. Before this trouble—this wretched Capitalist war—the Dutch of the Cape Colony were passionately attached to this country. Their belief in it and in the Queen was something pathetic. Their love for the Queen was shown by the fact that if one went through Dutch-speaking districts of the Cape Colony, one would find in the houses more portraits of the Queen than one would find in a similar number of houses in Great Britain, and that the people pointed to them with pride. They regarded her with the greatest affection as a Christian Lady who loved them, and always sought peace. This was the population which, if the Empire had had to go to war, were as good fighting material as any that could be had anywhere. Was it wise to alienate so brave, loyal, and devoted a people?. . .

He did not like to see any people dominated from the centre as old Rome dominated her provinces; he desired to see the Colonies governing themselves, as Australia now proposed to govern itself, and tied to the mother country by bonds of sympathy and love. That was the strength of a people—to be held together by affection. (Applause). It was true that to regard the matter from the point of fighting strength to the Empire was to look at it from a selfish and not a very high standpoint. But it was a high standpoint to regard it as an irreparable loss if the affections of a people are alienated. But there was a higher ground with regard to the Republics, and he appealed to them on that ground. . . . It was not for a free and generous people like the British to crush small Nationalities, which, if left to themselves, would grow and be a benefit to humanity at large. (Cheers.) He appealed to his hearers to stand together for the truest interests of the Empire and humanity. If they saw any party doing anything like sheer annexation and the subjugation of a free people, let them not help such a party. If such a thing had to be done let it be done against their protest, their most vigorous protest, by speech and action in every possible way. (Applause.) . . .

Reprinted from the Holmfirth Express *as a penny pamphlet (Holmfirth, 1900) and distributed by the Transvaal Committee, the Stop the War Committee, and the South Africa Conciliation Committee*

6:Petitions, Protests, and Politics

Convinced that the war was largely the product of Boer distrust, much of it justified, the leaders of the South Africa Conciliation Committee insisted that the promulgation of moderate war aims would bring an immediate end to hostilities. On March 12, they petitioned the Prime Minister against a punitive settlement.

An Appeal to the Prime Minister Against the Annexation of the Republics

SACC Pamphlet No. 30

My Lord,

The repeated victories of the British arms, the retreat of the enemy on many sides at once, with the capture of a considerable Army from the two Republics, open a new phase of the war. Whatever temporary successes may yet be achieved by the Boers, there is little reason to doubt the complete victory of the Imperial forces. In these circumstances it would appear inevitable, with a view to the restoration of confidence in the Cape Colony, and to a resettlement of South Africa, that the policy of the Government in respect of such resettlement should be presently declared.

We address you with reluctance, but we feel constrained to speak in view of the dangerous policy which has been advocated elsewhere.

We are now at the parting of the ways. Shall we continue the war until the last spark of resistance is stamped out, and then establish Crown Colonies in the two Republics, to be governed with the assistance of a large army of occupation? This must arouse the resentment of the majority of our fellow-subjects at the Cape, and must be continued until that far distant time when we are asked to believe that memories and aspirations will be forgotten, and the Boers will placidly submit to our authority; while in the meantime it is quite possible that some opportunity might be seized of upsetting a dominion founded on military superiority.

Or shall we, remembering your declaration that we desired neither goldfields nor territory, and satisfied that our strength and resources are understood by the Boers, as we understand their courage and determination, be content to secure within the two Republics political rights for white men of whatever origin, on terms such as were approved by her Majesty's Government before the war, coupled with the demolition of forts and the abandonment of all armaments not required for the maintenance of internal order, and therewith leave to the Republics the enjoyment of the national life within their own borders for which they have now, not for the first time, so bravely fought, in the assurance that by these means alone can the conditions of permanent peace be enjoyed in South Africa?

Our decision must depend on a just appreciation of the past as well as of the factors of to-day. British and Dutch have to live amicably side by side; the Dutch are now, and are likely to be, always numerically preponderant throughout South Africa. No choice is free from difficulty or even from danger. But common sense, not less than justice, must lead us to adopt the least dangerous course. In the height of our military triumph it is true wisdom to remember the permanent forces of political life, and to act on the truth that the path of generosity is the path of prudence.

LEONARD COURTNEY,
President

F. C. SELOUS,
Vice-President

FREDERIC MACKARNESS,
Chairman

The Most Hon. the Marquis of Salisbury

By mid-March, the tide had turned: a complete British victory was only a matter of time. After lifting the seiges at Kimberley and Ladysmith, British forces occupied Blomfontein, capital of the Orange Free State. May brought the invasion of the Transvaal: Mafeking was relieved on the seventeenth, and Johannesburg fell on the thirty-first. Five days later, Pretoria was taken.

On May 28, the Orange Free State was declared annexed. The following October, after Kruger had fled to exile in Europe, formal ceremonies marked the annexation of the Transvaal.

Some pro-Boers were more incensed than others by the government's action. At a dinner party on May 23, Morley responded with philosophic resignation. More surprisingly, most of his guests shared his mood.

A Note by F. W. Hirst   May 23, 1900

At first Mr. M. kept the talk on general subjects, and then it became a conference on the subject of the hour. What was to be the reply to Chamberlain's annexation policy? Spence Watson did little more than defend himself regarding the recent proceedings of the National Liberal Federation. J. M. said he had thought of going down to move the rejection of the Report. S. W. wished he had, and added that the motion would have been carried. To my surprise Dillon and Massingham—but they are both impressionists—were mealy-mouthed about annexation. After J. M. had skilfully elicited the views of the table he put forward his own idea. He would send out an impartial, wise, and trustworthy Commissioner like Pauncefote and recall Milner. Then he would consider the Commissioner's recommendations. We all agreed that it would never do to welcome annexation, or even to admit that it is inevitable. Lehmann made a great effort to get Morley to take more part in the fray. He touched his arm: "You are our leader, Mr. Morley." J. M. with a delightful smile: "Get on with your drinking, my dear Lehmann."

> *Quoted in Hirst,* In the Golden Days
> *(London, 1947), pp. 208–9*

A disparate group of individuals, among them the progeny of some of Liberalism's founding fathers, combined to issue a public appeal.

**The Purpose of Conquest, An Appeal to the Nation
Issued by The South Africa
Conciliation Committee** London, May, 1900

To England, for England, the memory of Englishmen appeals,
the spirit of our fathers, who through prolonged struggles on
the field and in Parliament, through consecrated martyrdom
at the stake and on the scaffold, have won for us our freedom,
and now conjures you by the present duty to humanity, and by
those hopes for the future of our race and of the whole world
which are the springs of greatness, to consider most deeply,
most religiously, the object of the war now being waged against
a small State by the forces of our Empire....

What are our sons sent to die for? Is it a cause consistent
with our great traditions, and honourable to the honoured defenders of national rights, freedom, independence?

For what gain must peace be refused? Not, surely, for mere
revenge, for a sorrowful proof that if in past combats the
peasants have bravely won, they can now be bravely beaten by
the weight of numbers. Here there is no glory, no honour,
but rather a fuller testimony to the qualities of the defenders,
a ruinous vaunt of power unworthy of a great people. Nor can
the object be the perpetration of a crime, the extinction of a
nation's life....

The way of force is the way of death, the way by which
Persia, Assyria, Carthage, Macedon, the Turks, and Spain expanded in conquest and sank into decline. Already we have
lost materially in Samoa and China, in Persia and Asia Minor,
and morally in the esteem of the best minds of all countries.
The loss of one or two hundred millions of money in this
trouble is nothing compared with the loss of our great inheritance of a reputation for justice, tolerance and humanity. This
will cripple our national life for generations and deprive us of
our former weight in International Councils. The hypocrisy
which rose from the Peace Conference to drive to death a
State which had been excluded from its benefits will not be
forgotten in a century. We have alienated the Dutch in South
Africa, who are the sturdiest people in the world, not easily

gained, not easily lost, but responsive towards consistent friendship.

The way of equity is the way of life. Therefore the true Briton, strong in the principles of his faith and the wisdom of the heart, and warned by the records of history, will do all in his power for the ascendancy of the spirit of life over the allurements of destruction. The patriot is the man who thinks and works for what is best in his nation, and thereby contributes to its enduring greatness. Not the supporter of any enterprise into which a reckless politician may cajole his country at the risk of moral and material ruin. Daily we read of "the enemy," of jealous Europe, of rifle ranges, and conscription. Who is the enemy? The country's worst enemies are within it. An iniquity foisted upon a free electorate may be sanctioned or repelled. To ratify un-English perfidy is anti-English, unpatriotic, disloyal. Loyalty is allegiance to the law of right. We want no conspiracies in the Queen's name, no infamy under cover of a Charter. The honour of the Sovereign demands good faith in her Ministers, and the future of the Empire will be served not by bluster but by sagacity and fair dealing. A patriotic people will be true to itself; the ends aimed at will be for country, for God and truth.

Charles F. Aked	Frederic Harrison
R. A. Armstrong	John Hunter, D.D.
E. S. Beesly	Agatha Russell
J. H. Bridges	Rollo Russell
J. A. Bright	T. Cobden Sanderson
Edith Bright	Annie Cobden Sanderson
G. L. Bruce	T. Fisher Unwin
Edward Carpenter	Jane Cobden Unwin
Robert J. Colenso	Alfred R. Wallace
Stephen Gladstone	

Leonard Courtney, professing not to believe that the government would persevere, appealed to the prime minister on May 18 "against the Suppression of Free Government in the

Republics" (SACC Pamphlet No. 45). A week later, he addressed a meeting at London's Westminster Palace Hotel on the same subject.

Leonard Courtney
Speech to the South Africa Conciliation Committee
(SACC Pamphlet No. 47)   **May 25, 1900**

We have met here to-day in order soon to follow up the manifesto published in the papers last week by a unanimous meeting, protesting against the annexation of the Boer Republics. Time is moving on, the military situation is changing rapidly, and, as some think, is drawing to a final conclusion in the Transvaal; and we may at any time have before us the question of the terms of settlement of the war in which we are unhappily engaged, and it is too evident that, unless we take action in time, there will come to be a kind of fatalistic conviction that nothing is possible except the extinction of the Republics which have so magnificently shown their right to exist. (Cheers.) Against that extinction we must protest as often and as loudly as we can, and we raise our voice here to-day not for the first time and not for the last, as the commencement, we hope, of a movement which may show—as Mr. Keir Hardie suggests in his letter—that the nation is not by any means divided, as writers in the press and some public men assert, into the bulk of the people on one side, and a few scattered fanatics on the other. We hold that the sound, sober, reflecting part of the nation has revolted against this war as it has been conducted (cheers) and still more repudiates the settlement which has been suggested. (Cheers.) . . . And, if we turn our eyes from South Africa homewards, if we think of what is involved in the other necessary consequence of the maintenance of an army of occupation, if you think of the cost not in money only, but in men, involved in that occupation, if you think how it would bring over our domestic policy the predominance of military considerations, how the poison which has already infected so deeply our public life would spread until our whole body politic became diseased—then, I

say, those who have at heart any of the traditions of the freedom of our country, those who desire to see it maintained in
the future, as it has been in the past, free from the curse of
militarism, must indeed deprecate, as one of the worst of calamities, the extinction of the Republics in South Africa. (Cheers.)
Do we want that this war shall be followed by a peace which
shall endure? Surely that is the desire of all. That is even the
alleged motive of those who advocate the extinction of the
Republics. They, too, desire a permanent peace, and they say
to themselves, "The only way to secure that permanent peace
is by the destruction of the power of the Republics that have
hitherto existed." We hold that this is a wrong and fatal way,
but then we are branded as speculative dreamers, as senti-
mentalists, as mere fanatics. However, in relation to this question of policy and wisdom, I would bring forward as a witness
a man who can be suspected of no sentimentality, a man whose
coolness and sureness of judgment is allowed by all the world.
I want you to recall for a moment the historic situation which
followed the battle of Sadowa, when the power of Austria
was broken by that of North Germany. What was then the
desire of the military chiefs who had succeeded in beating
down the forces of the Emperor of Austria? They wanted
annexation, they wanted to take away this or that province
from the beaten Emperor, but it was Bismarck who stood up
against them, and on grounds of mere prudence and worldly
wisdom, and not from any motive of sentiment but from regard to the future situation that might be created and would
certainly follow, strongly and successfully resisted the policy
of annexation which his colleagues pressed upon the King,
and which the King himself was only too desirous of carrying
into effect. Bismarck prevailed—the level-headed, the cool,
the contemptuous of morality. He prevailed and had his reward, for, in the struggle which followed with France, Austria lay perfectly content, sought not to recover provinces because no provinces had been taken from her, and allowed the
contest to go on between the rising Empire and the Emperor
of the French, who was courting the Emperor of Austria's alliance, without any interference.... Ah! but you may say—or

some may say—of what use is this inflammatory protest—"the thing is done, it is certain, it is inevitable. Say what you will, this annexation is a thing registered by the Gods, the Fates have ordained it; you may as well consent first as last." Have we to submit to this fatal conclusion? . . . We none of us know, even as this moment, with sufficient clearness, what is the temper of the nation, and if we don't know it, who will say what will be the temper of the nation if, as seems probable, this war is wearisomely prolonged and the demands of blood and money are continued? I will not despair of the majority coming to saner counsels. After all, in treating of the wills and determinations of men we are not handling fixed and immutable facts, we are considering fluctuating elements which move here and there according to the conditions of reason and which change as times progress and circumstances alter. If we, singly and collectively, are true to our opinions, cannot we go forth and move, with the assistance of the history that is going on about us, the minds of men so that their wills and affections shall be more like ours about a settlement promising of peace? And, if this were not possible, even if at the end we are outvoted, still we have the power and the duty of protest, though it be vain. (Cheers.) That power we will exercise; that duty, God helping, we will try to fulfil. Whatever the result, we will work towards it. But I for one do not despair that with a strong cause, with a cause such as that which is moving us, passing through a drama such as we are witnesses of, we may succeed in convincing others to hold the conclusions we hold ourselves, to join with us, and to bring the nation to agree in protesting against the annexation of the Republics as fatal to the peace of South Africa, fatal to our own interests, and, above all, to be condemned because it is abhorrent to the justice of God. (Prolonged cheers.)

With a dissolution expected at any time, it became all the more urgent for pro-Boers, especially those with parliamentary seats to defend, to establish their reputations as the custodians of an older, more noble tradition. Some Liberal M.P.'s, trying to stave off defeat, tried to out-jingo the jingoes. Others feverishly attempted to demonstrate that their actions had in no way been incompatible with patriotic ideals.

Sir John Brunner, reproved by one of his constituents for unguarded statements, took refuge behind Queen Victoria's skirts.

W. Blagg to Sir John Brunner   March 7, 1900

In a speech delivered by you last week at the Gladstone Liberal Club, Northwich, you are reported to have said: "Who was going to get any good out of the war? He did not believe any of the mineowners would, and he expected that before the British occupied Johannesburg the machinery in the mines would be smashed, and the mines themselves would be destroyed by explosives.

"He had not the shadow of a doubt that twenty millions of the capital expended in the mines would be utterly lost...." These remarks have been the subject of animated discussion by a goodly number of your constituents.

The interpretation put on them by some few implies that you have some knowledge of what is going to take place, or that by the use of the words imputed to you you intended to give some encouragement to acts of violence on the part of the Boers against the property of private individuals.

As one of your constituents and knowing that all such interpretations are contrary to any sentiment of your mind and absolutely foreign to your nature, I have ventured with great respect to call your attention to what you are reported to have said and the constructions which are being put upon it.

Brunner Papers, Letterbook

Sir John Brunner to W. Blagg   March 9, 1900

The American philosopher said "never prophesy unless you know." I prophesied without knowing. But I based my anticipation upon the well known fact that there are among the Boers many fanatics who hate the gold mines and everything connected with them, believing them to have been a curse to their country.

If these people do destroy the Mining Companies' plant we shall get no indemnity from the Companies, and shall have heavier taxes to pay; so we must all hope that the damage may be prevented.

The idea that I wish for so deplorable a catastrophe is very far fetched and need not be remarked upon.

What a memorable pleasure it was yesterday to join with the members of the two houses in attending in the great court-yard of Buckingham Palace to express our gratitude to, and our admiration and reverence for Her Majesty. She has, I assure you, touched all our hearts by her decision to visit Ireland and thus to render her thanks for the splendid valour of her Irish Regiments and her sorrow for their losses. This decision and the order that all Irish Regiments shall henceforth wear the shamrock on St. Patricks day are universally believed to have come, not from the advice of Ministers but from Her Majesty's own warm quick sympathies. God save the Queen!

Brunner Papers, Letterbook

Brunner's seat at Northwich, which he had held without interruption since an 1887 by-election, was comparatively secure. The reports he received as president of the Cheshire Liberal Federal Council indicated, however, that the party's chances were less favorable elsewhere in the county.

Cheshire Liberal Federal Council
Report to Sir John Brunner May 26, 1900

Eddisbury: Mr. Bate & Mr. Cooke reported registration better looked after. Cooke thinks possibly a Liberal majority in the Division if it can be got to the Poll. Pity not to fight. But does not think he is the man to fight.

Crewe: Mr. Darling reported. Registration all right. Register increased 1500. Many *new* voters, who generally vote Liberal first time. Gained on Municipal Elections. War Fever bad.

Hyde: Mr. J. F. L. Brunner [Sir John's son] selected to be candidate. Good fortune returning Conservative candidate not so popular. Win if not for War. Changing agent. Registration good.

Knutsford: Dr. Bowman reported. Registration and machinery improved.... Want candidate—not pro-Boer—absence of candidate discouraging.

Birkenhead: No attendance.

Macclesfield: Mr. W. Small reported registration well looked after. No candidate. Member's position strengthened by being at the War....

Northwich: Mr. W. Handley reported all in order. Member still popular. War fever might reduce majority. Don't fear defeat.

Stockport: Mr. Massey reported registration good. Gained at Municipal election. Sir J. Leigh will stand.

Stalybridge: Mr. J. F. Chatham elected to be Candidate, No proper agents. No attendance.

Wirral: No attendance. Mr. A. Mills looking after registration.

Chester: If War over every chance with right man. Mr. W. H. Lever would win the Constituency.

Brunner Papers

Philip Stanhope, prevented by illness from putting in a personal appearance at Burnley, appealed to his constituents by means of an open letter.

Philip Stanhope
Letter to His Constituents

Manchester Guardian   **April 9, 1900**

At the annual meeting of the Burnley Liberal Council the following letter was read from Mr. P. Stanhope, M.P.:

House of Commons, April 8, 1900.

Dear Mr. Armistead,—I see that the Burnley Liberal Association will hold their annual Council meeting to-morrow night, and will no doubt show that the Liberalism of Burnley is as consistent and determined as it has ever been; and although the moment is not a favourable one for the discussion of general political topics, I trust the Council will reassert its adhesion to the great causes to which we stand committed. It was to me a matter of sincere regret that ill-health prevented my attendance at the Liberal bazaar and from taking a personal part in that strikingly successful affair, but even to-day I have not regained the full use of my voice, and am obliged to exercise great prudence during the prevalence of the east winds. I hope, however, that with the coming spring I shall be completely re-established and restored to public activity, and I shall hold myself at the disposition of the Liberal Executive should it be decided to have ward or other meetings in view of the approach of a general election. Burnley is, happily, a centre where the right of free speech is cherished, and we are not confronted with the difficulties existing in so many places where the passions of the hour have given rise to discreditable scenes entirely alien to British custom. I trust that every occasion will be taken to protest, in the name of the Liberal party, against the growing intolerance which for the moment threatens one of the most precious of our liberties, and which, if continued, would bring shame and disgrace upon the nation as a whole. I wish the circumstances of the present time rendered it possible to speak with more precision as to the prospects of peace, but the military situation, brilliant as have been recent achievements of our troops, is still sufficiently serious to raise doubts as to the early conclusion of the war, and I therefore confine myself to the assertion of two fundamental principles which, in my judgment, must form the basis of our action in the hour of victory. First, it is obviously essential that the military position must be made perfectly secure against any possible recurrence of the present conflict. Second, the question of the future administration of the two South African Republics must be governed by the consideration that the majority of our fellow-citizens in South Africa are of the Dutch race, and that any scheme which failed to recognise this fact and which did permanent violence to their sentiments could only intensify racial hatreds and result in the creation of another Irish question at 6,000 miles from our shores. The approaching return of Mr. Rhodes to this country will certainly be followed by an active campaign in favour of extreme courses designed to obtain financial advantage for his group of cosmopolitan mining speculators and for the Chartered Company of South Africa. The powerful interests which he and his friends possess in an unlimited purse and a docile press will be brought to bear in full volume. Social and other pressure will be strenuously applied in Ministerial and other quarters, and, in spite of the ungenerous and vulgar taunts which he has showered upon the brave officers and men who maintained the defence of Kimberley and effected its relief, and his shameless declaration that the British flag was to him only the "greatest of commercial assets," the existing worship of Mammon and the blind pursuit of wealth are still such potent forces amongst us that it will require all the united energies and all the enthusiasm of the Radicalism of the country to combat and defeat his plans. I do not for a moment doubt, however, that in Burnley, at all events, we shall show a resolute front and pursue a course worthy of a great Radical constituency.—Believe me, sincerely yours,

Philip Stanhope

As a Liberal Unionist, Leonard Courtney was probably the most vulnerable of the pro-Boer M.P.'s. He exchanged a series of letters—most of them public—with party professionals in his division, who naturally took a dim view of his behavior. Throughout the winter and spring, strong pressure was applied to him, but he did not yield, and consequently he was not adopted to contest the seat again.

Lord St. Germans, Chairman of the Liberal Unionist Party in South East Cornwall

Letter to Leonard Courtney   **January 16, 1900**

As far as my own feelings are concerned, although I entirely differ from you in regard to the war, it would give me sincere pleasure to see you again returned for South-East Cornwall; but I cannot disguise from myself that at present your chances are by no means satisfactory. Some two and a half months ago the Conservative section of the Unionist party intimated to me informally that, while the leaders of the section retained unabated their loyalty to the party and were not trying to go behind the compact, they considered your attitude and vote on the foreign policy of the Government had alienated from you the confidence of the party, and that it would be impossible to secure for you the continued support of the rank and file at the next election. ... In that case you would have to rely exclusively on the Liberal Unionist vote, and I much doubt if you would get the whole of that. Of course if the war is happily ended some time before the next election, feeling may calm down, and then your prospects would improve.

Quoted in G. P. Gooch, Life of Lord Courtney
(*London, 1920*), *p. 397*

Lord St. Germans
Letter to Leonard Courtney   **March 9, 1900**

You will have seen in the Western papers an account of the meeting of the Executive Committee of the Liberal Unionist Association and its result. ... The members of the Committee present were, so far as I could hear, most moderate in their language. No heat was shewn, and strong admiration was expressed for your great abilities and fearless honesty, and also much personal respect and goodwill towards you. But there was a strong and universal feeling that, by the attitude of hostility you have taken up towards the Government in regard to South Africa, you have alienated from yourself the support of the Liberal Unionists as well as that of the Conservatives, and that you can no longer be looked upon as representing the views of the constituency in the House of Commons.

Quoted in G. P. Gooch, Life of Lord Courtney
(*London, 1920*), *pp. 401–2*

Leonard Courtney
Letter to Lord St. Germans   **March 10, 1900**

I do not see my way to accept the suggestion that I should at once resign my seat. I do not wish to break up the Liberal

Unionist party in South-East Cornwall; but party has never been to me more than machinery adopted to help bring about certain ends. . . . In my judgment public opinion is the result of many influences, among which the speeches and actions of Members of Parliament used to be as effective as articles in newspapers; and those who have the privilege of employing the power without conflict with any pledge, promise or expectation held out when they were candidates for election, ought in the interests of the nation to guard it most jealously. However disagreeable it may be to electors to think that their Member is supporting a policy from which they would themselves dissent and to a Member to find that his customary friends are no longer in agreement with him, these transitory annoyances should be endured in the interest of the nation at large.

Quoted in G. P. Gooch, Life of Lord Courtney *(London, 1920), pp. 402–3*

Manchester Guardian   **June 18, 1900**

The General Committee of the Liberal Unionist Association of the Bodmin division met at Liskeard on Saturday to decide whether to select another candidate in view of the course which Mr. Courtney has taken in regard to South Africa. Lord St. Germans presided over an attendance of fifty members. The following letter was read from Mr. Courtney:

"I have received your circular convening a representative meeting of the Liberal Unionists of South-east Cornwall to consider whether as a body they will, in view of my opinions respecting the war in South Africa, continue to support me or choose some other candidate to be supported by them at the general election. I do not propose to attend that meeting, but I trust I may be excused if I write this short letter to be submitted to it. In the first place, I would ask my Liberal Unionist friends to measure my services in the past apart from the present war. I have doubtless done and said many things which have not been satisfactory to all my supporters, but I think I may claim that in none of them have I departed from the

141

position of a Liberal Unionist; that is, of a man who, opposed to Home Rule, remains firmly attached to the progressive Liberal faith, which inspired the united party before Home Rule was adopted by any section of it. I believe I cannot be discarded by Liberal Unionists in respect of any action of mine apart from the present war. It may be forcibly urged that the policy of the war is at this moment of such paramount importance as to outweigh every other consideration. If I do not dispute this I must be allowed to claim the benefit of the same thought on my side. My judgment of the war has been founded upon the study of the facts consistently maintained for more than twenty years, and I have opposed the war because I held it injurious to the best interests of South Africa and of our own country. Holding this view, I must desire as strongly to exercise any influence I have as those who are opposed to me may desire to nullify that influence. It would be a great pain to me to find friends with whom I have been so long and so intimately associated resolved to espouse another candidate. It must be a still greater pain to contest their choice, but however painful the prospect of the future I cannot at once abandon any hope or choice of continuing to represent South-east Cornwall. Should another candidate be chosen, I should not underrate the gravity of the step, but it would not of itself determine me to retreat from the constituency when an election comes. I think it only fair to say so much in order that the Electors Committee may understand my position. I have no other purpose than to make this plain, and I trust to the kindness I gratefully acknowledge has always been shown me to prevent any misconstruction of what I am writing."

The Chairman said however much they admired and respected Mr. Courtney they could not support him on a policy which they considered most dangerous to the country. Mr. St. Aubyn moved and Mr. Buder Howell seconded that in view of Mr. Courtney's opposition to the South Africa policy of the Government the Liberal Unionists of the Bodmin division could not support him at the next election.—Mr. Churchward moved an amendment declining to pledge themselves to a

142

candidate in consequence of the diversity of opinion and for the sake of preventing a split in the party.—The resolution was carried by 42 votes to six, and it was decided to invite Sir Lewis Molesworth to meet the Committee, with a view to his adoption as the Unionist candidate. Mr. W. T. Snell, Mr. Courtney's agent, then tendered his resignation as secretary of the Association.—On the motion of Lord St. Germans it was finally resolved—"That this meeting, although they feel it their painful duty to withdraw their support for Mr. Courtney, assure him of the personal esteem in which they hold him and their gratitude for the great services rendered to the Unionist cause in the past."

A May by-election was occasioned at Manchester South by the succession of the sitting member—Lord Lorne—to his father's dukedom. The local Liberal association adopted Leif Jones (later Lord Rhayader), an ardent temperance reformer with well publicized pro-Boer connections. The candidate, trusting that the *Guardian* had sufficiently educated electoral opinion in the area, was hopeful; but C. P. Scott, more of a realist, confessed privately that he would be satisfied to avert "an utter rout."[1]

The relief of Mafeking, midway through the campaign, unleashed a frenzy that the Unionists did not hesitate to exploit. Voters were implored to "let their first message to gallant Mafeking" be the news of a Liberal defeat. When the votes were counted on the twenty-fifth, Jones trailed his opponent by 2,039. Khaki tactics were proved successful, and, by the time that M.P.'s returned from the Whitsun recess, it was clear that the government was preparing to go to the country at an early opportunity.

David Lloyd George, second to none as an indefatigable critic of the government, denounced its political opportunism no less than its South African policy. It is worth noting that, eighteen years later, the Welsh firebrand (then prime minister)

1. Scott to L. T. Hobhouse [May 1900], quoted in P. F. Clarke, *Lancashire and the New Liberalism* (Cambridge, 1971), p. 183.

himself incurred violent resentment for calling a general election under much the same circumstances that he deplored at this time.

David Lloyd George
Speech in the House of Commons   **July 25, 1900**

... The Prime Minister has declared that we entered into this war to revenge the humiliation of Majuba, and to restore the proper credit of this country. I ask hon. Members, will they venture to say that this war has re-established British prestige in South Africa or elsewhere? A force of 250,000 of the picked and trained men, not only of this country, but of the colonies, is required to crush 35,000 peasants. [HON. MEMBERS: Oh!] Well, I am taking as my authority Mr. Cecil Rhodes. At the present moment I do not believe that anyone would even assert that there are more than 20,000 Boers in the field. How does that re-establish our prestige or avenge Majuba? It is with regret that I speak of it; there is a sense of humiliation in it. My own countrymen have been captured, and who can think of that without a sense of shame? But in this war during the last ten months we have been beaten in battles in which the loss was greater than all the men engaged on both sides at Majuba. Why, we have had a dozen Majubas. Revenging Majuba! You have overshadowed Majuba with the ghastlier tragedies of Magersfontein and Spion Kop. You may have destroyed the Conventions of 1881 and 1884; you may have wiped out the humiliation attached to the memory of Majuba, but you have substituted for it a proclamation which turned women and children in the depth of winter from their own homes into the African desert; and you call that restoring British prestige in South Africa. On the contrary, British prestige has suffered, and no one will deny that this great war has done nothing more than to multiply grief and poverty. As for our military reverses, it is not for me to dwell upon them; but, at any rate, there is in them no restoring of prestige. I remember perfectly well the great cry at the last General Election was "Support home industries," and the Government, and above all, the Minister who got his party into power on the prohibition of foreign brushes, is now engaged in the task of restoring British prestige with guns made in Germany, soldiers fed on French vegetables and South American meat, Hungarian horses provided with American saddles, and foreign fodder carried by Spanish mules. That is how we are restoring British prestige and the credit of the country. The fact is that this war was based on a gross miscalculation—upon a series of miscalculations. It was calculated that with 47,000 men we could conquer these two Republics. It is rather unfortunate to consider what that miscalculation was based upon. It was not a miscalculation of the Intelligence Department. It was not that we were taken by surprise by the military preparations of the Boers. The Under Secretary for War declared that they knew perfectly well at the War Office the number of men that the two Republics could turn out, the number of their guns, and the amount of ammunition they had; in fact, that they rather exaggerated the power of the Boers than otherwise. The miscalculation was a miscalculation of statesmanship—a miscalculation as to the character, disposition, ideals, and tenacity of the men with whom we had to deal. And that miscalculation must rest entirely on the shoulders of the right hon. Gentleman himself. He has led us into two blunders. The first was the war. But worse than the war is the change that has been effected in the purpose for which we are prosecuting the war. We went into the war for equal rights; we are prosecuting it for annexation. That is a most serious change in the tactics of the Government from any point of view. There may be something to be said for a war so long as it is entered upon for an unselfish purpose. The influence of a war must always be brutalising, at best; but still, if you enter upon it for an unselfish purpose there is something which almost consecrates the sacrifices, bloodshed, and suffering endured. But when you enter upon a war purely and simply for the purposes of plunder, I know of nothing which is more degrading to the country or more hideous in its effects on the mind and character of the people engaged in it. Anyone who looks at the illustrated papers must see the horrible presentments given of incidents which were formerly relegated to prints like the *Police Gazette*—details which I cannot give to the House without a gross breach of good taste. Incidents of that kind are not given for the purpose of producing any disgust in the minds of the people, but with every circumstance of indication that they are there to invoke admiration. And all these are circulated broadcast in every household throughout the country. The right hon. Gentleman the Colonial Secretary in a speech quoted by the hon. Member for Cockermouth [Lawson] said ... a war ... to impose internal reforms upon President Kruger would be an immoral war. If that be so, I ask the right hon. Gentleman or any of his friends to find an adjective sufficiently expressive of the character of a war entered upon for the purposes of annexation. The right hon. Gentleman admitted that we had no right to meddle in the affairs of the Transvaal, and that there was only one possible justification for it—that our motive was an unselfish one. We have thrown that justification away now. It is exactly as if you had entered into a man's house to protect the children, and started to steal his plate. You entered into these two Republics for philanthropic purposes, and remained to commit burglary. In changing the purpose of the war you have made a bad change. That is the impression you are creating abroad. Our critics say you are not going to war for equal rights and to establish fair play, but to get hold of the goldfields; and you have justified that criticism of our enemies by that change. But, worst of all, a change has been effected in the character of the war. Up to a certain point it was conducted with considerable chivalry, and, so far as war can be so conducted, with apparent good temper on both sides. A war of annexation, however, against a proud people must be a war of extermination, and that is unfortunately what it seems we are now committing ourselves to—burning homesteads and turning women and children out of their homes. The telegram received from Pretoria, and which had passed the military censor, stated that fact, and I do not think he would have let it come unless it was true. It is also confirmed from Lorenzo Marques by information that 600 women and children have been turned out and sent to the hills. There has been the burning of the home-steads of the rebels, and this war will brutalise the people, and the savagery which must necessarily follow will stain the name of this country. It seems to me that in this war we have grad-ually followed the policy of Spain in Cuba. The action of the Spaniards in Cuba produced such a feeling in America that they could not tolerate it, and we know how that war degraded the name of Spain. This is the state of things into which the right hon. Gentleman has brought us. During nine or ten months warfare we have lost between 40,000 and 50,000 men, there has been enormous expense, and the end is not yet in sight. And this Government, the advent of which we were told would terrorise all other governments abroad, has been re-duced to the necessity of appealing to Japan to protect its own Ministers in China. The right hon. Gentleman has made up his mind that this war shall produce electioneering capital to his own side. He is in a great hurry to go to the country before the facts are known. He wants to have the judgment of the people in the very height and excitement of the fever. He wants a verdict before the pleadings are closed and before "discovery" has been obtained. He does not want the docu-ments to come, but he wants to have the judgment of the country upon censored news, suppressed despatches, and un-paid bills. The right hon. Gentleman may not be a statesman, but he is an expert electioneerer, and in his desire to go to the country before the country realises what the war means he is the one man who pronounces the deepest condemnation upon his own proceedings.

Parliamentary Debates, *4th series, LXXXVI, cols. 1209–12*

7:Khaki at the Polls

By late summer, partisan invective had drowned out responsible debate. Government propagandists asserted that three Radical M.P.'s, wittingly or otherwise, were guilty of "advising the enemy."[1] Henry Labouchere, one of the accused, replied in self-defense that he had communicated nothing vital, and, in fact, nothing since the inception of hostilities.

Henry Labouchere
In Truth   August 23, 1900

The correspondence which I print below speaks for itself. I had not supposed that I was one of the three M.P.'s whose letters had fallen into the hands of Mr. Chamberlain, as I did not think that I ever wrote to any one in Pretoria. But I did, before the war, both write and talk to Mr. Montagu White, the Transvaal representative in London, and it would seem that he sent some of my letters to Pretoria. What there is requiring explanation in either my conversations or correspondence I do not know. The advice which I gave to Mr. White was that his Government should make reasonable concessions, and should gain time, in order to tide over the false impression created by Mr. Chamberlain's appeal to the passions which had been excited by statements in regard to Boer rule derived from the "kept" Rhodesian press in South Africa and the correspondents of the English newspapers, who were nearly all connected with that "kept press" and with the Rhodes gang. Had my advice been followed, there would have been no war. The difficulty which stood in the way of its being adopted was that President Kruger and other leading Boers were fully convinced that Mr. Chamberlain had been in the counsels of the Jameson-Rhodes

1. The electors of Northampton were asked: "Are you willing to be represented by a RADICAL WHO corresponds with your country's enemies? . . . WHO advises the enemy to gain time to deceive your country even as he has deceived you?" National Union leaflet No. 123 (August 1900), quoted by R. McKenzie and A. Silver, *Angels in Marble* (Chicago, 1968), pp. 56–57.

conspirators of 1895, and that—no matter what concessions the Transvaal might make—he was determined to have his revenge for President Kruger having got the better of him on that occasion.

For neither the first time nor the last, the Unionists (their party label symbolic in more than one sense) claimed a monopoly upon patriotism and denounced their opponents as the agents of separatism and disruption. Jerome K. Jerome, the author and journalist (his best-known work is the novel *Three Men in a Boat*) wrote in bitter indignation to Herbert Samuel, a prospective Liberal candidate who was to rise rapidly in the party hierarchy.

Jerome K. Jerome
Letter to Herbert Samuel   **September 25, 1900**

Liberty of thought is to be denounced as treachery—to cosmopolitan stockjobbers and their lackeys, who have come to regard England as their own property. The British flag is to be their "Commercial asset." Our peasants are to be drilled into an armed horde and their blood spent on mere financial exploits for the sole benefit of the rich. And those who prefer the cause of England, her fair name and her prosperity, to the success of the gold mines on the Rand, are denounced by the German Jew Press as unpatriotic!
Lord Samuel Papers (House of Lords Record Office), quoted in Bernard Porter, Critics of Empire (New York, 1968), pp. 90–91.

However much he railed against "Hebrew" influences in the world of finance, W. T. Stead wrapped himself in the mantle of an Old Testament seer. Under the aegis of the Stop the War Committee, he published a sixpenny pamphlet designed to protect the children of Abel from the blandishments of the "Candidates of Cain."

149

The Candidates of Cain
A Catechism for the Constituencies
W. T. Stead

A Foreword to the Reader

"HAST thou killed and also taken possession?" was no doubt regarded by Ahab and Jezebel as a highly impertinent question to be addressed by a meddlesome prophet to a king of Israel. For, after all, was not the murder of Naboth a matter of ancient history? The man was not only stone dead, but buried. The question of the hour was not how and by whom he came to his death, but how his vineyard should be laid out for the greatest enjoyment of his murderers.

Nevertheless Elijah persisted in his interrogatory, and the electors who share so much of the faith of the Hebrew prophet as to believe that cold-blooded conspiracy to slay one's neighbour in order to seize his vineyard or his gold mine is not exactly the highest of Christian virtues, will do well, every one in his own constituency, to press this question home to the candidates who are appealing for their suffrages. They will have the less difficulty in so doing because our Naboth is still in the convulsions of the death-agony, his vineyard is a fire-blasted wilderness, and the bill for the bloody deed has still to be presented for payment.

There are many who will be scandalised at this attempt to describe in the plain and simple language of the common people the unspeakable infamies of which our rulers have been guilty in South Africa. But before flinging away this indictment as exaggerated and "much too strong," may I beg any such reader to read carefully the few pages devoted to an explanation of the part which Mr. Chamberlain played in the Jameson Conspiracy, before and after the Raid. Then let him ask, if he can bring himself to contemplate such a hypothesis, supposing that these things are the simple record of literal truth, can any language be too strong, any condemnation too severe for such treachery and crime?

But that which to the Reader is an utterly incredible calumny is to me alas, known only too well to be a plain statement of the absolute truth. And not to me only. There is not one member of the Group of Conspirators in or of the Administration who does not know it also. And some day all the world will know it. Then every one will marvel at the moderation of my language, and upbraid me not for the vehemence of my appeals, but for my failure to do justice to the unutterable infamy of the crime for which the nation is now asked to accept the responsibility. . . .

W. T. STEAD

Sept. 25, 1900

Chapter I

The Supreme Duty of the Hour

1. *Q.* What is the supreme duty at this Election?

A. To repudiate by our vote any responsibility for the wickedest war that has been waged in our time.

2. *Q.* How can this be done?

A. By refusing to vote for any Candidate of Cain, and by doing the utmost in our power to secure the return of candidates who are opposed to murder for gain, or conquest for the sake of empire.

3. *Q.* Who are the Candidates of Cain?

A. The Candidates of Cain are those who defend, condone, justify or excuse the war with the South African Republics.

4. *Q.* What are the reasons for this urgency?

A. Because the blood of our brothers unjustly slain in a wanton war, unjustly forced upon them, cries, like the blood of righteous Abel, to Heaven for redress, and the curse of Cain will rest upon every elector who by voice or vote consents to share in the responsibility for the crime of Cain.

5. *Q.* Then this is not a party pamphlet?

A. By no means. The Candidates of Cain are of both parties. The issue at stake is wider and deeper than any party difference.

6. *Q.* What is that issue?

A. The issue which each elector must face is this, whether any man or nation can justify the slaughter of his fellow-man until he has exhausted every possible means of avoiding so terrible an alternative.

7. *Q.* But do you mean to say that we did not do everything to avoid war in South Africa?

A. That is just what I do say, and what is more, I will prove it to the hilt. Instead of doing everything that could be done to avert war, it is as clear as day that we not only got up a dispute which need not have been raised, but that we obstinately refused, in face of the repeated entreaties of the other side, to adopt the peaceable means which were duly made and provided for settling the dispute amicably before a tribunal of justice and right.

8. *Q.* But if this is so then all who approve and support the war are guilty of aiding and abetting murder on an Imperial scale?

A. Precisely, excepting in so far as they have sinned in ignorance. Hitherto the electors have had no opportunity at the polls of repudiating or of accepting responsibility for this crime of Cain.

9. *Q.* Then what will be the result of the Election?

A. The result of the Election will be that every elector who puts a cross opposite the name of any candidate who approves and defends the war will stamp upon his own brow the bloody brand which blazed upon the forehead of the first murderer.

10. *Q.* But are we not already responsible for the war?

A. Nationally—yes; individually—no. And the importance of the General Election lies in this, that it affords each individual man amongst us who objects to slaying his brother before exhausting all means of peaceful settlement, the first chance of washing his hands of all responsibility in the matter, and of repudiating so far as in him lies all personal share in the worst war of our time.

11. *Q.* But if this advice is followed what will be the effect upon the polls?

A. That is a secondary consideration. The first is, that we must cleanse our own souls from blood-guiltiness. The differences between parties are mere affairs of Tweedledum and Tweedledee compared with the supreme question whether or not a nation is free to repeal the commandment, "Thou shalt do no murder"; and War brought about by the refusal of Arbitration is Murder pure and simple.

12. *Q.* Then you are not anxious to defeat the present Government?

A. The present Government should not only be defeated but impeached, and those members directly responsible for the war should be punished according to their deserts. But that is a very different thing from replacing them by others whose only complaint is that Cain's work was clumsily done, and who allege that if they had been in power they would have made a much quicker job of the murder of Abel.

13. *Q.* But why go into ancient history?

A. Because in the first place it is not ancient, and, in the second place, because the events of the Past enable us to judge how men are likely to act in the Future. A General Election is a Day of Judgment as well as the choice of a new Parliament. Everyone would laugh at the plea of a murderer at the bar who protested against wasting the time of the judge and jury upon such "ancient" history as the details which proved his guilt.

14. *Q.* What is your contention?

A. In one word this: that to insist on an appeal to the sword rather than an appeal to arbitration is a crime against civilisation and Christianity, the authors of which ought never to receive the vote of any civilized man. This broad issue overshadows all minor questions as to the merits of the dispute. A Government which defiantly refuses to refer a dispute to Arbitration in order to appeal to the Sword, is an Enemy of the Human Race, and all who support it are Candidates of Cain.

Polling, which began in the early days of October, was spread out over more than a fortnight. Among the first pro-Boer fatalities was Philip Stanhope, who lost Burnley (a seat that had not gone Conservative since 1868) by 600 votes, and Sir Wilfrid Lawson, who was defeated by 209 votes at Cockermouth. Lloyd George was returned for the Carnarvon Burghs with a shaky majority of 194, and Campbell-Bannerman for the Stirling Burghs with a majority half as large as the one he obtained in the previous General Election. C. P. Scott, who scraped by at Leigh by 120 votes (his previous majority was 677) was more fortunate than Augustine Birrell, Fred Maddison, T. R. Buchanan, W. C. Steadman, Dr. G. B. Clark, and (by various estimates) a dozen or so others, who had supported the Stanhope amendment and otherwise identified themselves as pro-Boers. In addition, there were a number of pro-Boer M.P.'s who had either resigned their seats (like Sir Edward Clarke at Plymouth), or who had retired (like Courtney) at the dissolution.

John Burns could afford to be complacent. Through thick or thin, he could count upon the devotion of his predominantly working-class constituents. Harold Spender, a journalist of varied skills, accompanied Burns on a last minute bicycle tour through the streets of Battersea.

Manchester Guardian October 2, 1900

I was in luck's way this afternoon [October 1]. Anxious to see Battersea on the eve of the greatest struggle in its history, I had ridden south-west to the silver Thames, crossed that beautiful park of Battersea, with its smooth roads, its ample playing fields, and large calm waters, and had emerged in the Battersea Road. The thoughts of a bicyclist are wonderfully calmed by a smooth road, and I had begun to think pleasantly of Battersea. But the city is the man; you cannot think of Battersea without thinking of Burns. His energy is writ large on every corner of this pleasant city—on the park, the public buildings, the cottages, the very roads. He has sweetened Battersea by the ceaseless infusion of ideas, and so it has become his city—the Battersea of Burns as well as the Burns of Battersea—the one poor suburb of London that has sweetness and light.

So I was thinking when I looked up, and there was the man himself. He was riding towards me on his bicycle, the handlebars decked with a bunch of blue and white ribbons; alert, robust, radiant with confident strength. He greeted me with a gay smile, and, riding side by side, we left the crowds of his too urgent followers and glided into a quieter street.

With that quick gift of intimacy he answered my unspoken question.

"We're going to win," he said.

We were riding along a row of new villa flats lately erected round Battersea Park. I looked up at them interrogatively. "They don't count," he said. "They are not on the register yet. The whole of these buildings have only 150 votes on the old register."

"So you actually score by the stale register?"

"That is so. In a year or two's time these people may be serious for me—but not now."

Few had window-cards, but I noticed that those who had were supporting Garton's.

He saw my eye on the cards. "Come," he said; "I will show you where my cards are."

We left the villas, crossed the main road and entered the working-class district with that swiftness of transition which makes life on a bicycle so vastly exhilarating and entertaining. As we moved he dwelt on the forces which were working on his side. The forces of progress were abolutely solid. The Social Democrats, who usually fought him, were now with him. The moderate "Jingo" Liberals did not count; they were gone already. And as for khaki, that had never caught on at Battersea. Burns analysed his chances simply and clearly, but I noticed that he was never over-confident, and he never hid from himself the chances of defeat. "Whatever happens," he always said, "I have done my best. I have held 56 meetings; I have spared myself nothing—I have fought the good fight."

We looked in at the committee-rooms, and saw Mrs. John Burns and her workers busy over envelopes, while Master John Burns, aged four, sat in a chair very silent and wise, saying nothing but thinking the more. Then we turned aside from the great Battersea Road and began to move through the real Battersea—the Battersea of the weekly tenant. There is little or no squalor in Battersea, and in this district in the Shaftesbury estate you have a model of how poor men should live well—small, neat cottages, prettily built, each with a gift of "home" for the occupants. The men were at work, but the women stood at the doors and smiled at Burns as he passed. Each street awoke for a moment from its dulness like a grey sky lit up by a flash of lightning. The boys and girls shouted, Burns passed quickly with a nod, a smile, or a pleasant word for all, but always reserving that terrible power of swift repartee for his foes. Two women at a street corner hissed as he passed, and cried "Traitor." Burns leant lightly from his saddle and gently murmured as he passed, "You are spoiling your faces." But we came to see the cards. Let me look. At first they all seem to be blue—for Burns. No, there is one for Garton. But let me count. Burns does it rapidly as we pass. "One, two, three—twenty in that street for me and three for Garton. One, two, three—thirty for me and four for Garton." The majority is overwhelming. The place is painted blue. That is the fact—whatever the result to-morrow.

"Cards are sometimes deceptive," I suggested.

"That is so, but they have no reason to conceal Garton's, and none to conceal mine."

We had passed through the district, and every symptom had gone to indicate victory.

Burns had to go off and pay calls on some doubtfuls, and we parted at the turning back into the main road.

"If they beat me," said Burns, with one of those splendid touches of egoism, "it will be a crime." And looking round on Battersea and all that he has done for it, no one can think otherwise.

One of the first towns to report was Oldham, a two-member Lancashire constituency, where there had been a hotly contested by-election in the spring of 1899. Winston Churchill, who then stood unsuccessfully in the Tory interest, now managed to edge out Walter Runciman, one of the Liberal incumbents, by 222 votes. Runciman was a supporter of the war; but the return of Churchill, celebrated for his exploits as a war correspondent in South Africa, was hailed as an imperialist victory.

Manchester Guardian   **October 2, 1900**

Oldham entered into the contest yesterday with characteristic fervour. Not the men only, but, very properly, the women and children too thought they had an interest in the affair, and many of the mills being closed for the whole or part of the day the whole population seemed to have turned out, and, adorned with favours of red or blue, imparted to the sombre streets a brightness in which on ordinary days they are sadly lacking. The protagonists in the fight were not behind in the matter of display. The borough covers so wide an area that they had to divide their forces, and each of the four candidates turned out in a separate equipage, smartly decked with appropriate colours. Thus while Mr. Emmott was in the west Mr. Runciman would be in the east, some five miles away, and Mr. Churchill would be in the south of the constituency while Mr. Crisp was paying his attentions to the north. In each case the candidate's carriage was graced with the presence of one or more ladies, Messrs. Emmott, Runciman, and Crisp being accompanied by their wives, while Mr. Churchill had the countenance of his mother, Mrs. G. Cornwallis-West, known on her former visit to Oldham as Lady Randolph Churchill.

The contest was conducted with entire good humour and with thorough earnestness on both sides, and as evidence of the interest excited in the election without as well as within the constituency came messages during the day from many distinguished politicians. Thus Mr. Chamberlain, taking the borough and the Empire under his wing, wired: "Every seat gained at this crisis by the Unionist party is a blow struck against enemies at home and abroad. I trust Lancashire will show she values the unity of the Empire and the affection of the colonies." Sir H. Campbell-Bannerman quickly responded with a message of encouragement to the Liberal workers. Every spare foot of wall bloomed with posters, red and blue. None excited more interest and amusement than a despairing blue placard appealing to the Tories not to split their votes. "Churchill and Crisp stand or fall together." The differences between the two candidates had been matter of common gossip. Since the bye-election of 1899 the electorate has increased by some 100 votes, the present number on the register being 29,253. Of these some 20,000 are in Oldham proper, and the remainder in Chadderton, Crompton and Shaw, Royton, and Lees. Crompton is the most Conservative part of the division, but its influence is supposed to be counteracted by the outlying district of Chadderton. Crompton, for instance, returns nine out of ten Tory members to the Urban District Council, while Chadderton has an equally predominant Liberal representation. It was in Oldham itself that the Liberal strength was thought to lie, but here, as elsewhere, the Liberals have been heavily handicapped by the staleness of the register. Over 1,000 removals had to be traced, and every possible effort was made in this direction by the agents of both sides, but with only moderate success. It is unquestionably true that in this vast constituency there are hundreds of householders who, by the Tory dodge of taking the election at the fag-end of the year, are robbed of the franchise.

The result of the poll was declared about eleven o'clock as follows:

Emmott (L)	12,947
Churchill (C)	12,931
Runciman (L)	12,709
Crisp (C)	12,522

At the bye-election last year the voting was as follows: Mr. Emmott (L), 12,976; Mr. Runciman (L), 12,770; Mr. W. S. Churchill (C), 11,477; Mr. Mawdsley (C), 11,449.

It will be seen that the Conservatives have gained one seat, and that while Mr. Emmott retains his position at the head of the poll, Mr. Churchill has polled 1,454 more votes than he did in 1899.

A. J. Balfour, having obtained his own return by a handsome margin, took to the road in support of less secure Unionist candidates. On the evening of the fifth, in a speech at

Kilmarnock, he commended the patriotism of the urban working classes, and defended the use of the epithet "pro-Boer."

Manchester Guardian   October 6, 1900

Mr. Balfour said that never before in the history of this country had the great centres of industry declared their adhesion to the policy of the Unionist and Conservative Government with a unanimity at all approaching or even comparable with the unanimity which had been shown in Manchester, Salford, Liverpool, Glasgow, Birmingham— (cheers) —London, and Newcastle—(cheers.) He would not go over the whole list, but never before in the history of this country had these great communities, in which the working men of this country not merely held the balance, who were nine-tenths or ninety-nine hundredths of the whole constituency—never had they shown themselves so solid and united in defence of a Unionist or Conservative Government.— (Cheers.) He saw that Mr. Morley in the second manifesto which he had just issued to his constituents told them that in this election the issues were more confused than they had been for 35 years. He had not seen so many general elections as Mr. Morley, though he had taken part as a candidate in more, but never did he remember any general election in which the issue was as defined, as clear-cut, as it had been at this election— (cheers) —and his conviction was that it was largely because the issue was clear-cut that the success of the Conservative and Unionist party had been, if possible, greater in these large centres of population in which by-issues were swept on one side and regarded as of no account in the battle that had been fought. Sir Henry Campbell-Bannerman thought that some of the successes which he, like the rest of the world, was obliged to admit they had enjoyed was due to misrepresentation on the part of the Unionist candidates. Well, he supposed that they had sorrowfully to admit that no general election ever took place without something in the nature of misrepresentation being used on the one or both sides. He himself had been represented in a widely diffused caricature as refusing assistance to the starving millions of

India while lavishing it on particular classes of the community. Criticism and misrepresentation he did not complain of. These things happened; but if one had 2,400 of a majority he did not mind criticism and misrepresentation.— (Cheers.) Of the two parties in the State it was not the Conservatives who had been in the past chiefly guilty of that. As a rule they had been the victims and not the executioners. They had been subjected to that kind of misrepresentation far more than they had ever indulged in it themselves.— (Interruption.) He saw there were one or two gentlemen who doubted that, but he would tell them that they had made a very imperfect study of electioneering literature.— (Hear, hear.) Sir Henry Campbell-Bannerman had been shocked—he had used strong language and "shocked" was the weakest word— (laughter) —at seeing a man walking about the Edinburgh streets with a placard which said "Vote for Agnew and defeat the pro-Boers." Well, they did vote for Agnew— (cheers) —and if there were any pro-Boers in Edinburgh they did defeat the pro-Boers. The question was—Was that a fair or was it not a fair placard? Personally he was not in love with this kind of placards, but the question was this— Had Sir William Agnew's opponent been returned of what party would he have been a member? The party to which he would have been returned numbered in the last Parliament 250 members, but more than 80, if his memory served him aright, were Nationalist members of Parliament. Every one of these Nationalist members was by his own confession a pro-Boer. He would not dispute, he actually boasted of it. Well, that was a third of the party that the opponent of Sir William Agnew hoped to support, and in his opinion the placard was perfectly fair, true, and just.— (Cheers.) When they added these Nationalists and those members of English constituencies —not so many—whose opinions could hardly be distinguished from those of their Irish allies, when they added these two divisions they had a very important and possibly dominating section of the present Opposition. And it was not a calumny to say, it was not pressing illegitimately any declaration they had made, it was not turning any chance phrase to a wrong account to say, it was a broad statement that they were pro-

Boers, and to this day were proud of being pro-Boers.—
(Cheers.) . . .

Sir John Brunner was accused by his "Imperialist" opponent,
C. L. Samson, of a willingness to sell out "the lives, the
liberty, and the property" of Englishmen in South Africa. It
was said that he belonged and provided financial support
to the Stop the War Committee, and, on better authority,
that he had chaired a May 30 meeting at Liverpool addressed
by "that prince of pro-Boers," Leonard Courtney.[1] His seat
endangered, Brunner defended himself on October 4 at an
election rally.

Manchester Guardian   **October 5, 1900**

The Middlewich Town Hall was crowded last night and an enthusiastic meeting was held in support of Sir John Brunner's
candidature. In the course of his address, Sir John said, in reply
to Mr. Samson, that he was not a member of the Stop-the-War
Committee; he did not attend the conference to form that
committee, and he did not subscribe to the funds. Mr. Stead
had asked him to subscribe, but he refused. He (Sir John)
was surprised that Mr. Samson had not taken the trouble to
verify his statements, and could not tell why he refused the
word of a gentleman. He, however, had asked Mr. Samson for
an apology, and expected to get one (applause). Much had
been said about his attending the Conciliation Committee.
Was anyone going to condemn him for that?— (No, no). When
our soldiers came back a few weeks hence, the British Empire
would be one vast conciliation committee.— (applause). Sir
John asked the electors to avoid the Tory policy of aggression
and militarism.

Last night a meeting was held in support of Mr. Samson's
candidature. The Conservative candidate said he now accepted
Sir John Brunner's denial that he was a member of the Stop-
the-War Committee and contributed thereto. He was sorry

1. S. E. Koss, *Sir John Brunner, Radical Plutocrat* (Cambridge,
1970), p. 188.

for having expressed disbelief. He still denounced his opponent as a pro-Boer.

Brunner held his seat at Northwich with a diminished majority of 699 (his 1895 majority had been 1,638), which was roughly the same margin by which his son was defeated at Hyde. As was the case with others who were castigated as pro-Boers, the drop in his vote was partly attributable to factors unrelated to the war. Campbell-Bannerman, for example, blamed his decreased majority at Stirling Burghs on the fickleness of Irish Catholic voters in that constituency.[1] In the case of Brunner, the largest employer in his locality, allegations of unfair labor practices probably hurt him more than insinuations about his patriotism.

Sir John Brunner
Letter to J. L. Hammond   **October 18, 1900**

I have had an awful job. When I, during the first week, addressed the Liberal organisation, I found that *nearly every* man believed the story that B[runner] M[ond] and Co. would not take on men over 30 years of age.

My reception by *them* was therefore deadly cold.

You may imagine how outsiders felt.

In the end I could not *kill* the lie. Many men had promised to vote against me before my canvassers went round to contradict what they themselves had said in good faith previously.

Luckily for me my opponent was a blunderer of the first order, otherwise I should have been beaten.

Hammond Papers, Bodleian Library, Oxford

J. E. Ellis summoned all his strength to save his seat from the jingo flood. Under the circumstances, he was not the least disappointed by his modest success. On October 9, he ex-

---

1. Campbell-Bannerman to Herbert Gladstone (copy), October 12, 1900, Campbell-Bannerman Papers, British Museum Add. MSS. 41,216, fol. 22.

pressed his gratitude to the faithful electors of the Rushcliffe division of Nottinghamshire.

Letter to His Constituents

J. E. Ellis   **October 9, 1900**

Gentlemen,

You have given your verdict. You have declared with an unmistakable voice that the man whom you send to the Commons House of Parliament ought to, and shall have the power to obtain, without interference, that "stream of facts" which is the only safe and sure foundation for correct opinion and right judgment.

You have protested against that throttling of the channel of intelligence from South Africa which has been practised by those charged with acts of maladministration at the time when they are seeking a vote of confidence for their conduct in relation to the war.

You have definitely pronounced for that policy of continuous striving for the betterment of our people at home, which demands that the spirit of justice and good-will shall underlie our relations with other people.

Gentlemen, rest assured I recognise with a grateful heart the extraordinary enthusiasm, the self-sacrificing and devoted work of the polling day. Do not think for a moment I regard the result of our work as having in it any element of personal triumph. No, Gentlemen, it is the deliberate but emphatic mandate of a great constituency to be taken by me to that supreme Council of the Nation to which I am proud to go for the fifth time in your service. I am, &c.

Quoted in Arthur T. Bassett, The Life of the Rt. Hon. John Edward Ellis, M.P. (*London, 1914*), *p. 180*

John Morley expended a minimum of effort to obtain his re-election for the Montrose Burghs. A throat ailment forced him to limit his campaigning to published manifestos, and he did not even appear on his own behalf. Two days after polling, he exulted to Frederic Harrison.

John Morley
Letter to Frederic Harrison   October 11, 1900

The *Scotsman*, I understand, plied them hard with exhortations daily to turn me out, and there was much underhand insinuation that I was malingering. It had no effect. The decrease of the majority just corresponds to the waste (deaths, removals, etc.) of the register.

Harrison Papers, British Library of Political and Economic Science

---

What was one to make of the results? The Unionists were returned to power with a few more seats than they had held at the time of the dissolution, but not as many as they had won in the previous general election. Despite the vehemence of the campaign—"A seat lost to the Government," Chamberlain had crudely put it, "is a seat gained (or sold) to the Boers"—Sir William Harcourt found "the result . . . better rather than worse than [one] would have expected."[1]

Yet to speak of the Liberal Party holding its own, either in parliamentary representation or popular vote, is to ignore the profound divisions in its ranks. Liberal Imperialists often fared significantly better than others within the party: thirty miles from Stirling Burghs, where Campbell-Bannerman's vote plummeted, Asquith at East Fife increased his majority from 716 to 1,431. But the situation remained sufficiently confused for antithetical conclusions to be drawn from the same evidence.

The Times   October 18, 1900

To the Editor of *The Times*
Sir—There is one fact in regard to the recent election which is worthy of note. For the first time within a century the peace

---

1. Harcourt to Campbell-Bannerman, October 18, 1900, Campbell-Bannerman Papers, British Museum Add. MSS. 41,219, fols. 144–45.

party have maintained their ground at a general election held during or shortly after a serious war.

In 1812 the "peace" Whigs who had protested against the Peninsular war were for the most part unseated. Romilly, Brougham, Tierney, Horner, William Lamb, the principal leaders of the Opposition to the war, lost their seats. The Government of Lord Liverpool gained between 30 and 40 seats.

In 1857, after the Crimean war and on the "khaki" appeal of Lord Palmerston upon the China question, the small "peace" party in the House of Commons were annihilated by the country. Cobden, Bright, Milner-Gibson, W. J. Fox, and Miall all lost their seats, and Palmerston came back with an increased majority.

In 1900, as far as can be at present ascertained, the peace party have kept their numerical strength practically intact, while some of their members have been re-elected with increased majorities. It is true that the *personnel* is slightly altered. Sir Wilfrid Lawson, Mr. Stanhope, Mr. Maddison, and some others have lost their seats; but, on the other hand, such strenuous opponents of the war as Mr. Keir-Hardie, Mr. Richard Bell, and Mr. Corrie Grant, besides less prominent "peace" men, have won seats from supporters of the war. It is the first occasion upon which the Government which is responsible for the war has failed to materially increase its majority. I deduce no moral; I merely state a fact.

> Yours, &c.,
> Allan H. Bright
> Gorse Hey, West Derby, Liverpool, Oct. 16

The Times (October 17), admitting that it was "difficult at this moment to make an absolutely trustworthy classification" of Liberals elected to the new Parliament, nonetheless contemplated the returns—not yet complete—with general satisfaction. Regretfully, it counted fifteen Liberals "understood to be in sympathy with the South African policy of the Government who will not reappear at St. Stephen's." But, on balance, the "Little Englanders" in the party had suffered far worse.

Two days later, *The Times*—without making clear the criteria on which it based its calculation—was pleased to note that the Liberal Imperialists had increased their membership in the House from 63 to 81.

The Times (leader)   **October 19, 1900**

Out of the 106 Radical and Labour members, who have not been described in our analysis as Imperialists, the opinions of more than one half are doubtful or unascertained. There is reason to believe that the majority of those in this category will repudiate the imputation that they are going to range themselves with Mr. Labouchere, Mr. Burns, Sir Robert Reid, and Sir William Harcourt. . . . At any rate, leading politicians on the Liberal side are confident that fully two-thirds of the regular opposition will refuse to take the Little Englander line.

The Labour Representation Committee, which put itself on the electoral map in the next general election, achieved results that were equally open to controversy.[1] It fielded fifteen candidates, only two of whom won seats: Keir Hardie and Richard Bell. Both, however, as Allan H. Bright had noted in his letter to *The Times*, were "strenuous opponents of the war." Other pro-Boer Labour candidates, most conspicuously Philip Snowden at Blackburn, polled surprisingly well; and pro-Boer Lib-Labs, including John Burns at Battersea, held their ground. Meanwhile, as the *Manchester Guardian* pointed out on the seventeenth, Havelock Wilson and Sam Woods, two Labour men who supported the war, were defeated in their bids for reelection.

Keir Hardie, in an October 28 speech at Manchester, made an appeal for Lib-Lab cooperation that the *Manchester Guardian* was happy to endorse.

Manchester Guardian (leader)   **October 29, 1900**

Mr. Keir Hardie, speaking in the Free-trade Hall yesterday, made a powerful appeal to all Liberals "who wished to remain true to the traditions and principles of their old party" to co-operate with the Independent Labour party in fighting the

1. Compare the report in the *Labour Leader*, October 13, 1900, with the account in Roy Douglas, *History of the Liberal Party, 1895–1970* (London, 1971), pp. 67–68.

common enemy, the "new Imperialism." He pointed out quite
justly that Liberalism and Mr. Chamberlain's Imperialism were
antagonistic and mutually destructive, and that Liberals must
choose between them and could not profess both faiths at
once. The war, Mr. Keir Hardie sees, is but an incident in
the general movement towards militarism, which the Government has done its utmost to foster during the last five years,
and when the Boers are conquered this sham Imperialism will
remain a standing danger to peace and progress. His advice to
all who regard it with apprehension, whether they are Liberals
or Socialists, to find a common basis for action is, therefore,
both wise and timely, although we do not share his fears lest
the Liberal party should be controlled in the future by those
who would be Imperialists first and Liberals afterwards. The
need for concerted action was shown clearly enough in the
late election. For while Mr. Keir Hardie himself owed his return for Merthyr Tydvil in no small measure to Liberal votes
and Mr. Ward came very near winning the seat for Gorton,
where Liberals and the Labour party worked harmoniously together, several seats were won for the Government simply
through disunion in the progressive ranks. It is to be hoped
that the conciliatory overtures of Mr. Keir Hardie will be
received by Liberals in the same spirit in which they are made.

Except perhaps in the short run, the distinction between
Liberal Imperialists and pro-Boers was less meaningful than
other, more basic differences among Liberals. To C. F. G.
Masterman, soon to launch a distinguished (and eventually
forlorn) career as a publicist and parliamentarian, the election
had done its greatest harm in deflecting attention from
domestic problems and in weakening the forces of social change.

"For Zion's Sake:
The Wail of a Social Reformer"
C. F. G. Masterman   In the Commonwealth, November, 1900

Smarting under the sense of inglorious defeat, it is difficult
for one who has been personally engaged in the conflict to
take an altogether dispassionate view of the present Election.

We had descended upon a prosperous provincial town. There, we argued, exhorted, entreated, lamented. We praised our soldiers in the war, talked proudly of the Empire, spread a Gargantuan banquet of social reform—housing, temperance, educational. We waxed pathetic over the million illegally overcrowded in London, six times the Outlanders of the Transvaal. We mourned over the children contaminated by the public house. We darkly prophesied the results of foreign competition and our imperfect education. Our opponent, like Gallio, openly protested that he cared for none of these things. He talked little, slapped his chest at intervals, and muttered concerning Lord Roberts and the British Army. And the result was that he was triumphantly elected, we were ignominiously rejected. . . .

The consolations faintly administered by the Liberal press fail to move those whose first interest is social progress. The numbers of the parties in the New Parliament may approximate to the numbers in the old. But the real result is here disguised by the success of those Liberals who in order to retain their seats were content to masquerade in any form of "Imperialistic" garments: "worshipping" (in a phrase now famous) the "new gods of the heathen amongst whom they dwelt." Only when we come to estimate individual losses can we appreciate the full extent of the debacle. Steadman has gone from Stepney: all his pertinacity in the cause of Housing Reform could not save him: a military person descended upon his constituency from afar and swept him away by an overwhelming majority. Augustine Birrell definitely appealed upon social reform: Mr. Chamberlain and myself, he continually asserted, are but shadows: fleeting shadows are the politicians of a day; but the condition of Manchester ten years hence is not a shadow. But Manchester would have none of it and his place knows him no more. Stuart, "the member for London," eager and passionate champion of all schemes for the welfare of the great city, is rejected of Hoxton: the man who would do most despised by those who most need. The personal popularity and ready humour of Sir Wilfrid Lawson could not help the veteran leader of the temperance party. Almost all those few distinguished by energy or enthusiasm for social reform have perished in the great disaster. Methyr Tydvil indeed returned the Independent Labour Party after he had been rejected by Preston: Derby has sent a welcome addition in Mr. Bell: and John Burns retained his seat at Battersea in a fight with the echoes of which South London is still reverberating. But in the first parliament of the new century the friends of Social Progress will be numbered on the fingers of one hand. . . .

The election itself may have been influenced by other causes. The total failure of official Liberalism to unite or to guide: sympathy with our colonists and those fighting in South Africa; the bewilderment and doubt of those not possessing capacity of clear thought in the sudden dusty turmoil of a precipitate appeal: all these doubtless swung thousands of religious and patriotic voters away from the party of progress. But the spirit, intensified at the moment of Election, but manifest during many past years, is a spirit which cannot bring to this nation good will or peace. Languid indifference to the condition of our big cities, refusal to grapple with housing reform or temperance reform, a crying of peace at home where there is no peace and boisterous arrogance abroad—what fruit but dead sea apples can grow from such a tree?

8: The Winter of Discontents

In the wake of the general election, there was the natural tendency for pro-Boers to slacken their efforts and reformulate their strategies. It was not clear how much incendiary rhetoric (such as Stead's) had worked to the disadvantage of antiwar candidates. Nor could one be certain how newly elected M.P.'s would align themselves. James Bryce encouraged Courtney to continue the agitation, but to concentrate upon a few well-defined objectives.

James Bryce

Letter to Leonard Courtney　　　　　　　　**October 22, 1900**

It is unluckily impossible for me to come to town on Wednesday for the Conciliation Committee meeting as I have engagements here. So far as I can judge there are only two things the Committee can now do. One is to continue to try to enlighten the public regarding the truth of the case in South Africa. It is astonishing how even intelligent people are still under delusions, such as the "great Dutch conspiracy," the arming of the Transvaal since 1881, etc. To remove these delusions so far as possible, if people will consent to listen to arguments on what they are coming to regard as *chose jugée*, would accelerate the reaction which may otherwise come too late. The other is to watch current events, and particularly the resettlement and appointments made in the conquered States. I confess to seeing no present alternative to Crown Colony Government except a provisional military government. Military indeed any government must needs be for a time; and to establish one under a good military man with some sensible civil assistants from home, not South African English, seems to me better than the mockery of a quasi-representative government which a Crown Colony would mean.

Quoted in G. P. Gooch, Life of Lord Courtney
(London, 1920), p. 416

Conquered, but by no means subdued, the Boers unleashed a guerilla war: their commandos would ambush British troops, then escape to safety in the veldt. Confronted with this new situation, the British resorted to drastic tactics that did them less than proud. Farms were burned in retaliation or to prevent their use as arms depots; civilian hostages were taken; and noncombatants were crowded into concentration camps (far different from the institutions later known by that name), where sanitation was inadequate and mortality rates were shockingly high.

The officers of the South Africa Conciliation Committee protested to the prime minister against "the Change that Has Come Over the War." (Successive pamphlets on the same theme were addressed to a wider audience.)

A Plain Statement of the Change that Has Come Over the War in South Africa: A Memorial Addressed to Lord Salisbury by the South Africa Conciliation Committee SACC Pamphlet No. 58

. . . The increasing rigour of the measures adopted by Lord Roberts is illustrated by each day's intelligence from South Africa. October closed with the news of the burning of all the Boer houses between Vryheid and Dundee, a distance of upwards of fifty miles, the complete destruction of Bothaville and Ventersburg, and the imprisonment of many Dutch Reformed Ministers, the effect of the last named step being to deprive infants of baptism, and grown-up persons of those spiritual ministrations which are so deeply valued by them.

A further advance on the road of severity is seen in a Reuter's special telegram of October 30th, which announces that every male Boer, over fourteen years of age, outside a radius of ten miles of Bloemfontein, is being "coralled" or "concentrated" into Bloemfontein. Their women and children are being carried away hundreds of miles into the Cape Colony. A still further development of this drastic policy is to be found in a proclamation stated to have been issued from Bloemfontein on October 24th, requiring all farmers to scour every night the vicinity of their farms to prevent "sniping." Failure to comply with this order subjects the farmers, first, to a fine of £200, and, secondly, to the burning of their farms. A moment's consideration of the large areas of the Boer farms and the mobility of the Boer commandos reveals the very difficult situation thus thrust upon the unfortunate farmers.

It is, indeed, difficult to realise how the character of the struggle has passed from phase to phase. As now developed it involves the burning of farms and even of villages, the denudation of whole districts of stock and crop, the deportation of the women and children left homeless, some of them over the borders, some into the remoter parts of the Transvaal, and some apparently about to be driven into the ranks of the companies of the enemy still in the field. No motive of cruelty is suggested in our soldiers, who are carrying out a policy for which they have no responsibility. When, however, it is said that all this is war, it must be added that it is not war as practised in Europe, and as regulated by the Conventions of civilised nations.

Only quite recently has the seal been set by the greatest European authorities to the well known principles of international law regulating the conduct of wars. The clauses of the Hague Convention which deal with the subject are clear and definite. . . . It is evident that they are at variance with the recent proclamations. And if it is pleaded that this variance is inevitable, we cannot but recall the words of a great English jurist that "the plea that every means is legitimate which would drive an enemy to submission is a plea which would cover every barbarity that disgraced the wars of the seventeenth century."

Another word must be said. Where a policy fails all pleas in support of it are valueless. It must be remembered that the persons subjected to the recent proclamations are the sons, the brothers, or the near relations of very many thousands of our own fellow-subjects in the Cape Colony, and that to passively witness the infliction upon their kinsmen of so much suffering and misery must be to those Cape Colonists a trial almost beyond endurance.

It is a historical fact that the severities inflicted upon our colonists by Lord Cornwallis during our struggle with the American colonies only brought recruits to Washington and made the colonists irreconcilable, and that the policy of Lord North—which was the same as that now being pursued in South Africa—was denounced by Pitt as "that impious curse of enforcing unconditional submission."

The peril of a similar experience is at least evident. Step has followed step, and the army and the nation are face to face with a wearisome and apparently endless war. The soldiers in the field are tired of it. The people at home turn from the daily record of harrying and burning and loss of lives with something approaching disgust. "Has it been all necessary?" is a question constantly arising, along with that other question, "When will it end?" These questions must force themselves all the more upon the national conscience when confronted with the testimony of the latest eyewitnesses of the war, one of whom, Dr. Conan Doyle, himself a supporter of the policy of the war, has written:

> Whatever else may be laid to the charge of the Boer, it can never be truthfully said that he is a coward or a man unworthy of the Briton's steel. The words were written early in the campaign and the whole empire will endorse them to-day. Could we have such men as willing fellow-citizens, they are worth more than all the gold mines of their country.

It is in the interests not less of policy than of civilisation and religion that we urge the offer of some terms to the Boers which may bring to an end the calamitous state of things to which South Africa has been reduced.

Leonard Courtney, *President*
S. H. Swinny, *Secretary*
Reprinted in the Speaker, *November 10, 1900*

It was not until after the war entered its second year that women's organizations, social and political, began to take official notice of it. This is not to imply that women had been indifferent to the war, but rather that they were now beginning, in a variety of ways, to conceive of themselves as an interest group.

Manchester Guardian October 24, 1900

The annual Conference of the National Union of Women Workers was opened at Brighton to-day [October 23]. There was a large attendance of delegates from various parts of the country. The President, Mrs. A. T. Lyttelton, occupied the chair, and there were also on the platform Lady Laura Ridding, Mrs. Creighton, Mrs. Henry Fawcett, Mrs. Bryant, Lady Louise Loder, &c.

At the inaugural meeting, which took place in the morning, Lady Louise Loder, president of the Brighton Conference Committee, offered a welcome to the delegates. She said that women were no longer expected to confine themselves merely to domestic duties, although the importance of home life and social calls was recognised. Women's capability was now a recognised factor in civilised life, and with it came new responsibilities.— (Hear, hear.)

Mrs. A. T. Lyttelton, president, in her opening address said that since they last met the whole nation had been passing through a period of great stress and trial. However much opinions might differ as to questions of policy, of strategy, and of organisation in connection with the South African war, on one subject they were all agreed; they all recognised the bravery and endurance of our soldiers, both in the field and in the still more difficult ordeals of sickness and privation, and they all recognised that throughout the nation there had been a great answering wave of enthusiasm and endeavour. There had been a great quickening of interest, which had stimulated the imagination and filled the minds of many who perhaps before had realised little outside their own immediate circle, with its pretty round of joys and sorrows and excitements. Whatever might be the dangers of the war spirit, the result of the sacrifice necessary in a time of war was unmistakable. It was seen in a strong unselfish spirit, a determined self-devotion, a quickening of interest and sympathy, an imagination which could understand the stress and the suffering of others. What was to be the result? Were we to look back upon the whole episode with a sense of relief that it was over, and return to our comfortable lives again, or were we to try and remain at the higher level to which we had risen, to hold fast to the self-devotion, the strengthened and quickened interest? These were grave questions, and much of the future of England depended upon the manner in which they were answered. For we were at the parting of the ways, and unless the good which the war had called out was held and confirmed the dangers which it had also called forth would predominate, and there would be a deterioration of the moral fibre. If we were to be better our soldiers must show in their ordinary lives something of the self-sacrifice and endurance which they had practised in time of war, and our citizens must exhibit in relation to their suffering and sinning fellow men and women the self-sacrifice and the imagination which they showed during the past year. England must throw into the great world struggle against impurity and evil the measured strength and determination which she had shown in the conflict she had just passed through. We must once again put forth our strength if we were to be equal to the task before us.— (Cheers.) It had become more than ever impossible to lead lives of self-indulgence or of a narrow pettiness in the face of this new realisation of the responsibility of our great inheritance.— (Cheers.) . . .

With the general election out of the way, and Rosebery temporarily no threat to his leadership, Campbell-Bannerman could afford to speak out more forcefully. Always "anti-Joe, but never pro-Kruger," C. B. decried the colonial secretary's virtual dominance of public affairs.

Sir Henry Campbell-Bannerman
Speech in the House of Commons   **December 6, 1900**

. . . The war in South Africa still engrosses our attention and interest, and what is the most remarkable circumstance when we think of it now? It is that the British public know so little about it. Never has a war, great or small, been conducted with so little communication of authentic information as to its incidence and policy. Since the earlier days of the war we have

not had a despatch published. We have had newspaper correspondence with stories not always to be relied on; we have had
private letters, some of which have been published in the
Press; we have had scrappy, hasty telegrams—I do not complain
of their being hasty and scrappy in the circumstances in which
they were despatched by officers in command—but we have had
no despatch whatever explaining or summing up any one incident in the whole of the campaign. Now, I hold that this is not
respectful to the British public or to the House of Commons.
We hear a good deal in these days about a thing called "Imperialism," and everybody is contending with everybody else
as to the best kind of Imperialism to profess. There is an Imperialism in the sense of devotion to and desire to maintain
our Empire. But there is an Imperialism which may have, and
does have, another meaning, when an Executive Government
takes on itself to manage all the affairs of the country and the
representatives of the people are ignored, when the country is
kept in the dark, when plans are laid to evade the interference
of the Legislature, when things are done and resolutions announced at the moment when the representative body has become dumb and when all doubters, critics, and scoffers are
classed together as discreditable persons guilty of a sort of *lèse
majesté* against the Executive Government. That is Imperialism as we have seen it in other countries; is there not a little
danger that we may drift into some sort of squalid, shabby
imitation of it here? . . .

Parliamentary Debates, *4th series, LXXXVIII, col. 114*

There were definite signs that pro-Boer propaganda had an
effect not only upon the mass public, but also upon uncom-
mitted M.P.'s. Edmund Robertson, by his circumspect
performance in the last Parliament, was one of those Liberals
whom *The Times* (October 17) had found "difficult to
classify." Weeks later, he was presiding at a meeting of the
League of Liberals Against Aggression and Militarism, to
which he introduced J. M. Robertson ("Scrutator" of the
Morning Leader). Those present included R. C. Lehmann and

Sir John Brunner, officers of the League, Leonard Courtney, Charles Molteno (a member of the Cape legislative assembly), and such M.P.'s as F. A. Channing, J. Keir Hardie, Thomas Burt, and H. J. Wilson.

The Speaker   **December 8, 1900**

A large and enthusiastic meeting of Liberals was held, on Wednesday, [December 5] at the Westminster Palace Hotel, when Mr. J. M. Robertson described the present state of affairs in South Africa. The chair was taken by Mr. Edmund Robertson, Q.C., who said that, during last Session, he was one of those members who voted supplies for the war, because he thought the Empire was in peril, and that that peril might be turned into catastrophe by military reverses. He now thought that the Empire was in danger from the continuance of the war under existing conditions and under the methods which had recently been pursued. Mr. Robertson went on to point out how the country had been misled through lack of information and the deliberate misrepresentation of those on the spot, and quoted as a last despairing attempt to stifle criticism the *Standard's* exhortation to Liberals not to give way to party feeling lest they encourage De Wet. Readers of *The Speaker* have already read an account of what Mr. J. M. Robertson saw on his visit to South Africa. The chief points of his speech were the intense racial feeling which the war is sure to leave behind it amongst the Dutch and the suicidal folly of an attempt to enforce unconditional surrender on men whom we are leaving no home to return to. The blame for such a state of things was not for the officers who had to carry out their instructions. It was rather for Ministers at home whose ignorant pride and obstinacy induce them to persist in an unreasonable policy. . . . Two resolutions . . . were carried the same day by the executive committee of the Women's Liberal Association calling for definite information and protesting against any aggravation of the already overwhelming difficulties of restoring the prosperity and contentment which the war has destroyed.

At a time when the English conscience was awakening to social distress, it was poignantly shown that war inflicted untold suffering, particularly upon women and children. Charity appeals, without passing judgment upon the politics of the war, were nonetheless a powerful argument against its further prolongation.

The Speaker   **December 15, 1900**

To the Editor of *The Speaker*

Sir—May we draw your attention to the formation of a committee for the alleviation of the widespread distress among women and children during the military operations in South Africa? In the most recent phases of the war those operations have entailed the burning of farms and the destruction of property, whereby, it is to be feared, many hundreds of women and children formerly in affluent circumstances have been rendered homeless and probably destitute. As after a battle the conquerors' ambulances pick up and tend the wounded, so we may claim to come in and do what we can for these sorely wounded women and children. It is with this object that our committee is to be formed. Its aim will be to get into personal contact with women and children, whether Boer, British, or any other nationality, who have been rendered homeless or destitute during recent military operations, to investigate the character and extent of their needs, and to administer such relief as may be necessary and as its funds may allow. It is the hope of the committee that, over and above the material relief, something, however small, may be done to soften bitter feeling and begin that work of reconciliation which every statesman recognises as the one hope for the future of South Africa.

The name and objects of the fund proposed are as follows: Name—South African Women and Children Distress Fund. (a) Character: Purely benevolent; non-political, non-sectarian, national. (b) Objects: To feed, clothe, shelter and rescue women and children, Boer, British or others, who have been rendered destitute and homeless by the destruction of property, deportation, or other incidents of the military operations. (c) Distribution: The distribution shall be placed in the hands of persons deputed by the committee, and shall not run counter to the requirements of the local, civil, and military authorities.

Yours, &c.,

K. E. Farrer

Frederick W. Lawrence

The growing revulsion against the war was not limited to the metropolis or its press. At the close of 1900, the *Blackburn Weekly Telegraph*, which boasted a healthy circulation in the cotton towns of central Lancashire, presented its readers with a sober review of the year's events. The anonymous author was A. G. Gardiner, who, fifteen months later, was summoned to London to edit the *Daily News*, which was acquired earlier that year by a pro-Boer syndicate.

"The Story of the Year"
by "The Tatler"

Blackburn Weekly Telegraph   **December 29, 1900**

"Happy is the nation that has no history," says the proverb. If the same test may be applied to time, 1900 will not rank among the happy years of our history. It has been as full of movement and incident as a dime novel. We have passed from one thrilling sensation to another, from joy to despair, from success to failure. "So foul and fair a day I have not seen," says Macbeth; and we may say that so foul and fair a year is witnessed only once in a lifetime. The experience of a generation has been crowded into the narrow limits of a twelvemonth.

> We live in deeds, not years—in thoughts, not breaths—
> In feelings, not in figures on a dial.
> We should count time by heart-throbs.

And "counting time by heart-throbs," 1900 is not a year but a decade. How vast a revolution in public sentiment has taken place during these weary months may be measured by one fact. Early in the year the land was echoing with "The Absent-minded Beggar." It was the battle song of an ebullient Imperialism, and no one was free from suspicion who had not the doggerel on his lips. "The Absent-minded Beggar" has passed into oblivion with the wave of sentiment that evoked it. We are a wiser and a good deal sadder people to-day. We do not want to sing Jingo ballads. Watts' hymns would be more agreeable to the national humour. We have begun to realise the cost of our picnic to Pretoria—that picnic which was to end with a display of fireworks by Christmas, 1899, and which is still in progress; which was to be accomplished by 50,000 men, and is still employing a quarter of a million; which was to cost ten millions of money, and has already cost a hundred millions; which was to settle everything, and has settled nothing, but has raised up for us an "Ireland over the sea" which we shall have to hold down with the iron heel of martial rule, and which will provide us with "hot water" far into the new century.

... We in this district have had our part in the mighty movement of events, both at home and abroad. The year had hardly dawned when, on the 18th of January, we turned out in our tens—I might almost say our hundreds—of thousands to witness the departure of the local volunteers to join the mighty stream of warriors ordered South. It was a bright afternoon and a brilliant "send-off," and it is calculated, if I remember correctly, that Blackburn sacrificed £800 in wages by making holiday on that occasion. Then we had a multitude of minor events of the same sort. With every batch of reservists called up there were new ebullitions of enthusiasm, more jollifications, more fireworks, more good-byes, more raucous renderings of "Soldiers of the Queen." Then came Ladysmith, as we, with the rest of the world, threw up our hats and drank ale with patriotic enthusiasm. And who will forget Mafeking night, when the long-expected tidings brought the whole town out of doors, and the streets were alive with people and ablaze with coloured lights far into the morning? That was on the 18th of May. A fortnight later the formal celebration of the event and of the Queen's birthday took place, the mills being closed for three days from the 2nd of June. That was the high tide of our exultation. Since then, with the exception of a Pretoria demonstration at Witton and a similar event at Wilpshire, we have ceased to jubilate over the war. The war, indeed, has long ceased to lend itself to jubilation. It has become instead an interminable tragedy, unrelieved by any of those dramatic episodes which gave it piquancy in the early days of the struggle. The district has contributed its share in blood and treasure to that tragedy. Many local men have fallen victims either to the bullets of the enemy or to disease, the most notable loss being that of Sergeant Candy, of Darwen, who was well known for his enthusiasm in all Christian work, and whose death created a profound sorrow in the Peaceful Valley. In treasure we have contributed much voluntarily and far more involuntarily. The mayor's fund in aid of the reservists amounts to-day to £8,541. What we have contributed in extra taxation and loss of business will never be told.

Genial, but unprepossessing, Sir Henry Campbell-Bannerman was easy to underestimate. Time proved him a more astute tactician than his critics, either to the right or the left, tended to suspect. His caution was dictated not by timidity so much as by a shrewd analysis of British character. "We must be very careful not to take any line which might seem to be anti-British," he told James Bryce, "for our countrymen, though sick at heart are all the more touchy and obstinate and if we are to have any influence, we must not run counter at this moment to the policy in which the national dignity seems involved."[1]

Morley, on the other hand, had other reasons for maintaining silence. Like many moderates, he was put off by the outrageous slogans spouted by certain undisciplined allies. "No—I cannot undertake to speak," he wrote to R. C. Lehmann, the interim editor of the *Daily News*. "Nor am I sure that I could come up to the mark of some of my pro-Boer friends. One or two of them seem taking a line that will drive me into the arms of [R. W.] Perks," M.P. for Louth and the driving force in the Liberal Imperialist Council.[2]

1. Quoted in J. A. Spender, *The Life of the Rt. Honourable Sir Henry Campbell-Bannerman* (London, 1923) 1:317.
2. John Morley to R. C. Lehmann, January 21, 1901, Lehmann Papers (courtesy of Mr. John Lehmann).

In retrospect, one can see that the moderates and extremists within the pro-Boer camp differed from each other more in style (which mattered a good deal to Morley and other politicians of the old school) than substance. By this stage, however they expressed themselves, all were eager to stop the war. A leader in the *New Age* justly argued that the only relevant question was whether one condoned the war or condemned it.

New Age   **January 27, 1901**

Between those who are able to persuade themselves that this is a just war, and those who condemn it as the worst of infamies, there is a great gulf too wide to be bridged. The question that divides us goes down far deeper than any party question; it touches the very strings of national existence. Between those on the one and the other side there can be no compact, no common action. Whether we deplore it or not, the fact is there.

While it would be farfetched to suggest that Liberal unity was restored, there evolved a consensus which was opposed to the war, if not in principle, then at least in practice. The senseless continuation of hostilities was blamed upon the government's refusal—perhaps its inability—to offer reasonable peace terms. On February 27, the general committee of the National Liberal Federation, "the parliament of Liberalism," met at Rugby and issued a strongly worded resolution.

General Committee of the
National Liberal Federation
Resolution passed at Rugby   **February 27, 1901**

That this Committee records its profound conviction that the long continuance of the deplorable war in South Africa—declared for electioneering ends to be over last September—is due to the policy of demanding unconditional surrender, and to a want of knowledge, foresight and judgment on the part of the Government, who have neither demonstrated effectively to the

Boers the military supremacy of Great Britain nor so conducted the war as to induce them to lay down their arms.

This Committee bitterly laments the slaughter of thousands of brave men on both sides; the terrible loss of life from disease, owing in no small degree to the scandalous inadequacy of the sanitary and hospital arrangements provided for our forces; and the enormous waste of resources in the actual expenditure upon the war, in the devastation of territory, and in the economic embarrassments which must inevitably follow.

The Committee calls upon the Government to announce forthwith, and to carry out on the cessation of hostilities, a policy for the settlement of South African affairs which will secure equal rights to the white races, just and humane treatment of the natives, and such a measure of self-government as can honourably be accepted by a brave and high-spirited people.

In an article facetiously entitled "The United Party," the *Speaker* weighed the significance of the N.L.F. decision.

The Speaker   **March 2, 1901**

Perpetual discord is not the best symptom of health in a party, and the delegates who met at Rugby on Wednesday arrived at agreement; but they did more than that, for they agreed on the only terms on which agreement can be effective or honourable. They adopted a resolution which brings them into direct collision with the Government's policy. The prolongation of the war was declared to be due to the demand for unconditional surrender. The distracted and divided sympathies of the Liberal party during the last two years would have made it impossible for anybody to rely confidently on securing the concurrence of every Liberal member in a definite protest against the identification of this country with that hateful demand. But the demand for unconditional surrender is only part of a general policy that aims at inflicting the maximum of humiliation on a brave enemy, and the whole of that policy was repudiated by the Liberal delegates at Rugby. . . .

The day before the delegates met at Rugby a still stronger resolution was unanimously adopted by the Liberal Twelve Hundred of Manchester. Mr. Dillon's amendment in the House of Commons, moved in a speech of passionate eloquence, but expressed in terms too indiscriminating to command a wide assent, was supported by no less than twenty-nine Liberal members, many of them men of conspicuously moderate views.

Recent events strengthened the position of Campbell-Bannerman, both in Parliament and in his party. In an address to a combined meeting of two distinguished Liberal groups, he tellingly recalled how the government had campaigned for reelection with fulsome assurances that victory was in hand. Just as the government was unable to perceive the nature of the struggle, so was its spirit inimical to a just and durable solution.

Sir Henry Campbell-Bannerman
Speech to a joint dinner of the
Eighty and Russell Clubs, Oxford   **March 2, 1901**

I have to make a few observations to you on public affairs tonight, and I find it must be on one topic alone, because there has been for many months one subject which is absorbing all our attention—a subject also which I hope will continue to absorb our attention—namely, the question of South Africa.

The war in which we have been engaged is, in some senses, a great war—not great, I fear, in any credit or glory it will have brought to this country, but great in the sacrifices involved, great in the efforts it demanded, great also in its consequences to the interests of the Empire. Its course has been full of vicissitudes and surprises, which have been followed with the intensest interest by our fellow-countrymen, usually in an equable and calm spirit, the interest sometimes, however, running into extravagant alarm or indecent jubilation. What I am afraid of is, that as hostilities continue, as they gradually become more tame and monotonous, and as there is a clearer prospect of a conclusion, interest may flag. Yet it is precisely now and after the conclusion of the war that events ought to be scrutinised by us nervously, anxiously, and closely, because it is upon these events that depends the future of South Africa. . . .

Now, precisely as the military elements of interest and excitement evaporate, so the things that are said and done in your name become of greater importance. Don't let us, therefore, modify, let us rather quicken, the interest that we show in the events as the end approaches, and even after it has been reached. But is that end approaching? How near are we to the end of the war? I would advise you to be very chary in attempting an answer to that question. The members of His Majesty's Government are exceedingly sensitive on this subject. They do not forget that in September last they gave the most positive assurances of the accomplished end of the war, and thereby they misled us all. . . .

But one thing is certain—the country almost unanimously wishes to see the war ended. Go into any society of men you like, be they Liberals or Conservatives; be they what are called "Imperialists," or be they—what is the opposite phrase to "Imperialists"?—let us say "Economists," selecting something which at all events will distinguish the class of men to whom I refer from the supporters and admirers of the present Government; be they civilians or be they soldiers—wherever you go there is but one desire, for peace. Not, indeed, a peace which would sacrifice anything that can be legitimately and advantageously claimed as the fruits of our sacrifices and efforts; not a peace which would fail in any degree to secure the acknowledgment of our military superiority or our immunity from the revival of old dangers; but an honourable and—may I not, as between brave combatants, say?—a friendly peace, upon which a friendly future in South Africa may be based. We may well be proud that it is the chief independent organisation of the Liberal party that has been the first in this country to give formal and open expression to this national desire.

After the memorable meeting at Rugby on Wednesday of the National Liberal Federation, there is no question what the Liberal policy is. That policy is directed to two main objects—

first, that we should clearly make known to the peoples of the belligerent States, not in vague but in definite terms, that our purpose is not conquest but conciliation, not humiliation but friendship and freedom; and in the second place, that these terms should include the resettlement in their homes of the burghers who by capture or the operations of war have been dispossessed, and the establishment, as soon as order is restored, of free self-governing institutions. Hitherto, when we have urged, as I and others have urged in public, the necessity of the earliest possible announcement of our friendly intentions, we have been met in two ways. We have been told that our intentions are perfectly well known already, to which my own sufficient reply is, that all that can have reached the Boers on the subject is some report of the vague utterances of Ministers and their agents on the spot, and they can have no knowledge, as we have here, of the general disposition and intention of the people of this country. Now, any confidence which you and I may feel, and any degree of equanimity which we can entertain, regarding the future of South Africa, depends not upon the utterances of our ministers, but upon our confidence in the right feeling of our countrymen at large. If we look to the words of Ministers, what do we find? We find here and there occasional vague declarations of humane intention, neutralised and belied by some reckless and mischievous phrases. Who can trust to hopes of clemency and generosity when we hear demands for unconditional surrender and bold threats of conquest carried to the bitter end, when we are told that not a shred of independence is to be left to our beaten foe, when an interval of years and even of generations, we are told, is to be necessary before even the form of self-government can be considered? And if we at home are thus puzzled and full of wonder in consequence of the words of our Ministers, and if we find it difficult to reconcile those words one with another, can it be said for a moment that the Boers out on the veldt in their laagers at the present moment are well aware of the intentions of the Imperial Government? . . .

Now it may be that the more truculent writers and speakers who have endeavoured to control the policy of our country—

they have not succeeded, and fortunately now we can see them becoming both fewer in number and milder in tone—will sneer at any such suggestion as this. We need not mind their sneers, because they only show that they have failed to apprehend that which is the true key of the problem in South Africa. Let us repeat it until it sinks deeply in the popular mind. If we are to maintain the political supremacy of the British power in South Africa—and this surely is the purpose and end of all we are doing—it can only be by conciliation and friendship; it will never be by domination and ascendancy, because the British power cannot, there or elsewhere, rest securely unless it rests upon the willing consent of a sympathetic and contented people. As regards the actual terms of settlement, there is much upon which I trust there will be no controversy. At least upon this surely we shall all be agreed—the restoration of the burghers to their farms, with such pecuniary assistance as may be requisite. Not that this, as I fear, will avail to mollify the exasperation caused by the mistaken and deplorable policy of burnings and confiscations, but we must for humanity's sake, and to prevent greater evils, do what we can to restore the country to its former condition.

When, however, the Colony has been cleared of the invaders and the hostilities practically cease, what social and political arrangements are to follow? There, I think, it is not unlikely that some considerable diversity of opinion may come in. I trust for my part that the Liberal party will adhere to and maintain and persist in its objection to the establishment of that which we know as the Crown Colony system of Government. Because I have raised this objection it has been imputed to me that I thought that a complete system of free institutions can be at once introduced—that, we will say, the last shot will be fired and the last bugle sounded on Monday, and on Tuesday a fully-equipped constituent assembly will march in and commence their functions at once. Need I say that I never thought or said anything so ridiculous? The disturbed state of a country which has been the scene of such a war as this, the dislocation of the machinery of government, and even of social habits and arrangements, makes it an absolute necessity that there should be established some provisional and temporary form of government. I have spoken of a military form of government taking this duty, and I did so because there would be plenty of capable soldiers on the spot, and because after all there is this advantage in a government by military men—that as long as soldiers exercise it you may be sure it will not be permanently continued. But whether under civilians or soldiers the one great essential is that it should be of a provisional and temporary character.

Our great object should be, as soon as the inhabitants have returned, as soon as order is fairly re-established, as soon as the organisation of society has been set up again—our object should be to introduce, in as complete a form as possible, representative institutions. Now a sort of autocracy, or semi-autocracy, such as we know under the name of Crown Colony Government, is very well suited to certain countries and certain conditions of society, but I can imagine nothing less suited to such a community as will be found in these two States when all this is over. I doubt whether in recent years we have ever attempted to establish such a system of Government over such a community, and if we did establish it the very first to call out against it would probably be the Outlanders, mostly British, but some of them of miscellaneous origin, gathered from all the quarters of the world, who will rush in to take advantage of the field for their enterprise and industry which these States will afford. It is not at all the phlegmatic Dutchman pursuing his lonely life on the veldt on his own farm that is likely to complain. It is the lively-minded and excitable Outlander from whom difficulty is almost certain to arise. To impose, in the feverish and excited condition of these communities, a fully-equipped and organised system of Crown Colony administration under the direct rule of London would be to court disturbance and disaster.

And, above all, it would be a practical impediment in the way of the recognition of self-governing rights, which we ought not for our own credit to refuse or to delay, and without which there can be no true stability for our power. The Outlanders, above all if they come from this country, will have been in the enjoyment of self-governing rights where they come from. The very Dutch burghers will have exercised the same powers before the war in the homes in which they will be living. Is it to be thought for a moment that we can refuse to give these powers again? With what countenance can we, who pose before the world as the special friends and nurses, if not the authors, of representative government—with what countenance can we tolerate any impediment being placed, after order is once fairly established, between these men and the rights we consider so necessary for them? And it is we who are to do it, we who have been waging this war on the ground of this very question of granting or refusing the suffrage. It is to the same people that we are to refuse to give it after the war is over. The thing is impossible. Therefore, whether with excuse or without excuse, there ought—if we are to keep in view the contentment and prosperity and safety of our Empire in South Africa—to be no delay beyond the pure necessities of order in granting those free institutions which are associated with the very name of a British colony, wherever the main portion of the inhabitants are of European blood.

I apologise to you for having treated you to so long and dull a disquisition, but this is the main question before the country. . . . Above all things, it is necessary . . . not to allow our attention to be withdrawn from the events in South Africa, because they are of infinite importance. But far more than on any forms of government, success and security will depend upon the tone and spirit in which those forms are introduced and administered. It is to these things, illustrated in the daily events of the weeks and months to come, that I invite your close attention: for it will be our duty as a party to exert all the power we possess in order to imbue our administration in South Africa with the generosity, the equity, and the reciprocal good feeling which alone can sustain, as they alone have created and fortified, the world-power of a freedom-loving people.

Predictably, Campbell-Bannerman's conciliatory statements gave rise to accusations that he was, consciously or otherwise, undercutting the government's initiatives. But it was not only his political opponents who credited him with the intention of comforting, indeed abetting the enemy. The editors of the *New Age* applauded his Oxford speech with an enthusiasm that he doubtless considered an embarrassment.

New Age   **March 7, 1901**

We expressed our belief that his [Campbell-Bannerman's peace] proposal would greatly embarrass the Government. We express now the further opinion that his proposal will vastly encourage the Boers. If after the fight they have so far made they may hope for such a large measure of self-government as the Liberal leader outlines, what, they will say to themselves, may they not hope for if they are able to hold out a little longer. . . . But presently the British Government of today will be overthrown and in its place will come a government pledged to the largest possible measure of self-government for South Africa.

9:Which Way Out?

At the end of February, Lord Kitchener, who succeeded Lord Roberts as commander-in-chief, entered negotiations at Middelburg with General Botha, the most formidable of his Boer adversaries. Their talks soon broke down on the question of what was to be done with the "rebels" (no more than three hundred in number) who aided the Boer invasion of Cape Colony. Pro-Boer opinion presumed, not unreasonably, that the failure of negotiations resulted from the government's refusal to accept anything less than complete and unconditional surrender. But it subsequently became clear that the culprit was Lord Milner, the high commissioner, whose "vindictive" policy—the description was Kitchener's[1]—precluded the granting of amnesty.

James Bryce
Speech in the House of Commons   **March 28, 1901**

. . . We are all agreed that the Government took an onward step when they allowed the peace negotiations to be entered into, and I think it is important to observe that not only Lord Kitchener but Sir Alfred Milner was personally persuaded that General Botha was sincere in his wish for peace. . . . Sir Alfred Milner was hopeful and Lord Kitchener was hopeful, and, therefore, I trust the House will bear that in mind, because it is our justification in asking the House to look carefully at the difference between the terms Lord Kitchener stated in his interview and the terms which ultimately went to General Botha. There may have been many causes and forces at work which we do not know, which are not disclosed in these Papers, and which made the negotiations to be broken off; but we have to go on the basis of these Papers. General Botha and Lord Kitchener parted in the belief that peace was probable. A letter was received a few days afterwards in which General Botha says: "You will not be surprised to hear that my answer

1. "We are now carrying on the war to put two or three hundred Dutchmen in prison at the end of it," Kitchener complained to St. John Brodrick (later Lord Midleton) on March 22, 1901. "It seems to me absurd and wrong." Quoted in Sir George Arthur, *Life of Lord Kitchener* (London, 1920), 2:26.

191

is in the negative." What are the reasons for the use of the words "You will not be surprised"? One of two things must have happened—either Lord Kitchener heard from General Botha a great deal that we have not heard of, or else General Botha was so much struck by the difference between the terms Lord Kitchener had discussed and the terms received in the letter that he conceived a distrust of us altogether, and believed that the Government at home would not implement what Lord Kitchener had offered. . . .

While I regret the failure of the recent negotiations, I earnestly hope the Government will resume communications when there is a chance of doing so, and whenever a fresh proposal comes from the Boers for negotiation. ["Hear, hear!"] Yes, but not only then, but when this country has gained another clear military advantage I think it will be to our own interests to propose that negotiations should be resumed. . . . It should be our object . . . to offer terms which will be acceptable, and bring about a settlement on the basis that a valiant enemy has been respected and an appeal made to the good feelings of these people to work out the terms on which they have consented to come in and surrender, and to endeavour to let bygones be bygones, and to effect that fusion of the races upon which alone the prosperity and welfare of South Africa depend.

Parliamentary Debates, 4th series, XCII, cols. 114–23

Bryce kept contact with Goldwin Smith, the veteran of many a political agitation, who emigrated (to accept a professorship at Cornell University) in 1868, and had since moved to Toronto. In his youth, Smith was a merciless critic of Disraeli, who had his revenge by savagely depicting him in his 1870 novel, *Lothair.*

James Bryce

Letter to Goldwin Smith   **April 12, 1901**

You can hardly imagine the moral and political declension of England at this moment. It will, I hope and trust, soon pass:

and it is largely due to the campaign of falsehood and misrepresentation about all South African affairs and events which has been assiduously carried on by a large section of the press. Even among Radicals, even among the Nonconformist leaders, clerical and lay, the old ideals of justice, liberty, humanity, as they were cherished from 1840 to 1880, seem to have become obscured. Scarcely an attempt to realize the passion for independence which animates the people of these Republics; little recognition even of their tenacious courage. Disraeli's influence was bad enough; but one is amazed to find one's self wishing for Disraeli instead of those who now direct the Jingo whirlwind.

> *Quoted in H. A. L. Fisher,* James Bryce
> *(New York, 1927), 1: 317*

On April 14, fourteen months after its inauguration, the League of Liberals against Aggression and Militarism reconvened at the Westminster Palace Hotel for its first annual meeting. There was a recapitulation of the previous year's activities: on July 28, "a largely attended" conference on the economic aspects of imperialism was held at the Memorial Hall in Farringdon Street; on December 5, J. M. Robertson testified on South African conditions; numerous leaflets and circulars were distributed; and qualified speakers were provided for party meetings throughout the country. In summary, the League prided itself in having achieved its primary aim: "to strengthen the existing Liberal Organisation in the only way in which it can be strengthened—by infusing activity where it has fallen into decay, and by making it, as it was in the past, the effective instrument of sound Liberal principles."[1]

An account of the session appeared in the *Speaker*.

The Speaker   **April 27, 1901**

The first annual meeting of the League of Liberals against Aggression and Militarism was held on Wednesday. Recent

1. League of Liberals against Aggression and Militarism, *Report* (London, 1902).

events, as Dr. Spence Watson observed in a letter he wrote to the meeting, have helped to teach the nation the wisdom of a crusade against a policy of adventure, and the large audience, drawn from all parts of the country, showed that the work of the League in maintaining Mr. Gladstone's principles through the darkest hours of Liberalism had not been thrown away. The chief resolution, protesting against annexation and welcoming the Liberal Leader's declaration against a Crown colony, was moved by Mr. Maddison with an eloquence now rare in public life. The feature of the meeting was the presence of Mr. [J. X.] Merriman and Mr. [J. W.] Sauer. The audience gave the two distinguished colonial statesmen a great ovation. Mr. Merriman recalled the conference which he attended for the inauguration of the Imperial Federation League, and pointed out that as Imperialism grew, Federation receded into the background. Certainly it would be impossible to imagine anything more fatal to any idea of Federation than such applications of Imperialism as Mr. Merriman described in the administration of Cape Colony. Mr. Sauer made a powerful speech, in which he brought home very effectively the disastrous consequences to Dutch confidence in British rule which must follow from converting a war for satisfaction into a war of conquest. Both these gentlemen, we are glad to know, are to address meetings in the country. Cape Colony is fortunate in her representatives, and England is in great need of such advisers.

But concerned Englishmen did not have to rely for their information upon visiting South African dignitaries. No one could have provided a more complete—and affecting— account of human suffering than Emily Hobhouse, who toured the concentration camps and interviewed military and administrative officials. Her findings were publicized by the South African Women and Children Distress Fund, "a small but influential relief committee,"[1] which sponsored her investigations.

1. R. C. K. Ensor, *England, 1870–1914* (Oxford, 1963), p. 346.

Which Way Out?

To the Editor of *The Speaker*

Sir—We venture to appeal once again to the British public on behalf of suffering non-combatants. There are undoubtably many persons who have not yet realised that under the special circumstances under which the war has been carried on a very large proportion of the women and children of the two Colonies, covering an area far exceeding that of the British Isles, have perforce been swept out of their homes and collected into large camps, where they have entirely to depend for maintenance upon the military authorities, whose hands and resources are already fully occupied with the necessary provision of the troops. Of these circumstances it has been an inevitable consequence that their hardships have become terrible. . . .

With the full sanction of Sir Alfred Milner and Lord Kitchener, our representative, Miss Hobhouse, has been able to do something to alleviate the worst cases of distress, and the military authorities have shown themselves willing to adopt some of the various suggestions which her woman's wit has enabled her to put forward on behalf of her suffering sisters. For instance, in one camp, where the only supply of water was impure, they consented to allow a railway boiler to be used to boil water for drinking purposes. They have also added her name to an official committee, whom they have appointed to discuss tenders for the supply of necessary clothing. We think it necessary to state that we are well aware that some of the camps are well cared for; but the needs of each camp must be considered on its own merits, as the conditions vary so widely; and even where the military may be doing everything in their power to alleviate suffering very much remains to be done. . . .

Signed on behalf of the Committee,
C. Thomas Dyke Acland, Chairman
April 20th, 1901

Probably the most effective propaganda was the simplest and most direct: a reminder of the cost in human—especially

British—lives. On May 7, the *Manchester Guardian* assiduously reported the latest War Office statistics on "British Losses in the War." Elsewhere in the same issue, a leader pointedly implied that the figures would be higher if full information were available.

The Manchester Guardian   **May 7, 1901**

The War Office issued yesterday a table of casualties in the South African Field Force, reported during the month of April, and the total casualties reported since the commencement of the war up to and including the month. The casualties in action reported during April were:

	OFFICERS	N.C.O. AND MEN
Killed	7	79
Wounded	21	249
Died of wounds in South Africa (included in wounded)	1	43
Missing and prisoners	3	93

The total casualties in action reported up to the 30th April were:

Killed	355	3,667
Wounded	1,333	15,876
Died of wounds in South Africa (included in wounded)	115	1,230
Missing and prisoners	*341	*8,830

The casualties other than those in action reported during April were:

Died of disease in South Africa	16	372
Accidental deaths in South Africa	—	36
Invalids sent home	85	2,228

The total casualties other than those in action reported up to and including April were:

Died of disease in South Africa	232	8,949
Accidental deaths in South Africa	8	326

Invalids sent home:

Wounded	—	6,337
Sick	1,977	37,754
Not specified which	—	1,671

The total reduction of the South African Field Force up to the end of April was:

Killed in action	355	3,667
Died of wounds	115	1,230
Prisoners who have died in captivity	4	92
Died of disease	232	8,949
Accidental deaths	8	326
Total deaths in South Africa	814	14,264
Missing and prisoners (excluding those who have been recovered or have died in captivity)	7	**774
Sent home as invalids	1,977	†45,762
Total South African Field Force	2,698	60,800
		††63,498

Total reduction of the military forces through the war in South Africa:

Deaths in South Africa	714	14,264
Missing and prisoners	7	**758
Invalids sent home who have died	4	314
Invalids sent home who have left the service as unfit.	—	2,493
Totals	725	17,845
		††18,570

*Of these 330 officers and 7,964 men have been released or have escaped, and four officers and 92 men have died in captivity.

†Of these 314 have died, 2,493 have been discharged from the service as unfit, and 924 are in hospital.

**This total includes a number of men reported "missing" who subsequently rejoined, but whose return has not yet been notified.

††The difference between these two numbers is due to the fact that the great majority of the men invalided home have recovered and rejoined for duty (see note †).

Miss Hobhouse, who was not permitted (ostensibly for her own safety) to enter the Transvaal, reported on conditions in six camps: Norval's Pont, Aliwal North, Springfontein, Kimberley, Mafeking, and Blomfontein. Her revelations—amply corrorborated by the testimony of other witnesses[1]—made a profound impact on the consciences of her countrymen and, particularly, her countrywomen. The *Speaker* was only one of many British journals that reproduced lengthy extracts from her report.

The Speaker   **June 22, 1901**

The Bloemfontein Camp, January 26.

The exile camp here is a good two miles from the town, dumped down on the southern slope of a kopje, right out on to the bare brown veldt, not a vestige of a tree in any direction, nor shade of any description. It was about four o'clock of a scorching afternoon when I set foot in the camp, and I can't tell you what I felt like, so I won't try. . . .

I call this camp system a wholesale cruelty. It can never be wiped out of the memories of the people. It presses hardest on the children. They droop in the terrible heat, and with the insufficient, unsuitable food; whatever you do, whatever the authorities do, and they are, I believe, doing their best with very limited means, it is all only a miserable patch upon a great ill. Thousands, physically unfit, are placed in conditions of life which they have not strength to endure. In front of them is blank ruin. There are cases, too, in which whole families are severed and scattered, they don't know where.

If the people at home want to save their purses (you see I appeal to low motives), why not allow those who can maintain themselves to go to friends and relatives in the colony? Many wish ardently to do so. That would be some relief. If only the English people would try to exercise a little imagination—

1. See, for example, *A South African Diary by An Englishman in South Africa*, reprinted from the *Daily News* by the South Africa Conciliation Committee (Pamphlet No. 70).

picture the whole miserable scene. Entire villages and districts rooted up and dumped in a strange, bare place.

To keep the camps going is murder to the children. Still, of course, by more judicious management they could be improved; but, do what you will, you can't undo the thing itself.

Now I must tell you their rations:

> Daily—Meat, ½ lb. (with bone and fat) ; coffee, 2 oz.; wholemeal, ¾ lb.; condensed milk, one-twelfth of tin; sugar, 2 oz.; salt, ½ oz.

That is all, nothing else to fill in. Once they sometimes had potatoes, seven potatoes for seven people, but that has long been impossible. Soap also has been unattainable, and none given in the rations.[1] Some people have money, and may add to the above by purchasing certain things at some little retail shops allowed in the camp, which charge exorbitant prices,[2] for instance, 6d. for a reel of cotton.

We have much typhoid, and are dreading an outbreak, so I am directing my energies to getting the water of the Modder River boiled. As well swallow typhoid germs whole as drink that water—so say doctors. Yet, they cannot boil it all, for—first, fuel is very scarce. That which is supplied weekly would not cook a meal a day, and they have to search the already bare kopjes for a supply. There is hardly a bit to be had. Second, they have no extra utensil to hold the water when boiled. I propose, therefore, to give each tent another pail or crock, and get a proclamation issued that all drinking water must be boiled. It will cost nearly £50 to do this, even if utensils are procurable.

In spite of small water supply, and it is very spare, all the tents I have been in are exquisitely neat and clean, except two, and they were ordinary, and such limitations! . . .

Next,[3] a girl of twenty-one lay dying on a stretcher. The father, a big, gentle Boer, kneeling beside her; while, next tent, his wife was watching a child of six, also dying, and one of about five drooping. Already this couple had lost three children in the hospital, and so would not let these go, though I begged hard to take them out of the hot tent.

Norval's Pont.

The population of this camp is about 1,500, and it is well laid out in rows and streets with numbers, so that you can find your way about. There are only a few marquees, and those are put in a row on one side to accommodate some of the true refugees. *As these people are quite in a minority, it is wholly absurd to call the camps by their name, "Refugee"; and even they can hardly be said to have come quite of their own free will, only they were told their particular town was to be emptied out, and they would starve if they did not come.* The people who were in reality taken as prisoners of war occupy the centre and great bulk of the camp, and beyond a broad space on the other side are pitched the tents of the single men, people who have surrendered, or such like. . . .

Instead of drinking the waters of the Orange, they use that river only for bathing, and the Commandant had pipes laid on from a farm, where a spring gives 14,000 gallons per hour, and this pure water is brought into camp.

Much to my delight, I found that there was much less overcrowding in Norval's Pont, and that each tent was supplied with a low wooden bed, a mattress, bench, table, utensils. Consequently, the whole aspect of the people was different. There was no violent outbreak of sickness, though I understand that almost all the cases nursed in the hospital had died. This I attribute (and so did the people) to bad nursing. They have no trained nurse. I hope one may soon be procured. There is no minister and they bury their own dead. . . .

Aliwal North, February 12

It was an awful journey from Norval's Pont to Aliwal North, but still I did get there at last. Poor little Aliwal, with only 800 inhabitants, had, within four weeks, to receive and provide for a population of nearly 2,000, nearly three times its own number. And it does them credit, for it is well organised, and, as far as that goes, the misery is alleviated. The Commandant could not speak highly enough of the people— their patience, good conduct, and uncomplainingness under their privations and losses. His camp can barely be called a prison; he has no soldiers or sentries, and most of the people are free to walk into the town, or to receive visits from the people in the town, without passes. The towns of Smithfield, Rouxville, and Zastron are all here, and, so far, only two deaths have taken place. But the camp has only been forming a month. Everything is beautifully arranged and provided for. He gives two tents to large families, and offers sail cloth to any who care to put up wooden framework to make extra rooms. He encourages them to come and state their needs. The rations here are better. Compressed vegetables were given, and 1 lb. of potatoes twice a week (and potatoes are 6d. per lb., or eight times as dear as in London) . . . .

Bloemfontein, February 18

We want a large supply of tents, so that there may be less overcrowding. At present it averages six to a small bell-tent, which, of course, means nine and ten in many cases. The capacity is under 500 cubic feet; so even for six persons, imagine the atmosphere at night.[4]

It is such a curious position, hollow and rotten to the heart's core, to have made all over the State large, uncomfortable communities of people whom you call refugees, and say you are protecting, but who call themselves prisoners of war, compulsorily detained and detesting your protection. . . .

An old man was arrested in the camp yesterday. It appears that a gossiping woman refugee went to the Commandant and stated that she had heard the old man say: "Perhaps the Boers will be in Bloemfontein again, some day." So he was arrested and sent in to prison. . . .

Kimberley, March 13

All to-day I have been in the camp—fortunately only twenty minutes' walk from my hotel. It is the smallest in area that I have seen. The tents too close together and the whole enclosed in an 8 ft. high barbed wire fencing, which is supposed to be impregnable, and cost £500. Sentries at the gate and walking inside. No nurse; an empty, unfurnished marquee, which might be a hospital; overcrowded tents; measles and whooping-cough rife; camp dirty and smelling; an army doctor, who naturally knows little of children's ailments; fuel, almost none. . . .

Bloemfontein, April 22

If only the camps had remained the size they were even six weeks ago, I saw some chance of getting them well in hand, organising and dealing with the distress. But this sudden influx of hundreds and thousands has upset everything, and reduced us all to a state bordering on despair. More and more are coming in. A new sweeping movement has begun, resulting in hundreds and thousands of these unfortunate people either crowding into already crowded camps or else being dumped down to form a new one where nothing is at hand to shelter them.[5]

About food, too. The superintendent of a camp is getting in rations for such a number, and suddenly 200 more mouths are thrust in upon him, and things won't go round. Last Saturday 200 or 300 families were without meat in Bloemfontein Camp for that day and Sunday. This would not matter if there were an alternative food, but there is only the ordinary supply of coarse bread to fall back upon, with black coffee and sugar.

But, in spite of the death-roll, I think your fund has saved and strengthened many children. It has provided brandy, maizena, Mellin's, and, where possible, fresh milk. *The Government clothing has hitherto come to almost nothing.* . . .

Among the things pressing hardest, and which tend to undermine the health and constitutions of the women, are the following:

Lack of Fuel.—Imagine three small sticks of wood 18 in. long, or small stony coal enough to fill the well of a soup-plate, for daily cooking. The weekly baking becomes almost impossible, and often the meat cannot be cooked, and the bread is sodden because underbaked.

In Kimberley charity has supplied the bulk of the fuel.

In Springfontein mist (dried manure) ekes out the scanty ration, and the women root up a small weed to try and heat their clay-built ovens. Oil stoves would help if oil in any quantity could be procured.

Lack of Beds and Mattresses.—Only a few have beds or mattresses—the great majority lie on the ground. Even if each tent had a bed, it would not accommodate more than one or two inhabitants of the tent. Meanwhile the damp of the ground, the occasional streams of rain that run through, the draughty night air coming beneath the flap of the tent, combine to lower the health of the children and to kill them off in convalescent and delicate stages.

Lack of Soap.—This necessary was not given in any camp. After much urging and requisitioning, a very occasional and quite insufficient quantity is now doled out.

Diet.—The food is monotonous, and does not suit children. Some vegetable diet is greatly needed. It presses hard when the meat (as often) is magotty and the coffee coppery and undrinkable.

Water.—In Bloemfontein the supply is insufficient, and it is also bad. The clothes of thousands have for months been washed in a small dam of stagnant water only occasionally freshened by rain. It is foul. Many other camps need washhouses.

Overcrowding.—This is very great. Privacy is impossible. In some camps two, and even three, sets of people occupy one tent, and ten, and even twelve, persons are frequently herded together in tents of which the cubic capacity is about 500 c.f. In Mafeking and Norval's Pont this trouble is not nearly so bad.

Shoes, Clothes, and Blankets.—At first khaki blankets were plentiful. Now they are getting scarce, and there is much need in various places. The nights are very cold.

Warm clothes are universally wanted. Those people burnt out are, of course, very bare, and have only been relieved by English, Colonial, and Dutch help. Recent importations have been allowed to bring more with them of both bedding and clothes. Quite recently the Government has provided a little flannelette and dress stuff. Shoes are needed everywhere.

Sanitary Accommodations.—This is very inadequate to the number of people. They are separate for men and women, but otherwise wholly without privacy, open to the sun and the rain. Where properly looked after by the authorities all is sweet and clean, but elsewhere, notably Bloemfontein, the effluvia is terrible, making it impossible to approach within fifty yards, unless with nose and mouth tied up. The effluvia reaching one side of the camp makes those tents at times unbearable, and has resulted in tonsilitis and various throat troubles. The people feel these places a terrible degradation.

Each camp has now rough but useful little hospitals. Many necessaries were lacking in these, which I have supplied. The death rate in most of the camps is high. In Bloemfontein it is terrible; 172 deaths had occurred up to the date of my leaving. On Sunday, April 28, fifteen persons died in that camp. It figures out to about 25 per cent.

The Camp life is felt to be purposeless and demoralising. Mothers are anxious to get young girls out of such an atmosphere if the means were forthcoming to place them in boarding schools.

Education is now provided in a partial way for some of the children in some of the camps. Accommodation cannot be got for all. This is due to the energy of Mr. Sargant, Education Commissioner. There have been a few abortive attempts at recreation here and there, but most lack heart to enter into them. Something should be done in this direction.

To sum up. There is no doubt that the general discomfort could be vastly alleviated by attention to the points mentioned, but it should be clearly understood that they are suggested only by way of amelioration. The main thing is to let them go. The ruin of most is now complete, but let all who have friends or means left go. Above all one would hope that the good sense, if not the mercy, of the English people will cry out against the further development of this cruel system which falls with such crushing effect upon the old, the weak, and the children. May they stay the order to bring in more and yet more. Since Old Testament days was ever a whole nation carried captive?

Recommendations

Having, by the kindness of Lord Milner, been enabled to visit various women's camps, and bring succour to the people therein detained, I venture to urge the following improvements:

1. In view of the hardening effect of imprisonment upon the hearts and resolution of the women—of the imperfect supply of tents or other shelter—of the scarcity of food—the difficulty of transport—and the appalling effect of camp life upon the life and health of the people, and in support also of recent statements made in the House of Commons, I urge:

That all who still can should be at once allowed to go:

(a) viz., those who, themselves penniless, yet have friends and relatives in Cape Colony;

(b) Those who have means and could support themselves in the Cape Colony, or in towns on the line;

(c) Those who have houses in towns to which they could go;

(d) Those divided from their children who wish to find and rejoin them.

2. Free passes into towns for all equally wishing to find work there.

3. Equality of treatment whether the men of the family are fighting, imprisoned, dead, or surrendered.

4. In view of the size of the camps, the sickness and mortality, a resident minister in every camp, or free access to anyone living close by.

5. That, considering the countless difficulties ahead, and the already overcrowded state of the camps, no further women and children be brought in.

6. That considering the mass of the people are women, and seeing the success in organisation of the matron at Port Eliza-

beth, a matron, conversant with both languages, be appointed in every camp. Many would undertake this voluntarily. I do not consider this so necessary in the case of Norval's Pont.

7. That, considering the congested state of the line, and the great lack of fuel, any new camp formed should be in a healthy spot in Cape Colony, nearer supplies and charitable aid.

8. That, because all the above, and much more, including the economical distribution of clothing, demands much careful organisation, detailed work and devoted attention, free access should be given to a band of at least six accredited representatives of English philanthropic societies, who should be provided with permanent passes—have the authority of the High Commissioner for their work—be absolutely above suspicion, and be responsible to the Government, as well as to those they represent, for their work. Their mother-wit and womanly resource would set right many of the existing ills.

9. That the doctor's report on the state of health of the children in Bloemfontein Camp be called for and acted upon.

10. That the women whose applications are appended be at once allowed to leave. Their health is failing under the long strain. All three are good, respectable women.

By request of the Right Hon. St. John Brodrick these recommendations were forwarded to the War Office.

I would like to add one more recommendation, which I consider of great importance, and which was unfortunately omitted from those sent to Mr. Brodrick:

11. That, considering the growing impertinence of the Kaffirs, seeing the white women thus humiliated, every care shall be taken not to put them in places of authority.

---

1. With much persuasion, and weeks after requisitioning, soap is now given occasionally in very minute quantities—certainly not enough for clothes and personal washing.

2. In some camps steps are now taken to prevent exorbitant charges in these shops in certain articles.

3. It was the recital of this story that was received with "laughter" on some of the Ministerialist Benches during Mr. Herbert Lewis's speech last Monday.—[ED. *Speaker.*]

4. Note the cubic capacity required by the Factory Acts: Factory and Workshops Act, 1895—

I. (1) A factory shall, for the purpose of Section 3 of the principal Act, and a workshop shall, for the purpose of the law relating to public health, be deemed to be so overcrowded as to be *dangerous or injurious to the health* of the persons employed therein, if the number of cubic feet of space in any room therein bears to the number of persons employed at once in the room a *proportion less than two hundred and fifty, or during any period of overtime four hundred cubic feet* of space to every person.—[ED. *Speaker.*]

5. Mr. Brodrick's figures of the population were partly for May and partly for March. The appended telegram in the *Times* of June 17 describes one of many clearing movements that have occurred since.

General Bruce Hamilton has thoroughly cleared the tract of country extending between Bloemfontein, Fauresmith, Petrusberg, and Abraham's Kraal.—[ED. *Speaker.*]

The attention paid to Miss Hobhouse was an index to the increasing prominence of women in the antiwar movement. Much to its credit, the Women's Liberal Federation revised its priorities and decided not to restrict its endorsement to candidates in favor of women's suffrage. Instead, after a spirited debate, it passed a resolution (by a majority of three to one) deprecating the demand for unconditional surrender and the conduct of the war.

The Manchester Guardian   **May 10, 1901**

The annual Council meetings of the Women's Liberal Federation were resumed yesterday at the Midland Institute, Birmingham. Lady Trevelyan presided, and the attendance was large.

Lady Trevelyan read a letter from Lady Carlisle, president of the Federation, warmly thanking the Council for the message of sympathy telegraphed to her on the previous day. If strength returned to her, and life were spared, she would try to serve the cause hereafter with redoubled efforts.—(Applause.)

On Wednesday the following resolution was proposed by Mrs. E. O. Fordham, seconded by Mrs. E. Stewart-Brown:

"This Council records its profound conviction that the long continuance of the deplorable war in South Africa—declared, for electioneering purposes, to be over last September—is due to the policy of demanding unconditional surrender and to a want of knowledge, foresight, and judgment on the part of the Government, who have neither demonstrated effectively to the Boers the military supremacy of Great Britain nor so conducted the war as to induce them to lay down their arms. This Council further protests against the burning of homesteads and wholesale destruction of crops, the deportation and imprisonment of non-combatants, and the lowering of rations to those women whose husbands and sons were engaged in the war. It also deplores the unnecessary suffering and loss of life in South Africa, due to the neglect on the part of the Government to provide an adequate medical department, and to their refusal to avail themselves to the services of civilian sanitary experts tendered at the commencement of the war."

Miss Agnes E. Slack had moved as an amendment that the resolution should run—"This Council regrets the long continuance of the war in South Africa and the failure of the recent negotiations for the restoration of peace. It also deplores the unnecessary suffering and loss of life," &c.

Mrs. Sheldon Amos, resuming the discussion yesterday, said the resolution and the amendment meant quite different things, although in the amendment regret was expressed at the continuance of the war. Those of them who were supporting the resolution were regretting that England had lost her ancient magnanimity, her honour, her prestige; had lost her humanity, had lost her old chivalry.—("No," and cheers.) When they met their foreign friends, and those friends spoke strong things about England, they had nothing to say in reply. There were those who took a different view, as Miss Slack did. They laid the blame of the war upon that splendid and gallant people, fighting to-day for the last shreds of national life.—(Applause.) She did not see what they could do other than to reject the amendment, which was drawn up in a spirit which suggested the subterfuges of the present Government.—(Hear, hear.) She did not wonder that someone on the previous day called out that Miss Slack was a Tory.—(Laughter and applause.) She hoped they would reject the amendment and hold to their own wording. Miss Slack had said that war was war. She was afraid that Miss Slack was trying to find an excuse for what had been done in this war when she said that. But the country knew now that the word "war" did not cover glory or anything that a Christian nation should have attached to its name. The amendment expressed regret at the failure of the recent peace negotiations. Under that expression they were not to speak about a future settlement. For herself, she did not see how an honourable people could have accepted even the terms which Lord Kitchener offered. Lord Kitchener had a bad record against him.—(No.) Well, she thought the story of the disposal of the Mahdi's head was a very bad record; but still Lord Kitchener offered terms not so impossible of acceptance as they were when they had been modified by Sir Alfred Milner and Mr. Chamberlain.—(Applause.)

Miss Clissold said that the passing of the resolution would be considered by their enemies as a sign of weakness and if that were so all we had done would have been useless. She thought there were far too many of them at home here who were wishful to put a halo round the heads of the Boers and the horn and tail, on our own people.—(Laughter.) The Boers were a brave people, but there were also many brutes among them, just as there were brutes in our own army. As to the farm burning she felt sure that it only took place when it became an absolute necessity.— (Hear, hear.)

Mrs. C. A. V. Conybeare (Chelsea) supported the resolution.

Mrs. S. Brown said there were no doubt many things to deplore on both sides. They deplored ruthless farm burning, equally they deplored the improper use of the white flag and the wreckage of trains. As to the farm-burning, they must, of course, bear in mind the fact that in many cases the farms were simply magazines for the enemy and that great explosions followed on the burning. There were generally two sides to a case and one side was not generally all black and the other side all white. There was no reason, she held, why we should paint ourselves and our army as black and the other side as white and as pure as the driven snow.— (Laughter and "Hear, hear.")

Mrs. Margaret Ramsay expressed her absolute and entire sympathy with the resolution. On hearing Miss Slack's speech for the amendment, she pinched her arm, to see whether or not she was asleep and dreaming that she was in an assembly of Primrose dames.— (Laughter and applause.) She would have Miss Slack to amend her ways and become a true Liberal.— (Laughter.)

Mrs. D. A. Thomas supported the amendment.

Mrs. George Cadbury said their only safe standing place was that held by the Society of Friends—namely, that all war was sinful.— (Applause.)

Mrs. Fordham replied on the debate, and said that, if the burning of farms might be called an act of war, then we might as well carry the thing so far as to say that well poisoning and other horrid things were acts of war. Such dealing with an enemy had never been resorted to in modern times.

The amendment was lost by a large majority, and the resolution was then passed.

Despite their callous statements—"War is war," St. John Brodrick, the Secretary of State for War, blandly philosophized—and public evasions, Chamberlain and his colleagues privately took steps to remedy a situation that was far more grave than they had realized. Their own inquiries, intended partly to disarm criticism, produced information as incriminating as any that Miss Hobhouse had brought to light.

Frederic Harrison was sufficiently infuriated by a parliamentary bluebook on farm burning to write a stinging letter to the *Daily News*.

Daily News   **May 30, 1901**

Sir,

My friends urge me to send you a letter about the "Return of Farm-burning, South Africa (Cd. 524)," but I doubt if you would print anything which could fully express my own feelings on studying it; and I know that this incident is merely part of a far larger whole. However, if your readers would care to understand something of "the panoplied hatred" with which my friends and I regard this very brutal episode in an infamous war, I will put our case before them in plain words. I am neither "Little Englander" nor "pro-Boer," nor "cosmopolitan crank," but a patriotic Englishman, who does not think his country's greatness needs to be eked out with more Klondikes and Ugandas, and refuses to applaud every folly and crime into which demagogues in office may contrive to delude the nation.

The official return has disclosed a barbarous, vindictive, systematic attempt to terrorise and crush a brave enemy in arms, by devastating a country which it was found impossible to conquer, by ruining the homes of soldiers with whom we were waging war, and by exposing their wives and children to misery and want. This was a violation of the recognised laws of civilised war, and was expressly forbidden by the Hague Conference. It was especially infamous when resorted to against an honourable body of citizens who were defending the existence of their country. It was insane folly in the case of a people whom it was designed to incorporate in the Empire, who had actually been proclaimed as our own fellow countrymen.

It was a policy so degrading in plan and so revolting in its consequences that any honourable soldier would have been justified in declining to undertake such butcher's work. But our commanders, accustomed to wholesale slaughter and devastation in warfare with savages in Asia and in Africa and unaccustomed to fight with any men of European race, were found willing to act on it. And Ministers at home were found willing to palliate it with cheerful indifferences and evasive sneers. Both soldiers and Ministers may count on this, that their names will live in history with those who ordered and executed the barbarities of the Thirty Years' War, the devastation of the Palatinate, and the dragonnades of Louis XIV. . . .

The horrible side of this war to us who retain some feeling for the honour of our country is that the nature of the task to which we were committed made violent and unlawful measures almost inevitable. To conquer and annex two free and proud nations of European race and most stubborn nature is an outrage which has never been attempted since the partition of Poland. Considering the vast extent of the land, the physical difficulties of the task, and the superb fighting qualities of the patriots, it was an undertaking of extreme peril. Since they were of the same race, language, and traditions as the Afrikanders of our own colony, it made civil war and rebellion almost inevitable. And yet to fail in sight of mankind, after all our Quixotic braggadocio, would be intolerable humiliation. Accordingly, they set their teeth, prepared "to fight it out to a finish" by whatever means, flinging to the winds considerations of public law, humanity, and the great name of England. Men curse in their hearts the Law of Nations, and sneer openly at the farce of The Hague. And women of the governing class do not blush to say that "what is wanted is more cruelty." The horrible part of this war, I say, is that it has brutalized public opinion, made public men desperate, and has unsexed the women whom they pervert. . . .

It makes me tingle when I witness these blatant Bardolphs in their carouses, got up by politicians with an eye on the ballot-box. Our men are brave, and resolute, and enduring. Yes! But what are the Dutch farmers, old men and boys together, who serve under Cronje and De Wet? Has not Lord Kitchener slaughtered men in North Africa as well as in South Africa as brave as the men he commands? No one doubts that our men are worthy of honour. But are honour and glory and admiration due only to one side of this long and sanguinary war? What disgusts sensible men is all this larrikin shouting over the very disasters and blunders and failures that they inflict on our name. One would think that a Viceroy has only to plunge his province into unutterable ruin by fanning civil war, by making peace within it impossible for a generation, to be received with the honours our fathers accorded to a Clive or a Lawrence. And a General has only to "fall into a trap," to lose his guns, to sacrifice brigades in unsuccessful "frontal attacks," to be regarded as if he were a Nelson or a Wellington.

"The war is now over" we are officially informed week by week by commanders, Ministers, and their friends in the press. We look on these brazen untruths with alarm, for it is thought to be the prelude to some new policy of rage and barbarism. But all is not "over." We are not "over" the deadly blow all this has struck at the Empire, the ruin and chaos it has spread through South Africa, the blood-poison it has infused into public opinion, nor the stain on English honour in the sight of the civilised world. There is another thing, too, which is not yet "over." And that is the nationality of the Boer Republics which, I believe, are not yet crushed out for ever—which, as a patriotic Englishman, I trust never will be crushed out for ever.

FREDERIC HARRISON

10:"Methods of Barbarism"

On June 14, Sir Henry Campbell-Bannerman intervened with greater force than the imperialists—Liberal and Unionist—had thought he could muster, and greater conviction than most pro-Boers thought possible. In an address to the National Reform Union—with Harcourt, Morley, and Philip Stanhope on the platform—he decried the "methods of barbarism" with which the war was waged. At once, he gave the antiwar movement a new slogan and a new direction: it was not necessary to condemn the origins of the war to condemn the way it was fought. Campbell-Bannerman's speech has been either celebrated as a stroke of genius or criticized as a tactical error that widened the breach within the Liberal Party.[1] If, as government spokesmen angrily alleged, he encouraged the Boers to hold out until the Liberals came to power, he also convinced the Boers that he was genuinely capable of magnanimity, and this had significant effects when Boer self-government was conceded five years later.

The Times   June 15, 1901

Sir H. Campbell-Bannerman was received with loud cheers as he rose. He said that it was only at the express desire of Sir William Harcourt that he abandoned the position behind him that through the greater part of his political life he had been glad to take. He wished to express his acknowledgements of the high compliment which to-night, in common with his right hon. friend, he was receiving at the hands of the National Reform Union, which . . . for many years he had known as an institution devoted, and successfully devoted, to the cause of the Liberal party and the diffusion of sound Liberal principles throughout the country. It was an additional merit of the

1. Many years later, Asquith recalled that Campbell-Bannerman had "often admitted to me" that the "methods of barbarism" phrase "was his worst *gaffe*." Asquith also disputed the popular view that Campbell-Bannerman had been instrumental in working out a South African settlement (Asquith to A. G. Gardiner, October 28, 1923, quoted in Koss, *Fleet Street Radical*, p. 105n). Lloyd George, on the other hand, was no less adamant that the concession of self-government to South Africa "was entirely the veteran prime minister's own doing." Ensor, *England, 1870–1914*, p. 390n.

Union that its work had been accomplished without official inspiration or supervision. He earnestly hoped that it would go on and prosper in its beneficent career. The celebration of the evening was a joint one, and he was proud to share the honour with such a colleague as Sir W. Harcourt. During the whole of his political life they had been associated more or less closely, and through the kindness of the party in the House of Commons he had been appointed to stand in the place of Sir W. Harcourt. He took that opportunity of gladly acknowledging the open and effective support which he had received from his right hon. friend (cheers), whose advice he had often sought and sometimes followed (laughter), though he had sometimes gone against it, and success and disappointment had indifferently followed either alternative course. (Laughter.) It would be admitted that these were healthy relations between two old friends, and it was a great gratification to him to be associated with his right hon. friend.

On a festive occasion like that it might be expected that the thoughts of all would be turned to light and pleasant topics. But they could not disguise from themselves that at every gathering there was present the spectre of this terrible war. (Hear, hear.) What would not all of our countrymen give, whatever party they belonged to, if they could be free from the fear and misgivings and the horrors associated with this war? He had been taken to task, and some writers in the Unionist Press had used great acerbity of language because the other day he had said that there could only be an insignificant fraction of the Liberal party who approved the policy—as he had said, the unwise and unworthy policy (cheers) —of pressing unconditional surrender on those who were opposing us in this war. He had been called upon to produce a single Liberal anywhere who had approved that policy. What was that policy? That now that we had got the men we had been fighting against down, we should punish them as severely as possible, devastate their country, burn their homes, break up their very instruments of agriculture, and destroy the machinery by which food was produced ("Shame.") It was that we should sweep—as the Spaniards did in Cuba; and how we denounced the Spaniards—the women and children into camps in which they were destitute of all the decencies and comforts, and many of the necessities, of life, and in some of which the death-rate rose so high as 430 in the 1,000 ("Shame.") He did not say for a moment, because he did not think for a moment, that this was the deliberate and intentional policy of his Majesty's Government, but it was the policy of the writers in the Press who supported them; and, at all events, it was the thing which was being done at that moment in the name and by the authority of this most humane and Christian nation. ("Shame.") On the previous day he asked the leader of the House of Commons when the information would be afforded, of which we were so sadly in want. His request was refused. Mr. Balfour treated them with a short disquisition on the nature of the war. (Laughter.) A phrase often used was that "war is war," but when one came to ask about it, one was told that no war was going on—that it was not war. (Laughter.) When was a war not a war? (Laughter.) When it was carried on by methods of barbarism in South Africa. (Cheers.) Then Mr. Balfour went on to give an account of numbers, and he made out that there were 17,000 men in the field against us. A good many things had been scattered to the winds within the last year. Prudence, justice, common sense, and consistency had gone, and now the venerable science of arithmetic appeared to be gone by the board also. When the war began we were told that there were 30,000 burghers who could come into the field against us. Since then a great many had been killed or incapacitated through wounds and disease, some 17,000 had been deported, and we never opened a newspaper without seeing that another score or two had been made prisoners; and yet 17,000 still remained in the field out of the 30,000! (Laughter.) Mr. Balfour went on to make two statements—very serious statements. One was that he was anxious—and the right hon. gentleman was evidently nervously anxious—to clear his character and he assured the House that there was no truth whatever in the rumours that the Government were encouraging peace negotiations.

216

The other thing he said was that they had no information as to what was going on beyond that which was communicated to the public. Could they believe it? They must believe it, because he had said it. But it left us in a worse plight than before; because were we then to believe that they were so callous and indifferent that they remained contented with the small amount of information vouchsafed to the public? What we wanted to know was how many of these camps there were, where they were, and the numbers in them, and what provision was made at each of them for nursing and medical supervision. (Hear, hear.) It would not be enough to say that Lord Kitchener ought not to be interrupted by inquiries. He admitted that plea in the case of any small personal matter or matter of small moment, but the character of our nation was at stake. (Cheers.) For many months a civil Government had been established in the two new colonies; they had nothing to do, and if Lord Kitchener was too busy the members of that Government might very well busy themselves in obtaining promptly the requisite information. If the present policy was to be pursued it was the duty of the Government—it was nothing less than the public conscience required—to send out a full staff of ladies and competent civilian medical men, so that the lot of these unhappy people might be alleviated as far as possible. (Cheers.) The inhumanity of what was going on was only equalled by its infatuation. It was to be condemned on the grounds of policy—on the grounds of the very policy of his Majesty's Government themselves. The people towards whom the insane policy of subjugation and obliteration was being pursued were not only going to be our fellow-citizens—they were our fellow-citizens already—their territories had been made colonies and incorporated in the British Empire. British colonies throughout the world were held without difficulty in loyal friendship with us. Why? Because we treated them as equals. The sentiment of the Boers towards us, as the result of the policy at present pursued, would not only be that of racial jealousy and of political antipathy; it would be a personal hatred and a sense—an ineradicable sense—of per-

217

sonal wrong. (Hear, hear.) He hoped that by some means the Government would be compelled to obtain full information on all these matters and to give it to the people; and he was altogether mistaken in the character of his countrymen and still more of his countrywomen if, when they realized these facts, they did not instantly demand the adoption of some wholly different method to that hitherto pursued of arriving at that settlement which it was the desire of us all to achieve. (Cheers.)

Reinvigorated, the pro-Boers stepped up their activity, which had been allowed to abate after the general election. Disruptions, which had declined in savagery as well as frequency, also revived. On June 19, a Stop the War rally at London's Queen's Hall—with Labouchere in the chair—was invaded and reduced to bedlam by counterdemonstrators. On this occasion, however, there is reason to believe that the pro-Boers were not quite the innocent victims of popular prejudice. Not only did they indulge in rhetoric which they knew to be provocative, but—according to an American who was deeply shocked by what he saw—they also showed themselves fiercely intolerant of dissent.

Letter to the Editor
The Times June 24, 1901

. . . Long ere the meeting opened I had seen a dozen gentlemen who had the temerity to express themselves in ordinary tones to their waiting fellows as against the pro-Boer agitation, isolated, surrounded, and pummeled. After the meeting started the lowest note of dissent was the signal for a gang of ruffians to drag out and punch the objector's face to a jelly. . . . What a travesty when universal fraternity and principles of peace are to be upheld by professional bullies and pugilists, and instilled with their fists and boots!

London, W.C. AMERICAN

Fearing violence, the decision was taken to cancel summer appearances by Emily Hobhouse at Leeds (where a pro-Boer meeting in July was stormed by "patriots") and Scarborough. Nevertheless, Miss Hobhouse was far from idle. The *Speaker* (August 3, 1901) was "glad to learn from the *Daily News* that she held twenty-three successful orderly meetings in four weeks; a plucky campaign which excited wide interest in the question of the camps."

The Colonial Secretary, given daily support in the leader and correspondence columns of *The Times*, complained that his British critics (inspired by base political motives) were keeping alive Boer resistance and thereby endangering further lives.

James Bryce would have no truck with such arguments.

James Bryce
Speech in the House of Commons   **August 15, 1901**

It has been the wish of the Government from the first to represent those who have condemned the war as having had a sinister influence on the progress of events in South Africa, and therefore we may be sure that if anything said in England had influenced the minds of the Boer leaders, that case would have been brought out and made the most of. The absence of any such evidence is the most convincing proof that nothing of the sort has happened. . . . If anything said here has influenced the war, it has been the intemperate speeches made on behalf of His Majesty's Government and the violence—I might say the ferocity—of some of the organs of the press.

Parliamentary Debates, XCIX, col. 1021

One of the more prominent victims of the "methods of barbarism" was Olive Schreiner, whose novels gave literary expression to the new feminism. She and her husband, who returned to Cape Colony from speaking engagements in England, suffered the indignities of martial law.

Daily News   **September 17, 1901**

A correspondent thoroughly acquainted with the facts of the case gives us the following account of the treatment of Olive

Schreiner under martial law. Our informant states the matter briefly, dwelling wholly upon the main incident.

In September, 1900, Olive Schreiner, in a very delicate state of health, went to the little village of Hanover, which lies in the Karoo, over 4,500 feet above the level of the sea. She is an almost incessant sufferer from acute asthma, and has a weak heart. She rapidly regained her health at Hanover, being joined there by her husband, Mr. Cronwright Schreiner, whose health, strong as he is, had been almost broken down by the treatment he was subjected to in England and Scotland. They were appointed by the district of Hanover as delegates to attend the Worcester Congress on December 6th, 1900, where Mr. Cronwright Schreiner was one of the chief speakers. At that time martial law was not in force in Hanover or Worcester, or anywhere in the Cape Colony except a few border districts. From Worcester Olive Schreiner and Mr. Cronwright Schreiner went on to Capetown. Olive Schreiner's health did not permit her to remain many days, so she returned to Hanover, whither Mr. Cronwright Schreiner, who had some work to do, was to follow her after a few weeks. After her return to Hanover, martial law was proclaimed practically throughout the Colony, including Hanover. In January, Mr. Cronwright Schreiner applied to the head staff officer of Permits, Capetown, to be allowed to join his wife at Hanover (to which place he had a return ticket), but he met with a curt refusal. The statement that he remained at Capetown to escape the restrictions of martial law is thus false. So he had to remain on in Capetown. Like all the prominent Worcester Congress men, he was marked down by the authorities, while she was marked owing to her protests both before and after the war began. Thus, while he was not allowed to join her, she was subjected to special persecution at Hanover. She alone of all people there was kept a close prisoner within the little village enclosed with barbed wire entanglements. Others were allowed to walk and drive out, but she was kept for several months a prisoner in the village. It will thus be seen that Ouida's statement is practically correct. Under this strain, her isolation from everybody who knew her intimately and her enforced severance from her husband, her sensitive organisation, coupled with her weak heart, gradually broke down, until towards the end of May she collapsed completely, and very nearly died. When this stage was reached the doctor attending her wrote for her husband to come up, and the local commandant, acting at the doctor's request, sent a permit for him to come at once and to avoid any delay at Capetown. Mr. Cronwright Schreiner then first obtained a permit, and left for Hanover (about thirty hours by train) the same night. She was then gradually nursed back to comparative health, but so severely had she suffered that she is still unable to do any literary work, and is physically still a wreck. A Dutch lady had given her a room in her house, and here, until her husband's arrival, she was nursed and tended day and night by the Dutch. Not long before her health broke down she had been granted a pass to walk out on the commonage, but was only able to avail herself of it a few times. From the time of her collapse the commandant (who, in keeping her prisoner, was undoubtedly acting under instructions which he could not disregard) did what he could to make her lot easier. He sent her husband a permit to keep a light burning at night, and allowed them to drive out, and even placed his cart and horses at their disposal (which, however, they did not use). The new commandant has been equally considerate. They were allowed to go to a farm near De Aar for Olive Schreiner's health; Mr. Cronwright Schreiner has been granted a permit to make a short visit to Capetown on business, and Olive Schreiner has been granted a permit to go to Grahamstown to visit her aged mother who was thought to be dying. Such consideration as can be shown them under martial law has been shown them since her breakdown. The pity is that the authorities only learnt sense by nearly killing Olive Schreiner.

J. S. Haldane, the Oxford physiologist, wrote to the press on the subject of "the very heavy extra mortality" in the concentration camps. His letter, reflecting humanitarian concern within the academic community, was especially significant, coming as it did from the brother of a leading Liberal Imperialist.

Westminster Gazette   **September 30, 1901**

SIR,—You call attention in the *Westminster Gazette* of yesterday evening to the very serious statistics which are month by month returned from the Concentration Camps. I venture to think that the apparent apathy with which these returns are received depends largely on the fact that to most persons the significance of a high death-rate is not easy to grasp. The following analysis of the figures for the last three months may therefore be of service as showing roughly the deaths among Boer women and children which may be put down to insanitary surroundings, as compared with deaths which might be expected under normal conditions:

	Actual deaths.	Deaths under normal conditions.	Deaths due to insanitary surroundings.
Women	606	96	510
Children	3,245	272	2,973

The deaths under normal conditions are calculated from the last decennial return for England and Wales, children being taken as under fifteen years and women as averaging about forty years old. The actual normal death rates are not, of course, available; but the figures given are more likely to be too high than too low.

Unfortunately the very heavy extra mortality (which also prevails, though to a less extent, in the native camps) shows no sign of disappearing or even diminishing. The death-rate among the Boer children, though it fell in June to seven times the normal, has risen in August to thirteen times the normal. The women and children have doubtless received, and are receiving, every care which, under the existing circumstances, can be given them; but it is evident that the camps as at present organised have turned out to be a most disastrous, though well meant, experiment. There is no definite prospect that the inmates can return to their homes for many months to come, and the outlook, if the camps remain as they are, is a very terrible one.

To judge from the short notes appended to the returns, two causes seem to have been largely responsible for the deaths. One is the abnormal spread of infectious disease—a condition usually due to overcrowding. The other is exposure to cold. Whatever the main cause may be, however, they must now be well known to the medical officers on duty at the camps, who are, therefore, in a position to suggest the remedies, and ought surely to be called upon to do so. Possibly the only feasible plan may be to deport the inmates of the camps to undisturbed positions on the coast, where they can be more easily provided for under sanitary conditions; but whatever measures may turn out to be necessary, I would earnestly urge that no time be lost in dealing with this most serious matter.—Your, &c.,

Oxford, September 28th   J. S. HALDANE, M.D., F.R.S.

The Churches

It was not until the war had entered its third year, and moral imperatives overcame considerations of strategy and national pride, that the churches asserted themselves. To be sure, individual religious leaders had spoken with vehemence and, sometimes, eloquence; but organized religion had remained mute. "The leading Baptist and Independent Ministers are all right," F. W. Hirst wrote in his diary on the eve of war. The Reverend Hugh Price Hughes, according to Hirst, was an important exception; and the Church of England's attitude was conveyed by the Bishop of Chester's nonchalant remark, "There are worse things than war."[1] Silas Hocking, himself a product of the Methodist ministry, counted upon the support of the Quakers "as a body," most Unitarian divines, "and a few Congregationalists. The Baptists," he recalled unforgivingly, "as a whole ignored us."[2]

1. October 3, 1899, quoted in Hirst, *In the Golden Days* (London, 1947), p. 191.
2. Hocking, *My Book of Memory* (London, 1923), p. 180.

The *British Weekly*, an influential "journal of social and Christian progress" published at London and Edinburgh, closed its columns to devisive debate (January 4, 1900). In the same spirit, clergymen, anxious to avoid discord when they met in synod or assembly, hurried toward adjournment before anyone could move an antiwar resolution from the floor. As time passed, however, dissidents within each sect began to agitate to commit their respective churches to collective action. Denied a place on the agenda of the Congregationalist Union at Manchester, a large minority of delegates withdrew—like the representatives of the Third Estate in 1789—and issued their "tennis court oath."

Manchester Guardian   **October 18, 1901**

A meeting was held last evening in the Cavendish-street Chapel which the ministers and delegates attending the Congregational Assembly "who disapprove of the war and are willing to pray and speak for peace" had been asked to attend. Mr. Halley Stewart, formerly member of Parliament for the Spalding division, presided. There was a good attendance.

A letter was read from Dr. Alexander Mackennal, in which he apologised for absence and said: "I should have gladly associated myself with those who are declaring that this present war in South Africa is a national sin, and that every step we proceed in it—inevitable as each step may be—is only adding up the burden of inevitable national chastisement and repentence. My greatest distress is that so many of us are doomed to silence in the church assemblies, which are dearest to us, if we would not still further embitter the political conflict. My heart is with you in your meeting."

The Chairman explained that the meeting was in no sense identified with the pastor and members of the Cavendish-street Church. No meeting of those held during the week was more important. All other questions sank into insignificance beside that of the war. It demanded consideration of Christian men, and if it had not been considered he for one should have felt heart-broken at the sense of unreality which had gathered round the Congregational Union meetings. He thought it re-

grettable that the Union in Assembly could not discuss and
resolve upon a question of such national and world-wide magnitude. Questions of the kind had not always been excluded
from the Union Assembly. Twenty years ago, at the time of
the retrocession of the Transvaal to the Boers, a resolution
was passed at the meeting of the Union in Manchester com-
mending that procedure, and before the retrocession a great
many of them were urging Mr. Gladstone's Government to
adopt that course. It was only natural then for the Congregational Union to give expression to the Christian sentiment and
feeling of the hour in urging their leaders to do what they
believed to be simple justice to the Boers. But now, they could
not discuss the subject. He did not say that a resolution on
the war ought to have been moved in the Assembly, but it
ought to have been possible to have moved one. If it was true
that to have brought forward a resolution would have intensified feeling and fostered political differences, it might have
been wise or unwise to have refrained or to have approved of
it. In the realm of expediency and the balancing of interests
he was a child, but he did know that in his heart he believed
the war to be unchristian, and he could not see why the Congregational Union platform should not give an opportunity
for expressing what he believed to be Christian sentiments,
and the obligations of Christian and natural duty. He believed
that their brethren were mistaken in not giving a distinct
and clear utterance and emphasis to the side on which their
influence was cast. It was no use pretending that they did not
think they were in the right—they were there because they did
believe so, and that they were obeying the simple dictates of
Christian justice. Nothing was more important to him than the
war. If he had to choose between allegiance to independency
and silence on the war, his independency must be in abeyance
to-day for he could not but speak in behalf of justice to the
Boers. The interests of our State were wrapped up in doing
justice to other States. Through history God was on the side
of the small peoples, and might there not be some great store
of service to come to the world in the future through the des-

pised Boer of the Transvaal? It was the passion of freedom in them which made them want to do justice to men who were fighting for freedom. They owed allegiance to the State, but deeper still lay that sympathy which God had set deep in the spirit's core:

> Before men made us citizens
> Great Nature made us men.

The Rev. T. Gasquoine, who had acted as one of the secretaries to the conveners of the meeting, said he felt this war to be the most heart-breaking war of the last century. Some of them at least felt the sin of this war, and they were there to confess that sin. They were there as Christians, as representatives of Christian churches, and they must not be afraid of the word "sin." They had to confess not national mistakes but national sins. In regard to that convenient adjective "inevitable," he for one believed that if the churches had only two years ago been true to the cause of Christ and had spoken not one word in favour of war but every possible word for peace, then the war would not have happened.— (Applause.) He confidently looked forward to the time when all the Christians of the country would think of the war with horror and shame. He moved that the following letter be sent to their Christian brethren in South Africa:

To the British, Dutch, and Native Churches of South Africa.

Dear brethren,—Gathered as we are in the city of Manchester, in the old home-country of some of you, being a number of the ministers and delegates, members respectively of the Congregational Union of England and Wales, Scotland, and Ireland, our hearts go out to you in affectionate sympathy in this dark day of trouble caused by the long-continued war. Especially at these meetings can we not be unmindful of the great hindrances and difficulties which have beset the work of our Congregational British and Welsh Churches; but not the less tenderly do we feel, in their desolation, for churches which must seem for the time to be so painfully separated from us.

We disapprove of the war as a national sin, and are sadly indignant at some of the methods of warfare which have been adopted, such as farm-burning and the consequent concentration camps. And we have earnestly longed that our Government would propose such terms of peace as could honourably be accepted by a brave people.

In the meantime we would assure you all of our fervent prayers that the churches separated by woful [sic] and unholy strife may be speedily led to a peace that truly abides, a peace in the service among the peoples of South Africa of Christ our Savior and King: We are dear brethren, in a common faith and hope yours most truly (signed on behalf of the meeting held in Cavendish-street Chapel, Manchester, October 17, 1901).

Halley Stewart,
Chairman

T. Gasquoine,
Stephen Massey,
Secretaries

Mr. Stephen Massey, Mr. Gasquoine's co-secretary seconded the proposition. We were living, he said, in a dark day, but he thought that meeting already heralded the dawn of brighter days. They were met there, he took it, not in opposition to anybody. What they had to do was not to judge between Boer and Briton and to see on which side the fault lay. Had they even known of any war since history began in which the fault was all on one side? They were not there to say that the Boers had not done wrong and cruel things in the conduct of the war. What they were concerned for was the good name of the country they loved so much. . . .

The Rev. J. P. Gladstone, of London, in moving a vote of thanks to the chairman and speakers said that when the war began those who opposed it believed that at least it would be conducted in the most humane manner possible. If the horrors of the war had been anticipated two and a half years ago the country would have brought the Government to its senses while there was time.

The Rev. W. Riley, of Heckmondwike, seconded the resolution, which was adopted.

On October 18, the War Office released the previous month's statistics on deaths in the concentration camps. The *Manchester Guardian*, in its coverage the following day, calculated an "appalling" rise in the mortality rate, which "works out to 264 per thousand per annum among the whites"; but *The Times* tried to minimize the significance of the statistics on the grounds that information was incomplete, and that, besides, disease and child mortality had always been serious problems in South Africa.

Leonard Courtney, in a letter to the editor published on the 22nd, replied that such "vain attempts to wriggle away from truth serve only to discredit the wriggler." But Courtney's letter carried less weight than one that appeared on the same page by Dr. John Percival, the Bishop of Hereford,[1] who, later that week, preached the same sermon to the Hereford Diocesan Conference.[2]

The Times   **October 22, 1901**

Sir,—Every month brings us the dreary record of the enormous death-rate among the children in South African concentration camps, and to-day you publish one of the worst that we have hitherto received.

According to your tabular statement there are 54,326 white children in those camps, and of these 1,964 died during the month of September. As men read these dreadful figures they cannot but ask, How long is this fearful mortality to be allowed to go on?

Meanwhile, the ladies sent out some months ago to inspect and inquire are, I presume, preparing a report. That report will doubtless testify that almost everything possible under the circumstances is being done by the officers, doctors, nurses, and other humane persons who are working in the camps.

1. On Percival's Liberal proclivities, and the late Queen's disapproval of him, see Owen Chadwick, *The Victorian Church* (New York, 1970), 2:334.

2. *Manchester Guardian*, October 25, 1901.

The Government and its friends have constantly reminded us that this is so, and we all believe in their general desire that it should be so. Your Elandsfontein Correspondent, indeed, has the hardihood to assert in your columns to-day that Miss Hobhouse "has tried her best to foster the supposition that those who have organized these camps are utterly callous as to their welfare," and that she is thus guilty of "fostering a base and malicious untruth." This libellous attack is itself an untruth; we will not call it malicious, because he may have been misinformed, or his pen may have run away with him in South African fashion: but it is certainly mischievous, and not very manly or creditable.

The point, however, for the English public to notice is this. All of us who know the humanity of English officers, doctors, nurses feel assured that they are endeavouring to do everything that personal devotion can do under the circumstances.

This unending death-roll of children is the result. Surely, Sir, we need no other condemnation of the camp system for children.

And these recurring reports, extending over all these dreary and death-laden months, amount to a very strong condemnation of the Government for their supineness in not attempting something better long before this time.

Is no system of distribution possible? Could not all mothers with children and all children without mothers be somehow distributed among the loyalist population of Cape Colony or Natal in healthy situations?

Are we reduced to such a depth of impotence that our Government can do nothing to stop such a holocaust of child-life?

We who ask these questions ask them in no spirit of political controversy; no man would seek to make any political gain out of the sad fate of these little ones.

It is in all sadness and in the name of common human pity that we plead with our authorities here at home—the Cabinet and the responsible heads of the great departments concerned —to do something and to do it speedily.

It is a dismal and hateful thought to multitudes of English men and women, without any distinction of political party, for we are all one in our pity for these little children; and the more truly patriotic we are the more hateful is the thought that England should through the death of these children be blotting out a whole generation, to say nothing of the root of bitterness which must inevitably grow out of their graves.

We also plead for immediate action, because the good name of our country is so deeply involved.

Of all the bitter and humiliating legacies of this war there will be none so bitter, none so sorely felt hereafter, as the untimely death of all these unhappy children.

Moreover, when the Boer exile returns, eager to clasp in his arms the little ones he left, only to find himself a solitary or childless man, is that likely to prove the seed of his future loyalty?

It may be different if the children are kept alive to tell him how tenderly and with what loving kindness they were nursed by English men and English women. It is because those who are now working in these camps are doing their best to save, and yet in spite of all death laughs them in the face as he goes on reaping his ghastly harvest month after month, that such camps stand utterly condemned as homes for children.

Therefore the hearts of English fathers and mothers on every side are crying to the Government to bestir themselves and make haste in this saving work, for the love of Christ to make haste.

> Your obedient servant,
> J. Hereford

October 19

Some of the most impressive examples of clerical agitation were interdenominational. During the summer and autumn months, some five thousand Nonconformist ministers affixed their signatures to a manifesto against the war.

Manchester Guardian   **October 25, 1901**

To the Editor of the Manchester Guardian
Sir,—Your readers will be interested in the following letter,

sent yesterday to the Marquis of Salisbury, similar letters at the same time going to Mr. Balfour and Mr. Chamberlain:

> My Lord Marquis,—On August 9 a document entitled "Free Church Ministers' Manifesto on the War" was forwarded to you, bearing the names of four hundred ministers, on whose behalf it was submitted to your Lordship. I am now requested by the Committee in charge of this manifesto to inform your Lordship, and I have the honour of so doing, that up to this date it has been signed by no fewer than 5,214 ministers of the country. I am also directed to enclose for your Lordship a printed copy of the manifesto, and to pray you to take some steps as speedily as possible in the direction of the suggestions made therein.—I have, &c.,
> Geo. P. M'Kay, Hon. Sec. of the Committee.

Your readers, further, will be glad to know how the denominations stand in the signing of this peace document. Approximately, then, the numbers are—Congregationalists, 1,100; Baptists, 1,000; Presbyterians, 950; Primitive Methodists, 800; Wesleyan Methodists, 500; Welsh Methodists, 270; Free Methodists, 200; New Connexion Methodists, 100; Bible Christians, 100; Unitarian, 100; Friends, 50; New Church (Moravian), 40.

A number of the signatories to the manifesto have written during the last few days asking whether we can do anything unitedly to protest against the horrors of the concentration camps. Nothing of this nature, nor indeed of any other kind, can be tacked on to the manifesto; but from the thousands of letters and other communications I have recently had from the ministers of the land I gather that there is growing and deepening the very strongest detestation of the present inhuman policy, and that soon some form of united protest and of action against it must be found. May God speedily show the way to this!

Yours, &c.,
GEO. P. M'KAY

October 23, 1901

The Reverend Stephen Gladstone, the late prime minister's second son and spiritual counsellor, used the correspondence columns of the *Speaker* for a plea to the nation's wives and mothers.

The Speaker   October 26, 1901

Sir,—Even allowing for the fallacies of figures, it is appalling to see that some of the camps, where we compulsorily hold the wives and children foes in the field (having destroyed their homes), are becoming veritable charnel-houses, and this in spite of local effort on our part. Circumstances so special demand special treatment.

Is it reasonable to say of such a people that surrender is the true remedy? What should we think of Englishmen who were for the unconditional surrender of their country, even to save the lives and fortunes of their families? We should rightly hold them in contempt, and in this case, as has been said, the men cannot, and the women will not, surrender. Why should not conciliation even now be tried? Have they and we not suffered enough? Why deepen the dark shadows of the future?

The bulk of the victims are helpless, innocent children. England is one of the most humane countries in Europe. Mothers of England! What sacrifice do you not gladly undergo for your own dear children? Where are your hearts to-day? Realise the meaning of the awful facts before us. Press urgently for conciliation. Press at least for the trial of such suggestions as doctors and nurses on the spot surely have to give. Who can doubt that one glimpse at these terrible, pathetic scenes, or into the future, would move all hearts to act together?

Yours, &c.,
STEPHEN E. GLADSTONE

Hawarden Rectory, October 24, 1901

Charles Gore, canon of Westminster (and successively bishop of Worcester, Birmingham, and Oxford) was one of the more controversial members of the Establishment: an

Anglo-Catholic with a particular concern for the social effects of Christianity. On October 28, *The Times* featured a letter which he had written in support of one that H. N. Brailsford contributed three days earlier.

The Times   **October 28, 1901**

Sir,—I cannot but feel that Mr. Brailsford's letter in your columns of Friday goes far to dispose of our last excuses for tolerating the awful infant mortality in the concentration camps. Surely this matter can be isolated from all other questions as to the policy or methods of the war. Hitherto the conscience of the country has been actively or passively as a whole supporting the war; but, unless I am very much mistaken, it must peremptorily require that immediate steps, however costly— whether by the speedy introduction of suitable nourishment into the camps in sufficient abundance or by the removal of the camps to the sea—be taken to obviate this unexampled and horrible death-rate among the children for whose protection we have, by a policy which may have been mistaken but is, at any rate, not now reversible, made ourselves responsible. Otherwise I believe the honour of our country will contract a stain which we shall not be able to obliterate and the whole Christian conscience of the country will be outraged and alienated.

I am, Sir, your obedient servant,
CHARLES GORE

Edinburgh, Oct. 26

It was common for individual congregations to put themselves on record against the concentration camps and all that they connoted. Each Sunday brought a flurry of resolutions, which the *Manchester Guardian* and other newspapers reported during the week.

Manchester Guardian   **November 5, 1901**

The following resolution was passed at the close of the evening service last Sunday at the Ashley Road Congregational

Church, Hale, Cheshire: "The members of the church and congregation, viewing with horror the mortality amongst the women and children in the concentration camps in South Africa, implore the Government to take every step immediately to remedy this condition of affairs."

At the Railway Road Wesleyan Chapel, Darwen, on Sunday night, at the request of the Rev. George Hack, a large congregation unanimously passed the following resolution: "That whilst expressing no opinion concerning the origin and justness of the war, this congregation is so deeply impressed with the appalling mortality going on in the concentration camps that it respectfully requests the Government to do all that its wisdom and power will enable it to do to lessen that mortality as speedily as possible."

At the Sunday evening service at the Crescent Road Congregational Church, Dukinfield, the following resolution was submitted to the congregation and unanimously adopted: "We, the members of the church and congregation worshipping in Crescent Road Congregational Chapel, Dukinfield, hereby express our pain and horror at the conditions under which the concentration camps are conducted in South Africa, and we would earnestly urge His Majesty's Government to do all in their power, and at whatever cost to the nation, to alleviate the suffering, and to arrest the terrible high death-rate prevailing amongst innocent women and children."

The following resolution was adopted by the members of the congregation at the Hallfold Congregational Chapel, Whitworth, on Sunday evening: "That this assembly, met for worship in Hallfold Congregational Chapel, Whitworth, on Sunday evening, November 3, 1901, deeply deplores the fearful infantile mortality of the concentration camps in South Africa, and earnestly begs His Majesty's Government to take without delay the steps necessary to put an end to this terrible condition of affairs."

11: The Last Phase

On October 4, for the first time since they had returned him to
Parliament the year before, the electors of Dumfries were
addressed by Sir Robert Reid. Unfortunately, "the cloud
which o'ershadowed the country" at the general election had
still not passed. His speech, which (in the opinion of the
Manchester Guardian) "combined hard sense and keen
patriotism," questioned whether the British people were being
told the full facts of the situation.

Manchester Guardian   October 5, 1901

We are entering upon the third year of this lamentable conflict. We have already spent in lives the best lives of our country, our bravest youth. We have already lost between 17,000
and 18,000 men—that is in killed alone or in deaths from
disease. That takes no account of the wounded or the suffering, the decrepitude or the decay of health. We have spent in
money something between £150,000,000 and £200,000,000
sterling—that is to say, we have added at least a quarter to the
national debt of this country,—and are spending now at the
rate, our Government tells us, of one million and a quarter a
week, and I tell you you will find it nearer two millions a
week. Now there is an uneasy feeling, or rather I would say an
uncertain feeling, in the country with respect to the dearth,
the scarcity, and the incomplete character of the news that we
receive. There is a censorship—no man recognises more fully
than I do that it is necessary to have a censorship—over the
press for the purpose of preventing military information being communicated to the enemy. But I am afraid that this
censorship goes a great deal beyond that. There is some influence which prevents this country from being fully ap-
prised of the truth of what takes place in South Africa. We
read reports of captures, large captures of men and ammunition, of cattle; we hear that the enemy is being driven off and
that there are great sweeping movements. We were told that
this autumn 60,000 or 70,000 of our troops were to be recalled.
I am sorry to say that the war still goes on. There are deadly
fights the same as before, our men are not returning home,
and notwithstanding all the captures the enemy seems to be in

abundant numbers and abundantly supplied. I think it was in June last that Lord Kitchener estimated that there were 13,500 men in the field against us. Since that time there have been recorded between 6,000 and 7,000 men captured, and if that were so there would be only 6,000 left in the field. It is manifest that nothing of the kind represents the truth. (Cheers.)

I do not wish to evoke undue complaint, but I think the Government might take a country more into their confidence with regard to what is going forward in South Africa.— (Hear, hear.) We are not children, we are men, and the people of this country have firmness, courage, and constancy enough to bear being told the truth so far as it can safely be communicated with reference to military considerations. . . .

There is no doubt that the position is serious and that is a reason for us to be cool and steady. This country has been in more serious positions before now, and it has come out of them honourably and successfully.— (Hear, hear.) It has come out of them because our forefathers were prepared to see facts as they were and not facts as they would like to see them.

Elsewhere on the "Celtic fringe," Lloyd George initiated a series of Welsh "peace meetings." The first, at Llanelly on the seventh, considered the high price that Britain was paying in terms of international esteem. Not everyone, of course, accepted his criteria. On the same evening, Winston Churchill at Oldham, yet to feel the stirrings of his Liberalism, proclaimed himself a "victory-at-any-price man."

Manchester Guardian   **October 8, 1901**

. . . He who shirks the task of pointing out whither we are drifting from dread of incurring the wrath of his neighbours is indeed recreant. He is the real traitor to his trust. If we had any better aim in this business than the gratifying of an infatuated pride I would say "Fight on," but now I say, and I say it in all earnestness that the time has come for sensible men of all creeds and sections who love Britain and hope

great things from her strength for the progress of humanity
to step in and save that strength for nobler ends. There is a
certain type of politician who thinks he has settled everything by calling those who criticise the war "pro-Boers." That
is the silly delusion of silly men. To answer every argument
against the war by calling out "pro-Boer" is not the device of
a statesman but the trick of a political cockatoo. When John
Bright urged his countrymen to abandon the foolish war with
Russia in 1855, was he a pro-Russian? That war was then
more popular with all classes than the Boer war has ever been.
We all know now that John Bright was right then and that
the Crimean war was a costly blunder. When Mr. Chamberlain denounced the Afghan war and accused Lord Roberts
and his troops of barbarities in its prosecution was he a pro-
Afghan and a traitor to his country? There is another favour-
ite cockatoo phrase. It is that which says that in condemning
the war you are encouraging the Boers. I say it is not a true
charge, it is not a genuine one. For instance, does this extend
to criticism of the military situation? If not, why not? Which
is the more likely, I ask, to hearten the Boers in their resis-
tence?—a speech from a member of the minority—a small minority at present—in Parliament urging the Government to
grant the Boers the same terms as the Empire has already conceded with such excellent results to the French in Canada or
a speech from a Unionist M.P. or an article in a Unionist
paper stating that our troops are played out and stale, that our
generals are no good, that it is difficult to get recruits, and
that the military outlook is very serious. After quoting the
"Spectator's" criticism on Lord Kitchener, and instancing
other and worse things in the extreme Tory papers, Mr.
George proceeded. Unless you intend to impose a rigid silence
about the war, to adopt Russian methods, and black out every
allusion to it in the press, except bare announcements of
British victories, you must extend freedom of speech to both
sides. I apprehend that the Unionist desire is to close our
mouths, not because they believe we are inciting the Boers to
protract their defence, but because they are uneasy lest what we
say should enlighten the people of this country as to the

whole scope and character of the conspiracy which has landed us in this African morass. I am not going to-night to argue with you as to the origin of the war. You have probably made up your minds about it, and it would be a futile endeavor on my part to seek to induce you to alter it. What I want to point out to you is that there are two wars, and all my arguments will be addressed to convincing you about the desirability of putting an end to the second. The first war was one which had for its objects—at least for its avowed objects—the repelling of an invasion of our territories—I will not now inquire how that was brought about or who was at fault—the second to establish equal rights for all white men in the Transvaal, the third to redress all the grievances which British subjects endured in that republic. Lord Salisbury said with regard to that war, just a month after it commenced: "We seek no territories; we seek no goldfields." That war came to an end when the Boer armies were overthrown after the capture of Bloemfontein. We could then have secured every object which we professed to seek before the war. . . . Our rulers chose rather to change the whole purpose of the war. They proclaimed their new purpose, which was to destroy every shred of Boer independence. Then a second war, a more inglorious, a more costly, a more disastrous war, and a war that no man can foretell the end of, was embarked upon, as I think recklessly and without due thought of consequences. . . .

With uncharacteristic theatricality, Sir Henry Campbell-Bannerman arrived unannounced on the twenty-fifth at the annual meeting of the Scottish Liberal Association, and gave a speech that highlighted the proceedings. Pausing to condemn again the "methods of barbarism," he reaffirmed his dedication to Liberal principles and, in the process, his claims to Liberal leadership.[1]

1. To no one's surprise, *The Times* considered Campbell-Bannerman's remarks irresponsible, if not subversive. "When a nation is committed to a serious struggle in which its position in the world is at stake," reasoned its leader on the twenty-sixth, "it is the duty of

That week, Scotsmen were treated to more than their usual
share of Liberal oratory. For the first time since the outbreak
of war, John Morley crossed the Tweed (and, in a sense,
the Rubicon) to address his constituents. He spoke twice—
at Arbroath on October 31, and at Forfar on November 4—
and more than justified his reputation. Without delay, his
speeches were published and circulated by the Liberal
Publication Department in connection with the National
Liberal Federation and the Liberal Central Association.

John Morley

Speech at Forfar   **November 4, 1901**

The sway of this island, both the northern part of it, to which
you belong, and the southern part, where I live—the sway of
this island is greater and more glorious than ever was ancient
Rome. Our sway rests not on pride of the sword, though the
sword cannot be laid aside—it rests upon industry and the arts
of peace. It springs not from the pride of a dominating race,
though race counts. It is rather the protection of the claims of
nationality and tradition, alien as they may sometimes seem,
recognising the sentiment of nationality as one of the most
honourable and noblest parts of human nature. Finally, the
rule of the realm to which we love to think that we belong,
claims to rest on strict adherence to the rules and principles
of justice, equity, good faith, honour, and the grand truth of
which Mr. Gladstone said, "Self-government is the great aim
of rational politics."

Now think, gentlemen, what a burden of high responsibility
does citizenship in such a Commonwealth as I have described
to you impose upon you and all who possess the citizenship.
It is the very magnitude, it is beneficence of this inheritance of
ours, that ought to nerve us to resist the mad outcries of the
hour, and to return to those maxims of sanity and of caution
which have built up the mighty fabric: and though you may

---

every citizen, no matter what his opinion about the political quarrel,
to abstain at the very least from hampering and impeding the
policy of his country, if he cannot lend his active support."

think sanity and caution no very heroic or high sounding virtues, they are virtues for which this part of the island has been pretty conspicuous. They are virtues to which I have no doubt that this part of the island, though for a moment in what I may be allowed to call rather a bad condition politically, if I can read the signs of the times aright, is pretty rapidly returning. They tell me that those who held the opinions upon contemporary events which I hold are blind to the change of the circumstances in which the Empire finds itself placed. They say to me, Do you not see the armaments of foreign Powers, how huge, how threatening? The colonies, which not so long ago no foreign Power grudged to us, and on which we ourselves did not set so high a value as we rightly do to-day, are now the objects of the envy and covetousness of the world. Our trade and commerce are exposed to new rivalries and hotter competition. Our legitimate and indispensable power at sea now faces revolutionised conditions. I for one am blind to none of all these changes in the circumstances of the world, all these changes in the position of this country in relation to the Powers of the world.

But I beg you to mark this. It is exactly these changes in our circumstances—the growth of forces outside, of new aims in foreign Powers—it is exactly this change that constitutes the peril of the policy of expansion and militarism, and it is because of this change that I preach, as more needed than ever, the gospel of sanity and caution. . . .

Have we not the right to ask who were the better friends of the Empire, who showed more of the Imperial instinct—those who two years ago warned the Government that patience—patience in the negotiations before the sword was drawn, was the quality required, or those who now to-day invite your patience, invite your patience as the ship of our great State is drifting slowly and heavily through dark and unsounded channels? . . .

We are talking to-night of the Empire. Everybody knows that one of the sources of strength and power, and confidence in our strength and power, is the certainty that we could raise even the gigantic sums necessary for a great war without seriously feeling the burden of taxation required to pay the interest. That was one of the sources of our strength compared with the position of one of the great Continental Powers— this was one of the elements of the conviction here and abroad of the immense and deepseated strength of the people of this island. Gentlemen, this vantage ground will be impaired, and there will be no margin out of which the interest on a great debt for a great war could be met. I do not want to use any exaggerated language. I do not for a moment say that the nation is bleeding to death. I do say that we are on the wrong track, that we have got ideas in our heads that will lead to grave embarrassment and widespread ruin. Mere territorial expansions, mere acquisition of barren territory in Africa or anywhere else is not Empire-making. That is not strengthening the Empire. The estrangement of the goodwill of the world—which is admitted by the King's present Ministers— does not strengthen the Empire, but weakens it. . . .

Let us sink our party manoeuvres. I do not appeal to you to-night upon abstract principles of conscience, although there is something to be said for conscience even in public affairs— I do not appeal to you upon maxims of humanity, though there is much to be said for maxims of humanity; but I invite you to consider what I have said to-night not in a vague way, but earnestly, vigorously, resolutely, for the sake of the strength, the health, the well-being, the power, and the good fame of the mighty Commonwealth, of which the people of this island are the centre and the heart.

Morley, Two Years of War—and After   *(London, 1901)*

With Campbell-Bannerman and Morley already on record, Sir William Harcourt was not long behind. Lacking Scottish constituents to whom he could proclaim his views, he settled for the next best thing, a letter to the editor of *The Times*.

The Times   **November 8, 1901**

Sir,—We hear a good deal of condemnation of pessimism, but of all the pessimistic utterances none has equalled the warning by Lord Milner at Durban, "that in a formal sense the war may never be over." Till the war is "formally" over there can never be peace and the "war to a finish" may never have an end. What the "sort of war" of the Lord Chancellor and the "informal war" of Lord Milner is has received a ghastly illustration in the casualty list of Colonel Benson's column. Lord Milner, indeed, tells us that "the conflagration is burning itself out, but it comes to nothing because there is nothing left for the flames to feed on." Is that the fact? Is there still no part of South Africa which has not been laid waste? Are there no men or women of the Dutch race still alive? The fires, he says, "keep breaking out over and over again first at one point and then at another, but the moment the hose is turned on they die out." Yes, and many good men and true on each side "die out" too. We are told 65 columns of this fire brigade 200,000 strong are at work (which it is admitted are too few), and yet it is only a "sort of a fire," an "informal conflagration," and, in the words of Lord Milner, "large parts of South Africa are still in a state of ruinous disorder." This, in the third year of the war, is the diagnosis and the prognosis of the "man on the spot." We are told that to bring the real truth of this disastrous business before the country is to encourage the Boers, as if the Boers did not know it themselves as well as we do. But was there ever a statement more calculated to encourage the Boers in their resistance than this anticipation by the High Commissioner of the indefinite continuity of this "informal" war with its reckless waste of treasure and of blood? The dragon's teeth which have been sown by the Cadmus of the Colonial Office in his fateful furrow bring forth crop after crop of armed men resolved to do or to die.

The significant part of this deplorable business is that from the first to the last the pessimists have been more than right and the optimists have been more than wrong. But even Lord Milner himself seems beginning to be alive to the real facts of the situation. We were first told that, if we would only show our teeth and menace enough war, there would be no war and the Boers would not fight, and so the war broke out. We were assured that the war would be a mere military promenade to be settled by 10,000 men and as few millions. We have sent out 300,000 men, out of whom the "unreturning brave" have been decimated by death and disease. We were informed on careful calculation that the whole fighting force the Boers could raise did not amount to 40,000 men—less than the whole number of the prisoners of war. Without doubt after the capture of Pretoria, the whole resistance was soon to collapse—and Lord Roberts returned to verify the prediction. But from that moment demands for thousands more men were so urgent that recruits—like those of Falstaff at Coventry —were hurried to the front. We were invited to be confident that, if we only burned farms enough, destroyed the flocks and herds, laid waste the whole country, and carried off the wives and families of the Boers and half-starved those who belonged to combatants in arms, the spirit of the Boers would be finally broken—but the resistance only waxed the fiercer. Forty-one futile proclamations were issued and still the Boers fought on. A final effort was attempted (the last and most imbecile of all) which menaced the leaders with banishment and the followers with confiscation—a threat which every man of sense predicted would be treated with contempt, as is now admitted to be the case—not to mention that they were bogus threats illegal in themselves and incapable of execution. How obstinate are these delusions continuously practised on the country, is proved by the latest declarations of the Government. On August 14, in the last moments of the Session, I invited Mr. Chamberlain to give to Parliament some information as to the condition of the war. His reply was: "I stated no later than Friday last all we knew of the present position and the grounds for anticipating that it would be within the power of the Commander-in-Chief to send home a considerable number of troops at the termination of the winter campaign." This was the accurate information, I suppose, derived from the "men on the spot" on whom the Government implicitly rely, and upon whom they are always very anxious to devolve all responsibility. I confess I shudder when I hear the Government proclaim they are about to bring home troops. The return of Lord Roberts and the C.I.V. was only the prelude for demands for fresh levies. Mr. Chamberlain, in the middle of August, expects to "send home a considerable number of troops at the end of the winter campaign." Well, the winter in South Africa was over in September, but not the winter campaign; it continues fiercer than ever in the spring and, so far from troops being brought home, large contingents of more efficient troops are peremptorily called for, and the "informal" war seems to be more deadly and further than ever from an end.

What has been the fatal feature of this unhappy war from the beginning to the present moment is the invincible ignorance of those responsible for it, both at home and in South Africa, of the conditions they had to deal with, both physical and moral. Of their acquaintance with the physical conditions of the war they were about to wage the preparations they made for it are sufficient indication. After two years they begin to apologize for their failure by the discovery, apparently recent, that it is a big job to transport an army of 300,000 men with its equipments 6,000 miles, and that South Africa is an extensive and difficult country for military operations, but there were even unprofessional people who tried to impress these facts on their minds, though in vain at the time. And, as has been justly remarked, the distance of South Africa and the extent and character of the field of operations have not materially altered since that time. But the most inexcusable of all the blunders which have brought us to the present situation has been the moral and intellectual obliquity of vision which has blinded those who have brought about and conducted the war to the real character and spirit of their opponents in arms. They seem to have believed that they were cowards who would not fight; that they were men who would succumb at the first defeat; that they could be intimidated by these silly proclamations; that they would shrink even from the shameful torture of being compelled to witness the execution of their relatives and friends—an outrage which has been justly denounced in the noble speech of Mr. Morley at Arbroath. They seem to have known nothing of the race from which these men are sprung; of the traditions which they

244

cherish; and of the cause to which they were prepared to sacrifice their lives, their families, and their fortunes. The Government ignored the terrible nature of the enterprise which is undertaken by those who set about to subjugate a brave and a free people. And yet the lesson is written large in the pages of history from the days of the Persian King, of Phillip of Spain with the Indies, of Napoleon at the head of countless legions. It is one which it is incredible that a British Government should not have learned, especially as under evil counsellors, 120 years ago, the same thing was attempted on our own race. It is still more deplorable that the British nation should seem to have forgotten the issue of that ill-omened contest, which for many years was as enthusiastically applauded as that in which we are now engaged. But at least those who profess and call themselves Liberals cherish with pride the memorable protest against that ruinous policy which found a voice of thunder in Chatham's "mother tongue," in the fervour of Fox, and the wisdom of Burke. They, too, in their day were assailed by Ministerial slander and popular clamour as pro-Americans, as traitors, as enemies of their country, and friends of its foes. But they knew the truth, they spoke it, and their record remains for the instruction and imitation of those who come after them. Adversity is a stern instructor. The voice of reason in the end makes itself heard, and the most thoughtless are beginning to ask themselves whether a policy which bears such bitter fruits is a wise policy conducted by prudent and farseeing men.

We have made some advances. The optimism of Lord Milner in the past has proved utterly fallacious; it is probable that his present pessimism may turn out to be only too true and that "this war in a formal sense may never be over," and that all the talk of an early and happy settlement with a contented people is either an hypocrisy on the part of those who know or a delusion on the part of those who are ignorant. We have before us nothing, even with hostilities come to an end, but the dismal future of racial hatred and cruel coercion. Those who believe that such a prospect is one which will ultimately commend itself to the genius of the British people do injustice to their conscience and their traditions. We ask with a troubled mind what is to be the end and how is it to be attained, and the hopeless reply from the Government is only more troops and greater severity. . . .

We have the confession of Lord Milner that as it has been and as it is now conducted "in a formal sense this war may never cease." Those who desire that by a spirit of conciliation on reasonable terms it may cease now and for ever must look for that end in other paths and by other men.

Nov. 3   W. H. HARCOURT

The Times was inundated with irate letters on the subject of the concentration camps, and, up and down the country, town meetings were held to publicize and protest the spiraling death rate. Many were organized by the League of Liberals against Aggression and Militarism, in conjunction with either local constituency associations or *ad hoc* agencies.[1] On November 9, as never before, the pro-Boer forces projected an image of fundamental unity. At London's Memorial Hall, Leonard Courtney presided at a meeting sponsored by the South African Conciliation Committee. The speakers included Sir Robert Reid (who deprecated the demand for unconditional surrender), Edmund Robertson (who likened Emily Hobhouse to Florence Nightingale), Lord Coleridge (who decried the illegality of martial law), the Rev. Stephen Gladstone (who thundered against the concentration camps as a consequence of "the policy of violence and fire and sword"), and Keir Hardie (who charged the government with "lying and deceit"). There were repeated calls for the removal of Lord Milner. The list of M.P.'s and clergymen who either attended or sent messages of sympathy reads like a Who's Who of the pro-Boer movement.

Manchester Guardian   **November 9, 1901**

. . . The Chairman said that, looking back upon the two years that had passed since the Committee was formed, he, for one, was proud of the small share that he had been permitted to

1. *Second Annual Report of the League of Liberals Against Aggression and Militarism* (London, 1902).

take in their work. He saw nothing to regret in what they had
done. He could not say that every step taken, every word they
had uttered, and every sentence they had written would be
approved by the calm judgment of posterity—they would indeed be happy if they had escaped every blunder,—but he did
claim that no band of men had been animated with purer
patriotism, with a sincerer love of their country, with a more
passionate desire to keep its history pure and its reputation
scatheless than the active members of the Conciliation Committee.— (Renewed applause.) They might be told that they
had assisted the enemies of the country, that they had helped
to strengthen the enemy's resistance to our arms, and that but
for their words the Boers would have yielded to the necessities of the situation. He for one did not believe in the least in
the suggestion that the men who fought so desperately, and
with such courage, had received encouragement from their
poor words. Something greater, something more stimulating
had urged the Boers in their unequal fight.— (Applause.) The
members of the Committee had not helped the enemies of
their country; they had waged eternal war against them. But
what enemies? The enemies that were within our own gates.—
(Applause.) Those who had brought the country to the pass
in which it found itself to-day; those to whose counsels, to
whose temper, and to whose unwisdom it was due.— (Renewed
applause.) We stood now aghast at the prospect before us,
and the multitude was going to and fro asking "Who will
show us any good?" The members of the Committee had
tried their best, but he could not boast that they had succeeded
in conciliating their opponents. The rift, the division, the
animosity had increased rather than diminished. But as their
consciences were clear in that they had done what they could,
so their consciences would not be clear if they did not persist in doing what they could, and though they had failed in
the past in the hopes which some of them too fondly entertained, there was some ground for fresh action to-day, because
all men and all women who contemplated the present situation in South Africa were perplexed, if not in despair. There
was a growl of discontent from the masses of their countrymen

which had revealed itself in their attitude towards the Ministers by whom they had been led, and by whom it might be
said they had been betrayed.—(Applause.) In that growl he
detected something of hope, and whilst some men would
find in the present situation fresh food for stubborn determination to fight the war to a finish to perish if need
be in bringing the enemy under their heel, he did not
believe that that would be the temper of the majority of their
countrymen.—(Applause.) He believed that not a few—
enough to turn the scale in the balance of popular judgment
—were beginning to ask whether there was not some better
way than that along which we had been led, whether there
was not some possible escape from the dilemma in which we
found ourselves. To that inquiry, which was now permeating
the masses of their countrymen, they replied to-day in the
words which were on their lips when that Committee was
formed—that an escape was to be found in conciliation and
in conciliation alone.—(Applause.) The contrary policy
which had been pursued had deepened animosities, and
widened the breach between the two peoples. It had done
more than that. Let them look over the miserable series
of expedients by which we were now pursuing the war—the
devastation of the land, the ruined homesteads, the burnt
crops, the destroyed cattle. The very mills, the instruments
of industry, the reservoirs of organisation and irrigation had
been destroyed, and where there was peace, where the valleys
were thick with corn, where the people were prosecuting
their industries in agreement with their neighbours and in
submission to law, there was nothing but red ruin and the
breaking up of law. In the pursuit of our policy towards the
Boers we had managed to estrange the Dutch in Cape Colony
from us, so that our hold upon that colony was now most
insecure, all these things had sunk deep into the minds of our
Dutch fellow-subjects, and we must not be surprised if what
he had heard that day was true. He was told that when the
Boer commandos first entered the Cape Colony last January,
in one particular district which was pretty well populated,
only some half-dozen of the younger men joined the Boer

forces. When the commandos went away we put our irregular corps in the district, and they so harassed the inhabitants, so punished them because half a dozen young men had gone away with the commandos that four months later when the Boers reappeared they had a great levy of recruits instead of half a dozen. Now when, after nine months, the Boers came back again, it was with great difficulty that young men were restrained from joining their forces. All these attempts made in the path of ruthless determination to have our way at whatever cost had only made the situation worse, and we were now in a more hopeless condition than we were in during the early stages of the war.—(Applause.) Whatever military progress had been made—(A voice: None)—and it had not been so considerable as some people would have us believe—politically we had gone backward, and the hope of reconciliation was less than it was before. But it was not absolutely abandoned. Still there was a path open. If it were not so the prospect was one of despair. But still he believed that the path was open for reconciliation if the right temper was shown and the right men were appointed.— (Applause.) The people with whom we were dealing were such that, unless we were prepared to go to the bitter end of ruin and destruction, we should not be able to stand the certainty of having to deal with the problem over again. Extirpation was something to which the British people would never consent, although here and there we had sundry voices speaking as if the notion were quite tolerable. There was no hope that way, and the country would not stand it. What, then, was to be done? Again he used the magic word "conciliation." By negotiation, by agreement, we must bring about a settlement if a settlement was to stand. He did not say—he did not deceive himself—that if this country could be supposed to have the heart and the will to go on fighting with the determination to wipe out every inhabitant who persisted in opposing our supremacy we might not effect our purpose. He did not say that we might not induce a sullen submission to our power, but he was certain that that way safety did not lie, and that the only possible safety was through conciliation, through negotiation, and arrangement—(Applause.) Those people who were in favour of the war talked vainly of a distant future when self-government was to be conceded. What was this distant future, the date of which was never stated, and which Lord Salisbury himself said might be generations to come—what was this future compared with the frightful present? It was the present that was working upon the men who were resisting us, and until that present was changed they would continue to resist. —(Applause.) . . .

Prodded by his confederates, Lord Rosebery emerged from the shadows on December 15 to address a meeting at Chesterfield. Flanked by his Liberal Imperialist lieutenants, he called upon the party to attune its policies to the new century, to shed the albatross of Irish Home Rule, and "not [to] disassociate itself, even indirectly, from the new sentiment of Empire which occupies the nation." Yet even Rosebery, whom no one would categorize as a pro-Boer, publicly urged the Government to resume negotiations—his private initiatives in July had no effect—and he absolved the pro-Boers of the charge of prolonging the war.

Lord Rosebery
Speech at Chesterfield   December 15, 1901

. . . We hear much now of the war being protracted by misrepresentations, and, failing to find any other stick with which to beat the poor Opposition—the poor, weak, distracted Opposition—it has been discovered that they are responsible for the prolongation of the war. Well, that to me is a very remarkable allegation; but, if anybody seems to me responsible, or if any body of men seemed to be responsible in this country for the prolongation of the war, it is those who announced that every Liberal who was returned to Parliament was returned as a Boer, and that every seat lost to the Government was a gain to the Boers: for thus, on high authority—the highest in the Government—the Boers in the field, who are very well informed, were made to understand that, in addition to the eighty Irish members who were returned as avowedly the friends and supporters of the Boers, there were a large number of Liberal members who were returned to represent Boer ideas and advance the Boer policy in Parliament. I say this —that that was a scandalous misrepresentation, which, if any representation from England could encourage the Boers, would encourage them twenty times more than anything that has been said by any member of the Opposition. Sir, this is a grave matter. I do not think in all my lifetime, or in all my political recollections—certainly not since the Reform Bill of 1867—that there has been anything that struck so deep to the roots of political morality as the General Election of 1900. But there is a Nemesis that waits on operations of that kind. And fourteen or fifteen months after that general election took place you see the war flagrant, unabated, raging, and the Government, like the lean kine that swallowed up the fat kine, not a whit stronger for the majority it obtained in consequence of those misrepresentations.

> *Reprinted as* National Policy (*London: The Liberal Publication Department, 1902*), *pp. 7–8.*

Never shy of heroics, David Lloyd George took it upon himself to reply to Lord Rosebery, much his senior in party councils, and, at the same time, to unfurl the pro-Boer banner in Birmingham, which was Chamberlain's fief. It is difficult to say which action was the more audacious. A riot ensued, and Lloyd George had to be spirited from the Birmingham Town Hall in the borrowed garb of a police constable. Interviewed the next day on the platform of New Street Station, Chamberlain declined to blame his Birmingham neighbors for their response, but "deeply and sincerely deplored" the damage done to "the grand old Town Hall."

The special correspondent for the *Manchester Guardian* furnished an eyewitness account of the disturbances.

Manchester Guardian   **December 19, 1901**

Mr. Lloyd-George, M.P., arrived here this afternoon to address a meeting in the Town Hall arranged by the Birmingham Liberal Association. He went straight to the Town Hall, and at eight o'clock appeared on the platform. The audience would listen to nobody. The chairman and Mr. Lloyd-George made speeches to the reporters, and a few minutes before nine o'clock, while Mr. Lloyd-George was still speaking, there was a rush for the platform and the meeting was broken up with much disorder. Many things that happened before the meeting was held tended to foment rowdyism. Two days ago an attempt was made to persuade the Lord Mayor, Mr. J. H. Lloyd, who is a Liberal Unionist, to refuse the use of the Town Hall. Mr. Lloyd did not see that there was any reason for such interference, and when his decision was made known the leaders of those who desired to stop the meeting sent all over the city imitations of the official ticket of admission. Mr. W. Finnemore (the secretary of the Liberal Association) promptly withdrew all the first issue of tickets and to-day a new ticket was distributed. In spite of the exercise of all possible discretion, many of these tickets got into the hands of the peculiar persons who think the best aid to their own side is to prevent the sound of speech on the other, and an hour before the meeting was to begin it was evident that there would be trouble. Thousands of people swarmed around the Town Hall building, and those inside heard "Soldiers of the Queen" and "Rule, Britannia" sung with boisterous good humour. Cheers for Mr. Chamberlain were alternated with shouts of another description for Mr. Lloyd-George.

At half-past seven the Town Hall was filled, principally by well-dressed young men. These had come provided with flags and whistles, and having distributed themselves in all directions, they began to encourage merriment. The hall organ was played by way of introduction for a Liberal song, but the song was never sung, and the organ music was drowned with "Soldiers of the Queen" and cheering. Presently another tune was started in the Hall, to words that were greeted with roars of laughter. The refrain was, "Chuck Lloyd-George into the fountain and he'll never come to Brum any more." There was a special significance in this, because behind the Town Hall there is a square named after the Colonial Secretary, and its principal feature is a fountain with a large trough. The leaders of the Liberal party in Birmingham were greeted with cheers by some and with shouts of derision and laughter by others as they took seats on the platform, and Mr. Lloyd-George was hailed with a tumult of the most strangely sounding noise. His reception might almost have been one from a sympathetic audience, for everybody was applauding and flags and hats were waved. There was very little hissing and plenty of well-intentioned cheering, but lusty and long-drawn shouts predominated. The generally accepted cue was to make much noise and to do it as good humouredly as possible. Mr. Osler, the chairman, stood waiting for silence a full five minutes. He might as well have waited for a silent Niagara. At last he sat down, and Mr. Finnemore stood up. This was the signal for a crescendo in the hubbub. Mr. Finnemore took no notice of it. He read a letter of apology for absence from Mr. Alderman Cook, the president of the Liberal Association who should have taken the chair. Mr. Cook had anticipated some disturbance in the meeting, but his absence was because of indisposition. He wrote: "In some quarters I have noticed an inclination to blame the Lord Mayor for granting the use of the Town Hall to the Liberal Association for the meeting. The Liberal Association is a body of Birmingham men and women, peaceable, law-abiding, tax-paying citizens, who love their town and their country and are as anxious for their welfare, prestige, and honour as anyone residing therein. To suggest that the Lord Mayor should not grant them the Town Hall on the same terms as to other similar bodies is to suggest a method of procedure which I trust will never be tolerated in Birmingham." Mr. Cook added some comments on Lord Rosebery's speech. With the speech he is in accord. But none but the reporters who stood within a yard of Mr. Finnemore while he read heard the contents of the letter. The meeting proceeded in what, by the use of paradox, may be called "dumb show." People who wanted to hear the speakers only saw them speaking. The triumphant cries of the disturbers were deafening. Mr. Osler was on his feet for some minutes. What he had to say was this: "I take the chair more willingly because freedom of speech seems to have been challenged here by the disgraceful incitements to disorder of which an influential part of the Birmingham press has been guilty. One would think from all this hubbub that we had invited some criminal to be present to-night, or a man who had planned a raid on a friendly country, instead of one who pleaded for peace when the war spirit was high."

When Mr. Osler sat down Mr. Lloyd-George came quickly to the front of the platform. It was scarcely possible to say that the hubbub grew louder, but the cheers of friends gave it still another crescendo. Mr. Lloyd-George with a good-tempered smile watched the unfurling of flags and listened to the Fountain Song. Then he addressed himself to the reporters. "We are told," he began, "that speeches delivered in this country reach the ears of the Boers. If it is so the Boers will to-night learn how to interpret Birmingham Unionist promises of free institutions. I have been called an enemy of my country because I have, in common with thousands of others, declined to allow my judgment to be swept away by the unthinking clamour of the multitude." Then Mr. Lloyd-George rapidly read some notes that he had prepared on the subject of Lord Rosebery's speech. Of these notes I have telegraphed a summary.

Mr. Lloyd-George had nearly finished reading—only the reporters heard the sound of his voice—when a stone came through one of the high windows. I went to one of the police-guarded doors and looked out on a crowd of many thousands. At that moment a man scaled the new statue of Queen Victoria opposite the Council-house and fixed a flag on the top. Another man at the base of the statue shouted, "Come and let's break the doors. We are not afraid because there happens to be a traitor there." Thereupon there was a rush to the doors, and some of them were smashed in. Reinforcements of police barred further progress, and I returned to the hall just in time to see four stalwart young men climb on to the reporters' platform. Others were about to follow, but the police (there were 400 of them on duty inside and outside the hall) interposed, and very quietly the chairman and Mr. Lloyd-George retired from the speakers' platform. At the moment of triumph for the rowdies inside the hall those outside—where it was snowing heavily—increased the vigour of their attack. Glass from broken windows fell amongst the audience in the galleries, and stones—some of them evidently shot from catapults, others thrown by hand—and brick ends came crashing through from the street. This sort of thing soon became general. An evening newspaper had announced that the Liberal Association had guaranteed to the Lord Mayor that all damage would be paid for by the Liberal Association. Word to the effect was passed through the crowd, and the stones began to fly like hail. Soon the windows were riddled. The crowd appeared to glory in this diversion the while they waited for Mr. Lloyd-George. All the police outside were afoot. For a long time they were content to guard the doors of the Town Hall and to keep the crowd broken up, but after an hour of excitement the disorder became a riot, and at last an angry assault was made on the Town Hall doors by men who said they wanted to "get at that traitor Lloyd-George," who was believed to be still in the building. The angry development on the part of the crowd was so marked that the police were finally ordered to draw their batons and to charge. This they did, and at the moment of telegraphing there is a man with a badly bleeding head in the Post-office doorway, and there are many in a similar plight in doorways on the other side of the street. A policeman has been so badly injured in the head that an ambulance has been sent for, and it is reported that in the mêlée at least a dozen policemen and many civilians have been more or less seriously knocked about.

Telegraphing later our correspondent says: I have had some conversation with Chief Constable Rafter. He tells me that he was anxious to avoid ordering his men to charge the crowd, but that soon after ten o'clock a scaffold pole was brought up. Using this as a battering-ram, the crowd smashed in one of the doorways. It was then that the Chief Constable overcame his reluctance. Before the batons of the police the people rushed away in panic haste. In bodies of thirty the police swept the square, and the side streets were instantly filled with a flying mob. The Chief Constable says that one of his men had been nearly killed by a brick-end which crashed through his helmet. The man is now lying in the hospital. From other sources I gather that no disorder to equal that of to-night has been seen in Birmingham since the Murphy riots thirty years ago. At eleven o'clock there were many hundreds of people marching to and fro through the square shouting offensively against Mr. Lloyd-George and all "pro-Boers." Mr. Lloyd-George got safely away from the Town Hall a few minutes after he left the platform.

Like the outgoing year, the war staggered to an end. The Boers in the field remained capable of inflicting occasional embarrassments, but their defeat was a foregone conclusion. For the last time before he graduated to the editorship of the London *Daily News*, A. G. Gardiner wrote "The Story of the Year" for his readers at Blackburn. Like the *Manchester Guardian*, in its review three days later of "Trade and Finance," he was most concerned with the country's relative economic decline.

Blackburn Weekly Telegraph December 28, 1901

The sands of 1901 have nearly run out, and the time has come to take a rapid inventory of its career, to balance the account of good and evil, and to write its epitaph. In our national life two events have overshadowed all others. The first of these was the death of Queen Victoria after a reign extending over sixty years, and constituting a record in English history. She lived to witness the close of the century of which she was the foremost figure and to see the dawn of a new era, and then, full of years and honour, she passed away, amid the lamentations of the whole English-speaking world, leaving her son to fill the vacant throne as Edward VII. Side by side with this sorrow we have had the South African tragedy always with us. The whole year has been darkened by that giant shadow. The death of a beloved Queen under whom men had passed from youth to old age was, after all, a passing grief. The loss was natural and inevitable. But the war has dogged us day by day, and now at the close of the year it does not seem appreciably nearer an end than it did at the beginning. Indeed Lord Milner has declared that in "a formal sense" it may never be over at all, so that England has before it the prospect of having for years to come to spend its energies in holding down a territory half as big as Europe by military force. Lord Roberts, when he told us that the war was over in September, 1900, said that we should need a permanent garrison in South Africa of 30,000 men. But if Lord Milner be right, and there be a state of chronic rebellion, we shall probably need 100,000. Meanwhile we have still 200,000 engaged, and no prospect of any reduction in the number being possible. And every week adds a million and a quarter sterling in respect of the war alone to the burden under which the British taxpayer is groaning. Apart from this, taxation has enormously increased, while, on the other hand, the trade returns of the year have been distinctly on the down grade, and the United States have suddenly revealed their stupendous possibilities as commercial rivals. Hitherto we have feared the Germans as our most dangerous industrial foes, but this year has made it clear that America is to have the commercial crown of the world. This wonderful development has come about not merely as the result of the gigantic natural resources of the States, but because the Americans, like all States founded on modern ideals—Australia and New Zealand for example—have realised that the most valuable commodity of the nation is its sons and daughters, and that to educate them to the fullest extent is to make the soundest investment for the future. England has been left behind in the education race, and it is now paying the price.

12 : Retrospect

Despite their daring in isolated skirmishes, the Boer armies
were exhausted, and their escape routes were effectively cut.
It was nonetheless a war to the bitter end, exactly what the
advocates of conciliation had most wished to avoid. Leonard
Courtney self-searchingly asked whether the agitation had
been worth the time and trouble, and he concluded that a
significant purpose was served.

Leonard Courtney
Speech to the annual meeting of the South Africa
Conciliation Committee (Liverpool Branch) January 10, 1902

Mr. Courtney, who was received with great enthusiasm, said
the chairman had exhorted them to be strong in opinion but
moderate in language, and if he had at any time erred in for-
getting the latter part of that injunction, certainly he came
to that meeting in no spirit of contention, but to endeavour
as far as possible to strengthen themselves in the work they
had undertaken, in a temper of forbearance towards those
who differed from them, and in a temper of charity towards
all men. Nor did he think that anything had happened which
should alter this attitude of his. So far from exulting over the
too terrible evidence which experience had given of the accuracy of the forecast made, he would wish to put the memory
of all that, if possible, away, and to address himself only to
the problems of the present and see whether they could not
even now arrive at some resolution which should put an end
to the terrible spectacle which was presented to them not
only in South Africa but at home. It was impossible not to
remember some things which had happened, but he would
say as little as he could of the past and as much as he might
of the possibility of action in the future. (Applause).

There was one reason why he, for one, did not come to a
meeting like that with any feeling of exultation. On the contrary, looking back on the two years during which they had
been endeavouring to do something, he had been sometimes
tempted to ask in despair—"Have we done any good? Is there
any evidence whatever that we have touched the minds of any
of our countrymen and led them to a better appreciation of

258

the problem with which we are compelled to deal? Have we in any degree brought them back to counsels of moderation and of peace?" There were many who would say they had not done good, but evil; that they had made things worse instead of better—(cries of "No"); that so far from assuaging the temper of the controversy through which they had been passing they had made it more bitter. He was not disposed to accept in any degree the accuracy of the reasoning thus employed. (Applause). He was somtimes forced, however, to ask the question, "Have we done any good?" Although a man might be excused from saying that, after he had tried all he could do, it could not be accepted—Cobden would not so have accepted it—as an excuse for not trying. In all these matters there was no alternative. If a man was a patriot—if he had any respect for the character of his country, if he was proud of the traditions of the past, and would like to see preserved all that had made the record of his national life illustrious, all that had made it receive and deserve the admiration of the other nations of the world—if a man was animated by these feelings, and saw the bulk of his fellow-countrymen running into error, and embarking upon a policy which must bring mischief upon themselves, degradation of their own characters, deterioration of their own condition, and inflict uncalled-for injustice upon those outside our nation—that man, the more patriotic he was, the more necessary did he find it to speak.—(Cheers). They might be derided as "traitors to their country," and as assisting those who were at war with our national forces: That was an accusation which the majority would always bring, and always had brought, against the minority who were contending for right, and who so frequently in the end were found to be rightly contending for the right. They must make up their minds to submit to this experience, without resentment. . . . "I spoke of Cobden and Bright. I might go through the whole record of human history, sacred and profane, and show that the men in whom we affect to believe, whose teaching we claim to have made part of our own lives, were 'traitors to their country' in their day. When we are abused in the same way, shall we not rather think it a privilege than a punishment to be marshalled in the noble army that had gone before us?" (Applause). Yes, in spite of all discouragement, the supporters of the Conciliation Committee had done good. They had, Mr. Courtney added, done good to themselves. They had caused people to come together, and by so doing to strengthen one another. The strongest man was feeble in isolation.

Those who belonged to the Conciliation Committee knew what good had been done by calling into demonstrative existence people who might otherwise have remained unknown and inactive. This was a thing of which he could speak with special authority, because in the position which he had had the honour of filling, he had had the opportunity of meeting all over the country people in sympathy with the Conciliation Committee who were only eager to be shown some way of being more active and efficacious in the future. It was something to have realized themselves, even if they had secured nothing else. But they had done more. By their constant action —annoying as it had been to many—they had forced the perception of some facts upon an unwilling public. The facts themselves had too often followed to back up their arguments with a logic much greater than any they could employ. Their representations of fact, coupled with the growing accumulation of fact behind those representations, had compelled people to realize things which at first they refused to believe, and they were bringing the public into an attitude of mind which would make them capable of something very like a preparation for peace in no distant future. (Cheers). . . .

Having condemned the imposition of martial law in Cape Colony, and especially the dragging out of men and women to witness the execution of their friends, Mr. Courtney went on to ask how were we going to get out of the difficulty? Was there any prospect before us of an improvement? (A voice: "Dismiss Judas," and applause). No, no, that might do something, but there was something more than that. They must change the hearts of their countrymen. (Applause). Do not let them deceive themselves. For good or evil, the truth must be spoken. The majority of the nation had, he feared actively, and most certainly they had tacitly, approved of everything that had been done. Throughout England one could scarcely fasten upon any constituency in which one could say there had been a direct repudiation of the policy pursued by the Government. Wales to its honour (cheers) had done well, and so had Ireland. But in England, if they excepted two or three constituencies, one that of Mr. John Burns, and another that of Mr. Channing, it was not so. They could not disguise the truth that up to recently if not now, the majority of the nation tacitly, and, he feared, openly, approved of the war. Their task was to get their countrymen, before it was too late, to come to a better mind, and realize what they were about. The war was a blunder at the beginning, the ways in which it had been pursued had been mistaken ways, and was not the policy of "unconditional surrender," the demand that these people should be put under our feet and remain there, also a mistake, which must be given up if we would make peace.

They might have peace through subjection, but what trust could be put in a peace like that? (None). They wanted peace with righteousness and equity, otherwise it would crumble to pieces. We felt already something of the terrible strain put upon us. We would feel more of it in the near future through further taxation and draining of our resources, scantier employment, and worse times. The time would come—in fact it had come already—when throughout these islands the story of the Boer resistance to our arms would be related as a fitting companion to that of the Swiss in the maintenance of their freedom, to the story of the Greeks against the barbarians who sought to override them, and that of the Scotch who refused to submit to the power of Edward. The generous boys of all countries had rejoiced in these stories of the past, and had felt their pulses quicken and their blood become warmer as they heard of Bruce and Wallace, although it may have been they were fighting against the country from which they themselves had sprung. A time would come when the boys of England, in the same way, would read the story of De Wet, and would know that De Wet was a pattern and example of the mass of the Boers in the field. (Cheers). We must try to make our countrymen feel that the Boers were men to be made brothers of, not enemies to be grappled on to us with hooks of steel. We must live with them side by side, and not impress on them a form of organization which they stubbornly resisted, and not make "unconditional surrender" and the denial of "a single shred of independence" conditions of negotiating with them. (Cheers). Let us make peace as men with men, and brothers with brothers. He was sure if we approached them in that spirit and could persuade them of our sincerity we should establish a peace that would be lasting and well secured. (Loud cheers).

Manchester Guardian, January 11, 1902

Sir Henry Campbell-Bannerman emerged from the ordeal with a vastly enhanced reputation. His survival as party leader was itself no mean feat; but, more to his credit, he had won the respect of Boer politicians, to whom he held out the promise of generous imperial statesmanship. Writing one of his first leaders in the *Daily News* (March 6, 1902), A. G. Gardiner acknowledged that "Campbell-Bannerman would not himself claim to be a Bright or a Gladstone. But there have been times," Gardiner continued,

> when men of simple, straightforward honesty and transparent clearness of purpose have been more necessary to the salvation of the people than any great orator. Sir Henry belongs to that type—the type which, across the water, produced a Washington at one moment of national crisis and a Grant at another.

The National Reform Union held its annual session on Wednesday, March 12, in the Memorial Hall, Manchester. Richard Barlow, chairman of the executive committee, presided, although Philip Stanhope was present. There were delegates in attendance from nearly a hundred local branches. Copies of the executive committee report were made available.

Retrospect

The Annual Meeting
National Reform Union   (Manchester?, 1902)

... On the all-absorbing question of the day—the War in
South Africa—the attitude of the National Reform Union has
never wavered. Believing that the appeal to arms could have
been averted by a wise and tactful diplomacy, free from the
coarse and provocative methods of Mr. Chamberlain, and
that the economical and social conditions of the Transvaal
and Orange Free State were all naturally and inevitably tend-
ing towards the establishment of a South African Confederation under the acknowledged supremacy of the British Crown,
it protested against the policy which has resulted in the
devastation of that once happy and prosperous land. Nor
has it feared to condemn those "methods of barbarism" in the
conduct of the War—the farm-burning, the Concentration
Camps, and the execution and banishment of the Boer leaders—for which, not the Army, but the Government must be
held responsible, and which have proved to be as futile for
military ends as they have been prolific in suffering to innocent non-combatants. Above all has the Union raised its voice
against the scandalous suspension of constitutional government and the tyrannous suppression of the Civil Law in Cape
Colony.

With regard to the ending of the War and the settlement to
follow it, the Union had ranged itself with the Leader of the
Opposition in protesting against the policy of insisting on unconditional surrender, which would either result in the ruin
and annihilation of the Boer race, or, if it fell short of that,
would leave the remnant of them morally free to conspire to
regain their liberty at the first favourable opportunity. Inasmuch as this policy appears to be inspired by Lord Milner,
his recall, or his supersession in any negotiation for peace, is
imperative.

The spirit which has prompted and dominated the actions
of the Government in South Africa has been lauded by its
supporters, and defended even by some of its opponents, un-

263

der the specious title of Imperialism, and those who have condemned that spirit and its manifestation have been accused of
disloyalty to the Empire.... [Yet] the Imperialism which is
now made the badge of a party and the war-cry of a section
is synonymous with ... the curtailment of liberty at home
and abroad. It subordinates the welfare of the people in
Great Britain to the interests of cosmopolitan adventurers in
South Africa. It holds patriotism to consist in a contemptuous
disregard of all other nations. It fosters militarism, and talks
lightly of conscription as inevitable. It lavishes millions of
money and sacrifices thousands of lives without thought of the
sorrow and suffering entailed thereby. Against this spirit—
which is not patriotism but Jingoism—the National Reform
Union has fought and will continue to fight.

In the conflict of passions which the War has engendered,
the abiding principles of Liberalism—that great gospel glori-
ously propounded and established in the teachings of Cobden,
Bright, and Gladstone, the full and unbroken conservation of
which the Union has ever placed high above the personal
rivalries and political antagonisms which have from time to
time distracted the Liberal Party—have been in danger of
being forgotten. Embodied in the time-honoured formula
of "Peace, Retrenchment, and Reform"—the motto inherited
by the Union from its very founders—these principles may
perhaps be regarded by some as musty shibboleths of an
ancient faith; but they are still, and ever will remain, the
fixed and permanent creed of the National Reform Union,
and in its estimation the essential conditions of all genuine
Liberalism. To the sordid and flashy Imperialism of to-day it
would oppose the noble patriotism of a past, which held it to
be its paramount duty to uphold with dignity and pride the
position of the British Empire as the champion of the weak
and the oppressed, the friend of freedom, the moral guide of
the whole world. Then, as England's influence and territory
expanded, so also grew the respect which was rendered to her
by other peoples. Now, it is one of the constant boasts of
her present rulers, that as a nation she has come to be an object
of almost universal hatred abroad. They boldly employ this

as the basis of their demand for further armaments and ever-increasing military expenditure. The old rules of conduct in Foreign Affairs have been openly abandoned. The policy of non-intervention has been set aside for an alliance with an Eastern Power, which may at an inopportune moment plunge this nation into a European war for Asiatic interests. Protection, under the guise of Imperial Federation and Colonial Union, is in the air. Conscription is openly advocated by responsible statesmen. Public extravagance and profligate expenditure are the order of the day.

It is in circumstances like these that the National Reform Union renews its appeal to all true Liberals to stand firm by their traditional democratic principles, and not to allow temporary conditions of perplexity to sway their judgment or modify their action.

Sir Henry Campbell-Bannerman merits the praise and sympathy of every right-thinking Liberal for the strenuous efforts he has made, in spite of the abuse of opponents and the coldness of some of his party, to steer the Liberal ship in the right direction, and to save it from being wrecked in the breakers of reaction. Especially valuable has been his declaration of fidelity to the principles of Home Rule for Ireland. That policy was accepted by the Liberal Party in the firm conviction that it was the only alternative to that constant coercion which had formerly been regarded as the sole cure for Irish discontent. That was the belief of Mr. Gladstone, and that belief, consecrated by his death, Liberals still hold, and no considerations of party expediency will induce them to surrender it.

The alarming growth of public expenditure, which is the natural outcome of a profligate public policy, and the absorption of the time and energies of Parliament by the War, render it futile to discuss any of those urgent reforms which the National Reform Union has advocated for so many years. The simplification of registration, the abolition of the plural vote, the reduction of election expenses, the removal of every bar to the possession of the franchise by all duly qualified citizens, the disestablishment of State Churches, the reform of taxation both imperial and local, the granting to the people the power to control the drink traffic in their own districts, the housing of the working classes, the taxation of land values, the reorganisation of national education on a truly popular basis, and the abolition of the legislative powers of the House of Lords—these are still vital and urgent problems, which can only be solved thoroughly and effectively by Liberal methods and on Liberal principles. To these the Union declares its unshaken fidelity, and though hopeless of their near fulfilment, it will not abate its advocacy of and demand for them. The time for their realisation will come when the country has learnt the full lesson which the present administration seems bent on teaching it, and has to pay the full and bitter price for the luxury of having a Government whose policy is turbulent abroad and reactionary at home. The benefits of a peaceful policy, the necessity for stringent economy, and the crying needs of social reforms will then again come home to the people, and they will recognise that the old banner of Peace, Retrenchment, and Reform still remains the symbol and the inspiration of a living and illuminating political faith.

> *Signed by order of the Executive Committee,*
> RICHARD BARLOW, *Chairman*
> ARTHUR G. SYMONDS, *Secretary*

February 25th, 1902

By March, the war was, to all intents and purposes, over. On the twenty-third, the Boers sued for peace, and Lord Kitchener opened negotiations with them at Vereeniging, where a treaty was signed on May 31.

On the whole, it proved easier to restore confidence between victor and vanquished than between Englishmen who had divided over the war. A former friend wrote without forgiveness to Leonard Courtney's wife.

Lord Mount Eddy-Combe to "Kate" Courtney March 16, 1902

I cannot help regarding him [Courtney] as one of those leading men who, by their speeches, have done more to encourage the Boers to prolong the war, and are therefore responsible for more loss of life than any other individuals, and I felt that on that account I could not renew our acquaintance. One can shake hands with an enemy if he is fighting for his own people, but not if he is one's fellow countryman.

*Courtney Papers, British Library of
Political and Economic Science, London*

The Colonial Secretary, as one might expect, proved more willing to grant amnesty to the defeated enemy in South Africa than to his opponents at home.

Joseph Chamberlain
Speech in the House of Commons   **March 20, 1902**

[A pro-Boer was one who] thought that the Boers were right and that this country was wrong, and who supported the Boers in every incident of the campaign—who found no fault with them in anything they had done, who has never once lifted his voice against any of the crimes that have been brought to their charge, while he has never ceased to take every possible opportunity in order to bring insinuations against his own countrymen.

Parliamentary Debates, *4th series, CV, col. 578*

Cecil Rhodes, like the Queen in whose name he had acted, did not live to see the peace; and Lord Salisbury's premiership did not long survive it. Kruger lived out his days in embittered exile. In 1903, Chamberlain resigned office to proselytize for Imperial Preference; three years later, he suffered a stroke that ended his public career. There was, therefore, a change of personalities, from the monarch down, that seemed to relegate the war more quickly to the past.

The change became more pronounced at the close of 1905, with the arrival in office of a Liberal Government, led by Campbell-Bannerman, that proceeded to restore self-government to the Transvaal. On July 31, 1906, Winston Churchill, the under-secretary of state for the colonies, presented the government's proposals to the House of Commons. Opposition spokesmen angrily denounced the settlement as a sellout, and repudiated all responsibility for it. This hardly mattered to Sir Charles Dilke, who tartly reminded the House that "The great majority of those who sat on the Ministerial side repudiated all responsibility for the war out of which this settlement arose, and for the many evils which Sir William Harcourt prophesied would come from the war, with many of which this settlement was itself consistent."[1]

It is perhaps ironic that the task of promulgating the Transvaal constitution fell to Churchill, who first attained national prominence as a war correspondent in South Africa, and who had initially criticized the logic and prudence of Campbell-Bannerman's position.[2] The prime minister was not, however, a man to bear a grudge.

Sir Henry Campbell-Bannerman
Letter to Winston S. Churchill   **September 9, 1907**

Now that we have a little breathing time, I feel impelled, on looking back over the Session, to send you a special line of congratulation and recognition of the large part you have had in our success. There cannot be two opinions on one point, viz. that the most conspicuous event in the year is the creation of a self-governing state in the Transvaal and in the Orange Colony. It is not only the greatest achievement of this Government (which is a comparatively small matter) but it is the finest & noblest work of the British power in modern times. And you have so identified yourself with this courageous & righteous policy, and so greatly contributed to its successful enforcement that a large part of the credit of it must be always attributed to you.

I cannot thank you too greatly for the help you have given in this and in other matters, and the constant readiness and effectiveness with which you have upheld true principles of

1. *Parliamentary Debates*, 4th series, CLXII, cols. 764–65.
2. Letter to the editor of *The Times*, June 28, 1901.

government amid the debris and wreckage left by the blunders
and crimes of recent years.

Quoted in Randolph S. Churchill, Winston S. Churchill
(Boston, 1969), companion vol. 2, pt. 1, p. 667

The Boer leaders proclaimed the fact that the British dissidents who befriended them, or simply who showed concern
for Boer women and children, made it possible for them to
find a place within the Empire, and, indeed, not long afterwards, to bear arms in its defense. In the spring of 1910,
General Louis Botha, who had defeated the British at Colenso
and Spion Kop, became prime minister of a newly created
Union of South Africa. His cabinet included two other Boer
commanders (Smuts and Hertzog); a fourth member (Malan)
had been imprisoned during the war; and a fifth (Fischer)
had been kept under military surveillance, and was prevented
from returning after he had gone to Europe. Herbert Gladstone (now suitably dignified as Viscount Gladstone) was dispatched as the first governor-general and high commissioner.

The wheel had turned, and the pro-Boers were gratified by
events. Some, however, were disturbed by the reluctance of
South African politicians to entertain proposals for a native
franchise. "We are afraid," H. W. Massingham wrote in the
Nation (August 13, 1910), "this does not look as if the
vaguely liberal promises, made to British statesmen and
the British public when the Union Act was being passed,
would bear much fruit."

But it was still too early to despair of South African race
relations, and British Liberals were perennially hopeful.
Botha, after his election, visited London, where J. A. Spender
interviewed him for the *Westminster Gazette*. Inevitably,
their conversation drifted to less happy days.

J. A. Spender
Interview with General Botha   **1910**

Just as I was leaving he [Botha] stopped me for a moment and
said: "After all, three words made peace and union in South

Africa: 'methods of barbarism.' " Softening the epigram a little, he went on to speak of the tremendous impression which had been made upon men fighting a losing battle with an apparently hopeless future by the fact that the leader of one of the great English parties had had the courage to say this thing, and to brave the obloquy which it brought upon him. So far from encouraging them to a hopeless resistance, it touched their hearts and made them think seriously of the possibility of reconciliation.

J. A. Spender, The Life of the Right Hon. Sir Henry Cambell-Bannerman, G.C.B. (London, 1923), 1:351

Further Reading

Not surprisingly, much of the best anecdotal material about the pro-Boer agitation is to be found in memoirs or biographies written by journalists, some of whom graduated to careers in politics or literature. These include G. K. Chesterton's *Autobiography* (1936); A. G. Gardiner, *Life of Sir William Harcourt*, 2 vols. (1923); G. P. Gooch, *Life of Lord Courtney* (1920), and his own *Under Six Reigns* (1958); J. L. Hammond, *C. P. Scott* (1934); F. W. Hirst, *In the Golden Days* (1947); John Viscount Morley, *Recollections*, 2 vols. (1917); H. W. Nevinson, *Changes and Chances* (1923); G. W. E. Russell, ed., *Sir Wilfrid Lawson* (1909); and J. A. Spender, *The Life of Sir Henry Campbell-Bannerman*, 2 vols. (1923).

There is also information to be gleaned from the following books by or about participants: A. T. Bassett, *Life of J. E. Ellis* (1914); F. A. Channing, *Memories of Midland Politics* (1918); Sir Edward Clarke, *The Story of My Life* (1918); H. A. L. Fisher, *James Bryce*, 2 vols. (1922); Silas K. Hocking, *My Book of Memory* (1923); S. E. Koss, *Sir John Brunner, Radical Plutocrat* (1970) and *Fleet Street Radical: A. G. Gardiner and the "Daily News"* (1973); Sir James Marchant, *Dr. John Clifford* (1924); and A. L. Thorold, *The Life of Henry Labouchere* (1913).

There are two scholarly articles of seminal importance: J. O. Baylen, "W. T. Stead and the Boer War: the Irony of Idealism," *Canadian Historical Review* 40 (1959):304–14; and J. S. Galbraith, "The Pamphlet Campaign of the Boer War," *Journal of Modern History* 24 (1952):111–26.

General assessments are provided by Elie Halévy, *A History of the English People in the Nineteenth Century*, vol. V (1961), and R. C. K. Ensor, *England 1870–1914* (1936). There is detailed analysis of the imperial situation in R. Robinson, J. Gallagher, with A. Denny, *Africa and the Victorians* (1963), while A. P. Thornton, *The Imperial Idea and Its Enemies* (1959) offers further insights. On electoral questions, there are excellent interpretations in K. O. Morgan, *Wales in British Politics*, rev. ed. (1970), and Henry Pelling, *Popular Politics and Society in Late Victorian Britain* (1968).

Further Reading

A. J. P. Taylor helpfully roots the pro-Boers in the context of British Radicalism in *The Troublemakers* (1957), while Bernard Porter's *Critics of Empire* (1968) gives a thoughtful analysis of intellectual themes, some of which are discussed in Bernard Semmel's *Imperialism and Social Reform* (1960). More recently, Richard Price has made a valuable investigation of social factors in *An Imperial War and the British Working Class* (1972), and H. C. G. Matthew has attended to *The Liberal Imperialists* (1973).

Jeffrey Butler, *The Liberal Party and the Jameson Raid* (1968) supersedes all previous work on this vexing subject. Like D. M. Schreuder, *Gladstone and Kruger* (1969), it helps to explain the issues that generated wartime tensions and antagonisms. On the South African side, with which this volume is not directly concerned, one must make special mention of C. T. Gordon, *The Growth of Boer Opposition to Kruger* (1970); F. A. van Jaarsveld, *The Afrikaner's Interpretation of South African History* (1964); J. S. Marais, *The Fall of Kruger's Republic* (1961); and Leonard Thompson, "The Compromise of Union," in M. Wilson and L. Thompson, eds., *The Oxford History of South Africa*, vol. 2 (1971).

More specific references appear as footnote citations.

Index

Index

Davies, M. V., 46
Davitt, Michael, 33–34, 46
DeBeers Consolidated Mines, 56,
101
Derby, Lord, 51
Dewar, A., 46
DeWet, C. R., 177, 212, 261–62
Diamonds, 56. *See also* DeBeers
Consolidated Mines; Kimberley
diamond mines
Dilke, Sir Charles, 46, 91, 96–98,
268
Dillon, John, 38, 46, 129, 184
Disraeli, Benjamin (Earl of
Beaconsfield), xxvii, 192, 193
Donelan, Capt. A., 46
Doogan, P. C., 46
Doyle, Arthur Conan, 173
Dreyfus case, 18–21
Duckworth, J., 46

Echo, 11, 68
Edward VII, King, 256
Edwards, J. Passmore, 3
Edwards, O. M., 46
Egypt, British occupation of, 52, 57
Eighty Club, 184
Eliot, Sir John, 116
Ellis, J. E., xviii–xix, 44–45, 46, 48,
162–63
Emmott, A., 157–58
Ensor, R. C. K., xx
Evans, Sam, 44, 47
Exeter Hall meeting, 105–8, 113,
114, 118

Fabian Society, 58. *See also*
Beatrice Webb; Sidney Webb
Farquharson, Dr. R., 46
Farrer, K. E., 179
Fashoda crisis, xix, xx, 103
Fawcett, Mrs. Henry (Dame Milli-
cent), 174
Fenwick, C., 46
Field, W., 46
Fife, Duke of, 94
Fischer, Abraham, 269
Fisher, Sir John (Baron Fisher), xv
Fitzmaurice, Lord Edmond, 91
Flavin, M., 46
Fordham, Mrs. E. O., 207, 210
Fox, Charles James, 245

Fox, Dr. J. F., 46
Franco–Prussian War, 133
Free Speech, controversy over,
xxviii, 89, 105–26, 138, 147, 235,
237

Galbraith, J. S., xxix
Gardiner, A. G., xxxi, 179, 256–57,
262
Gasquoine, Rev. T., 226, 227
General Elections: (1895), 154, 164;
(1900), xxxii, 148–69, 170, 218,
235, 251; (1906), xv, xxxvii, 166;
(1918), 143
George III, King, 53
Gibney, J., 46
Gilhooly, J., 46
Gladstone, Herbert, 101, 269
Gladstone, Rev. J. P., 227
Gladstone, Rev. Stephen, 131, 232,
246
Gladstone, W. E., xv, xvii, xxii,
xxvii, xxviii, 8, 21, 34, 63, 96,
100, 194, 225, 239, 262, 264, 265;
Morley's biography of, 15, 98
Glasier, J. Bruce, 14
Goldfields, xvii, 7, 8, 21, 39, 56, 62,
71, 124, 135–36, 139, 146
Gooch, G. P., xx, xxi, xxii–xxiii,
xxv, 81
Gore, Canon Charles, 232–33
Grant, Corrie, 165
Grant, U. S., 262
Great Trek, xvi–xvii, 55, 63–64
Green, J. R., xxxv
Greene, Conyngham, 35, 36, 51
Grey, Sir Edward, xvii, xxvi, xxx,
32
Guerilla warfare, outbreak of,
170–71
Gurdon, Sir W. Brampton, 46, 100

Hague Conference, 18, 69, 102, 172,
211, 212
Haldane, J. S., 221
Haldane, R. B., xv, xxvi, 32
Halifax Liberal Association, 24
Hammond, Hays, 56, 59, 61
Hammond, J. L., xxxv, 81, 99, 101,
162
Harcourt, Lady, 44
Harcourt, L. V., xxxvii

275

Index

Index

Index